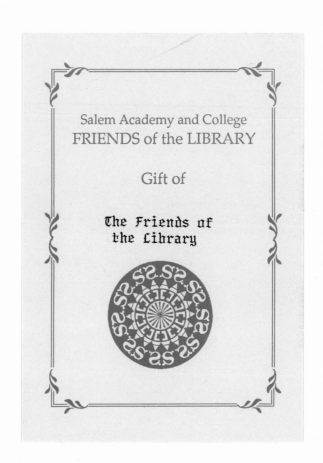

Intruders
in
the Play World

Intruders
in
the Play World

The Dynamics of Gender
in Molière's Comedies

Roxanne Decker Lalande

Madison • Teaneck
Fairleigh Dickinson University Press
London: Associated University Presses

Associated University Presses
440 Forsgate Drive
Cranbury, NJ 08512

Associated University Presses
25 Sicilian Avenue
London WC1A 2QH, England

Associated University Presses
P.O. Box 338, Port Credit
Mississauga, Ontario
Canada L5G 4L8

The paper used in this publication meets the requirements of the American National Standard for Permanence of Paper for Printed Library Materials Z39.48-1984.

Library of Congress Cataloging-in-Publication Data

Lalande, Roxanne Decker, 1950–
    Intruders in the play world : the dynamics of gender in Molière's comedies / Roxanne Decker Lalande.
        p. cm.
    Includes bibliographical references and index.
    ISBN 0-8386-3592-X (alk. paper)
    1. Molière, 1622–1673—Criticism and interpretation.   2. Sex role in literature.   3. Women in literature.   I. Title.
PQ1860.L27   1996
842'.4—dc20
                                                            95-32324
                                                            CIP

For my sons
Eric and William

Contents

Acknowledgments

I would like to thank the National Endowment for the Humanities for a Fellowship Grant providing financial assistance for this book. I would also like to express my appreciation to Lafayette College for further financial support.

I would like to thank the following people for their active encouragement and assistance: Dr. June Schlueter for her support, Dr. Janet Altman for her valuable suggestions in the early stages of my work, and Dr. Larry Riggs for his positive comments and suggestions for revision.

Chapter 8 is a revised version of an article originally published in *Cahiers du dix-septième siècle* 3, no. 2 (fall 1989): 83–104.

Intruders
in
the Play World

1

Introduction: Comic Theory and the Delineation of Ludic Space

Le divertissement sera agréable: il y en a qui donnent la comédie à leurs maîtresses; mais donner une dissection est quelque chose de plus galant.

—*Le Malade imaginaire* II, 5

Toinette's sarcastic admonishment to Thomas Diafoirus rings true to any critic wishing to undertake the dissection of comedy. Much as one might like to avoid the problem of semantics, any study that includes theoretical reflections on the comic must begin by defining a number of pivotal concepts, in view of the linguistic ambiguity surrounding terminology in the field. What may initially appear to be elementary notions such as laughter, the laughable, the comic, the joke, the ridiculous, and the ludicrous—not to mention comedy itself—must be examined in relationship to one another in order to afford a sound and intelligible basis for the ensuing analysis. I shall take the necessary time in this introductory chapter to pass in review the important critical doctrines of comic theory, accepting some points, rejecting others, until I have extracted the premises on which to base my own considerations.

Those who have made major contributions to the field of comic theory can be roughly divided into three broad groups: psychoanalysts, social philosophers, and formalist critics. The former have a vested interest in determining what laughter is and what circumstances favor it. The second category of thinkers is more concerned with the social function of laughter and of ludic activity generally, while the latter have contributed to our understanding of the morphology of the literary genre of comedy. As widely diverse as these interests may be, they all have certain points in common and have helped shape the current project.

13

Among the first group, findings of Sigmund Freud and Ernst Kris have provided the framework for the present study. In order to elaborate any theoretical considerations on comedy, one must first attempt to define the cause of laughter: both the inner psychic mechanism and the outer stimulus. Although laughter itself is not vital to the attainment of comic effect, a certain feeling of amusement or lightheartedness is. This feeling can be as subtle as it is occasionally raucous: it can generate outright laughter or a fleeting smile. Thus, the degree of amusement may vary, but the conditions necessary for achieving it are the same. One can view laughter as the strongest but not necessarily the optimal response to comic perception, and because it is the most obvious outward sign, it has also been subject to the greatest amount of interest. By examining what makes us laugh, psychoanalysts such as Freud and Kris have uncovered certain clues as to the nature of comic response generally.

According to Freud, laughter results from the sudden release of psychic energy, which has been brought to the surface in anticipation of a serious mental effort or expenditure, be it for ideation, inhibition or emotion.[1] Motor preparations are an expression of anticipation or expectation of any effort, physical or psychological. Freud uses the example of a person who reaches for a glass, believing it to be full. This person prepares a quantity of energy suitable to the anticipated effort. Should the glass be empty, its lightness will surprise him and his energy expenditure will reveal itself to be superfluous. An outburst of laughter is similarly caused by the same type of mechanism within the psyche: the damming up and sudden release of what Freud terms "cathetic" energy due to an economy of psychic expenditure, which in turn is caused by the sudden perception of the unsubstantial or non-serious nature of the object of ridicule. (It should be noted that Freud uses the terms "psychic" and "cathetic" energy interchangeably.) The superfluous energy thus raised to the surface for serious consideration must be discharged into laughter unless the mind has the time or the inclination to channel it elsewhere. This process is referred to as "cathexis." According to Freud, it accounts for the importance of tempo or timing in jokes and comedy. The comic perception must be sudden and disorienting, not allowing time for emotions, inhibitions, or rationalizations to reemploy and divert the cathetic energy. Therefore, a strong intellectual (analytical) or emotional (affective) response will neutralize the cathetic energy of the listener. A spectator who has difficulty unraveling a complicated plot, or a listener who finds a joke abusive or obscene will have very little urge to laugh. Nervous laughter can be discounted here as a response to embarrassment or fear, which does not reflect the comic spirit.

It must be observed that Freud's main purpose in writing *Jokes and Their Relation to the Unconscious* was to examine the specific relationship between laughter and the unconscious, and that he limits his study to the type of response elicited by jokes. He did not seek to apply his findings to literary or other art forms. Freud does, however, propose a distinction between jokes *(der Witz)* and the comic *(das Komische),* which he rightly perceives as belonging to two different orders. The term "comic" here is no longer taken in the broader sense of the word—a general category of effects with the potential to create laughter. Therefore, to avoid confusion, I shall refer to this Freudian subcategory of the comic as "the comic*al.*"

Freud postulates that the joke is the result of an action, a conscious and willful creative activity: the listener is not the object of ridicule, but is rather the joke-maker's accomplice. The comical, in opposition to the joke, can be simply perceived as a fortuitous occurrence to be found in nature: it is accidental, for the observer comes across it by chance. As a further distinction, a joke invites the active participation of at least three people: the joke-maker, his or her audience, and the butt of the joke. To make this distinction clearer, let us take an example of each. A mischievous school child affixes a humorous note to her teacher's back. Unaware of the prank, the instructor wonders why her students begin to laugh every time she turns around. This is a classic example of a practical or nonverbal joke in which the joke-maker or prankster enlists the support of an audience against an unwitting victim. As Freud explains, hostility on behalf of the prankster or his or her audience is not a necessary attribute of the joke, but is frequently present. The joker is, however, absent from our perception of the comical as an incidental occurrence. For example, a name such as Roméo Lamoureux might strike us as comical. A strange appearance or an accidental action—such as Bergson's example of a man slipping on a banana peel—might cause us to laugh.[2] In similar cases the object of ridicule causes laughter because of a characteristic or action stemming from his or her *own* being. In a sense, the fool strikes us as comical in and of him- or herself, even though certain conditions of receptivity must be present within the spectator for a comic perception to occur. According to Elder Olson, such an inherently foolish character can be termed "ridiculous," whereas the unwitting victim of a prank is merely "ludicrous."[3] We laugh at the latter's situation rather than his or her character. The comical as perceived in nature is essentially a bipartite relationship, for it involves an object of ridicule and a passive observer: any creative effort by a third party is absent.

Although Freud confined himself mainly to the study of verbal humor in jokes and probed into the psychic phenomenon that accompanies the laughter response, his conclusions have directed me to a literary question of the same order: "What are the fundamental characteristics of comedy that allow one to recognize it as such?" The comic perception itself—in other words, the relationship between the observer and the object, between the spectator and the play, between the laugher and the laughable—is of primary interest to the present study. In order to determine what is essential to the comic genre and its effect upon the audience, it becomes imperative to explain the relationship between a joke, a comical incident, and a comedy. Like a joke, a comedy is an artifact, the result of a conscious creative effort. Furthermore, the comic author has very much the same type of intent as the joke-maker: to enlist the support and the laughter of his or her audience. It is more difficult, however, to determine the object of ridicule. I would argue that on this external level of perception, which includes the author-spectator's reality as a framework to the inner workings of the fictional play, the laughter is directed against the collective dramatis personae—that is, the entire cast—for none of the fictional characters is capable of sharing the author's or the audience's global perspective. On the other hand, the tripartite relationship between the joker, the audience, and the butt of the joke can be present within the dramatic structure itself. In comedy, characters can generally be divided into three distinct groups: tricksters, laughers, and ridiculous figures. Thus, the external framework author/audience/object-of-ridicule is reflected onstage by a similar division. In this manner, inclusion and exclusion from the comic locus occur as natural results of the comic process.

The complexity of audience response to a comic play does not stop there. On the level of theatrical convention at least, the spectator is called upon to suspend his or her disbelief and to disregard the artificial nature of the action s/he is witnessing. Submersion in the dramatic illusion affords an occasional glimpse at the comical when the spectator momentarily forgets the author's presence and experiences the more intimate bipartite relationship between him or herself and the play. Because the spectator never truly forgets that s/he is witnessing fictional events, one might claim that a comic play affords the very rare merging of the joke and the comical as defined by Freud. This simultaneous experience of the bipartite and the tripartite may indeed be one of the keys to the pleasure yielded by comedy.

Aside from the structural attributes of comedy examined above, there exists a qualitative factor, which is far more elusive and difficult to define. The term "comic" in its most general application is a broad category that can, but need not, contain the laughable. Laughter and comedy have always been closely associated and there is a justifiable temptation to equate the two terms, yet there are some comedies (notably those prescribed by George Meredith) to which the laughter response is either minimal or non-existent, not by some miscalculation of the author's, but intentionally so. For this reason, one is forced to view laughter as a highly desirable accessory to comedy, but not as a determining factor.

Freud noted that in the longer, more fully developed jokes, which tend to resemble brief narratives, the joke-maker often carefully creates a comic atmosphere that serves as a facade for the joke. He terms the resulting audience response, which would parallel the creation of a comical contextual dimension within the framework of the joke, comic fore-pleasure. Its purpose is to elicit a state of pleasurable amusement at the outset, which serves to initiate a larger release of pleasure. "The result is a generation of pleasure far greater than the supervening possibility."[4] This occurs because the comic fore-pleasure principle combats successively reason, critical judgment, and suppression (inhibition), which are, all three, destructive of comic pleasure or cathetic release. "A comic facade encourages the effectiveness of a joke in more than one way; not only does it make the automatism of the joking process possible by holding the attention, but it also facilitates the discharge by sending ahead a discharge of a comic kind."[5] Akin to sexual foreplay, which heightens the final orgasmic release, fore-pleasure awakens our attention and heightens our anticipation, thus preparing for the cathetic release.

We have seen that Freud attributes laughter to a sudden increase and release of cathetic energy. Ernst Kris has contributed enormously to the elaboration of Freudian comic theory. His terminology differs slightly from that of his predecessor, for rather than using the terms "der Witz" and "das Komische," he distinguishes between "the comic which we invent or call into being" and "the comic which we find in life."[6] Though such a classification does not take into account the fundamental differences between a witticism and a comedy, which both belong to the first category, he does bring up an important distinction that Freud had overlooked.

For Kris, the comic and the laughable are by no means identical, for the comic is a broader category that can contain the laughable. Here Kris is interested primarily in the specific relationship between a comic incident and the more durative notion of comic atmosphere, as well as their effect upon spectator perception. He attempts to discover the qualitative element (not merely the quantitative factor discussed by Freud: the quantity of energy saved) by determining the nature of comic pleasure. He focuses his attention on the relationship of tempo or comic timing to the economy of cathetic expenditure: the speed at which tension is released. Speed can be perceived as a qualitative factor because it determines the type of response elicited: will the comic perception cause a sudden outburst of laughter or a durative comic mood? Freud had already examined the mechanism that is activated when the energy repressed by inhibition, ideation, or emotion suddenly becomes superfluous and is ready to be discharged into laughter. This definition takes into account the punctual occurrence, but avoids the issue of the durative nature of comic atmosphere. Freud certainly approaches the subject in his discussion of comic fore-pleasure, but does not consider timing to be the differentiating factor. For Kris "time plays no part in the psychic economy of humor; thus its achievement is more lasting."[7] A closer reading will reveal that the word "humor" describes an emotional response to the comic, somewhat akin to joy: "We often express our pleasure at humor not in laughter but in a quiet smile."[8] It is obvious that he wishes to juxtapose the sudden laughter *reaction,* dependent upon comic timing, to a pleasant *feeling*— and this feeling seems to be analogous to the Freudian fore-pleasure principle: a joyous, light-hearted and smile-provoking emotion that prepares the ground for a potential discharge of cathetic energy. The pleasurable and longer-lasting emotion or slow release serves as a prerelease for the stronger but briefer laughter expenditure.

Kris' work is of vital importance to comic theory, for he was one of the first to envision the possible relationship between Freudian theory of the comic and aesthetic forms of comedy, as well as between psychoanalysis and art in general. Charles Mauron was to carry on the work by narrowing his scope and by focusing on the personal myth of the comic author through a study of his metaphorical obsessions.[9] He applied the theoretical findings of his predecessors to the comic genre, limiting himself to the study of Old and New Comedy, as well as a brief examination of Molière. Mauron felt that the recurring patterns and plot structures of the comedies under investigation were so conventional that rather than conveying the author's personal obsessions, they reveal those of a whole society or generation. He therefore subjects a number of comic plots to a reduction process, finds the simplest common denominator, and arrives at a few basic archetypal comic situations, which all happen to show some form of reverse Oedipal pattern and represent the overcoming of the preternatural fears of patricide and/or incest. Mauron attempts to explain the secret of comedy as the displacement of tragic guilt from son to father. This discovery of archetypal plot patterns is very similar to studies undertaken by formalists such as Northrop Frye and Vladimir Propp. However, verifying his conclusions with personal data and life history whenever available, Mauron translates recurring patterns into personal obsessions with which to psychoanalyze the author or the generation of authors.

Although Mauron has contributed greatly to the study of the morphology of certain types of comic plot, his approach raises several objections. First of all, his theory makes virtually no distinction between a witticism and a comic play: "la comédie bien construite n'est qu'un vaste et complexe trait d'esprit."[10] [a well-made comedy is nothing more than an extended and complex witticism.] (Translation by author) This statement can be explained in part by Mauron's heavy reliance on Kris' findings. As seen earlier, Kris divides the comic into two categories: that which is accidental and that which is created. A joke and any type of comic art form would thus fall into the same category and would contain an implied triangular relationship between the artist (or joke-maker), the witness, and the fool. Indeed, comic art presupposes the will to cause laughter and in this it resembles the joke rather than the comical. The two have in common an artificial aspect and both have aesthetic unity with beginning, middle, and end. However, Mauron's opinion that comedy is nothing more than a complex joke requires further examination. Does not the time span of the play (its vastness) negate the idea of tempo so vital to the joke-work? Of course, it is possible that Mauron is using the term "vast" to imply that a comedy contains a series of sudden shifts and reversals, yet it is altogether more probable that he considers the final reversal of the Oedipal situation as the ultimate aim of all comedy and as the moment at which cathetic release, or what he terms "fantaisie de triomphe," [fantasy of triumph] would occur. By concentrating on those sporadic moments in which cathexis occurs, Mauron pays little attention to the durative element within a comedy. Still, he briefly mentions the background of comedy which forms "un canevas banal [qui] ne provoque pas le rire en soi, [mais] en est la prémisse favorable."[11] [a banal background [which] does not provoke laughter in and of itself [but] is conducive to it.] (Translation by author) Thus, he discerns something undefinable akin to the comic fore-pleasure principle, in which timing plays no part: a mood-setting context.

When Freud studies the joke mechanism, he considers its effect on the author of the joke as well as on the spectator and examines the relationship between the two. Any theory that does not take into account this double factor is not probing deeply enough into the possibilities of Freudian theory and its relationship to literary criticism. Mauron does indeed recognize the importance of the psychological reactions involved in the spectator's comic perception, yet his main interest lies in psychoanalyzing the author himself. Furthermore, Mauron seems to believe that the triumphant reversals that occur in anguishing archetypal situations are the basis for all comedy because they create comic catharsis by eliminating an unconscious fear, yet many plays do not fit easily into that mold. For example, Diderot's domestic drama Le Père de famille presents a prime instance of the displacement of tragic guilt from son to father, yet it is definitely not a comedy. The contrary is true of Corneille's Le Menteur, which presents no displacement of guilt, yet who can dispute its comic nature? Essentially, Mauron examines plot structure too narrowly, without asking himself what effect this might have on the spectator's appreciation of the comic.

The vital generic difference between tragedy and comedy lies not so much in the presence or absence of laughable incidents, but in the creation of a comic contextual dimension conducive to a durable sense of enjoyment or amusement. In order for the fore-pleasure principle to be operative within the paradigmatic and syntagmatic structures of comedy, the author must construct a play world favorable to cathetic release.

In order to determine in what manner playful perception can occur, it is necessary to spend some time examining the writings of such prominent sociologists, philosophers, and essayists as Jean Paul Richter, Schlegel, Lamb, Meredith, Hegel and Huizinga. Some concentrate their efforts on the social function of play, others examine the respective socio-historical roles of comedy and tragedy, while still others view comedy primarily as a social corrective. The first question to be answered is whether comedy is, or should be, a moralizing agent based upon the principle of poetic justice (follies justly chastised). It is always difficult to determine what is meant when a critic states that art ought to be moral— and equally difficult to decide what the opposite statement means. Normally, however, art without a moral or art for art's sake is defined as a form of estheticism in which the work of art belongs outside the realm of ethics and didacticism.

Ever since Horace wrote that art should be both delightful and useful, critics have endeavored to find some type of moral message in all genres of literature, and comedy has been no exception. Among these critics, one can cite such prominent names as Trissino, Minturno, Macaulay, Johnson, Heywood, Thackeray, Fielding, and Molière himself in his defense of *Tartuffe*.

For Meredith, comedy passes moral judgment, but ideally its moral lesson does not "hang like a tail, or preach from one character incessantly cocking an eye at the audience . . . but is in the heart of the work."[12] This novelist-critic maintains, however, that the idea contained is of greater value than the aesthetic form. Though he feels a certain reluctance to promote outright didacticism, the principle of poetic justice is dear to him. But Meredith soon alters his reflections on this ideal in favor of a slight variation: laughter resulting from comedy is the ultimate civilizer, because it allows us to sublimate our hostility and because it censures vanity and folly. Thus, Meredith's thoughtful mirth can be seen as a premise for civilization and a social corrective founded upon implicit moral value.

Bergson's theory also deals with the social implications of laughter. His view of laughter as a social corrective is surprisingly conventional, though he seems somehow to perceive the shortcomings of this statement when he concedes that if we fear ridicule, we may perhaps adjust our outward behavior but not necessarily our inner attitude to conform to social conventions. "Mais un défaut ridicule, dès qu'il se sent ridicule, cherche à se modifier, au moins extérieurement. Si Harpagon nous voyait rire de son avarice, je ne dis pas qu'il s'en corrigerait, mais il nous la montrerait moins, ou il nous la montrerait autrement. Disons-le dès maintenant, c'est en ce sens surtout que le rire 'châtie les moeurs'. Il fait que nous tâchons tout de suite de paraître ce que nous devrions être, ce que nous finirons sans doute un jour par être véritablement."[13] [But a defect that is ridiculous, as soon as it feels itself to be so, endeavors to modify itself or at least to appear as though it did. Were Harpagon to see us laugh at his miserliness, I do not say that he would get rid of it, but he would either show it less or show it differently. Indeed, it is in this sense only that laughter 'corrects men's manners.' It makes us at once endeavor to appear what we ought to be, what some day we shall perhaps end in being.]

Bergson considers the comic author in some ways akin to the moralist; however, this view rests somewhat uneasily alongside his main premise: that the comical is the perception of something mechanical encrusted upon the living. He claims that we laugh at what is rigid, codified, and lacking the living flexibility to adapt to unpredictable changes. Since Bergson views society as an ever changing, living organism, he sees no contradiction in viewing laughter as a form of chastisement for rigidity, on the one hand, and an incentive for conforming to social norms on the other.

In an earlier age when it was a generally accepted notion that art should both teach and please, few dared to contradict popular wisdom. Aristotelians such as Castelvetro and Robortello found it unnecessary to deal with the issue of didacticism because they limited themselves to the study of artistic forms and were committed to the supremacy of *delectare* over *docere*. Many critics, and among them mostly authors, accepted the notion of a useful moral lesson, but stressed the importance of pleasure over ethical considerations. Corneille himself felt that the primary aim of the poet was to please, and Dryden went even further by venturing that there was no such principle as poetic justice to be found in comedy. Tragedy's purpose was to instruct, but comedy existed in his view merely to delight and if by chance comedy should contain some edifying message, then this was secondary.[14]

Charles Lamb's argument was even more daring. His essay on the artificial comedy of the early eighteenth century can be seen as a very early and isolated instance of estheticism. He was reacting against a development at the end of the eighteenth century (which had its parallel also in French literature), which was to put an end to classical comedy and to replace it by various forms of melodrama and domestic drama, sentimental, humanitarian, and heavily moralistic.[15] Lamb despised this "insipid, levelling morality . . . a puritanical obtuseness of sentiment, a stupid infantile goodness."[16] Lamb's anger is turned, not so much against the principle of poetic justice per se, as against those who, like the Jansenist critic Nicole, were unable to see the distinction between the real world in which moral values apply and the play world, and who consequently objected to any portrayal of vices, even if these were duly chastised on stage. Lamb considers comic characterization to be preeminently neutral, standing at some point between vice and virtue. The characters of comedy do not offend moral sense because they do not appeal to it. He describes comedy as "that happy breathing-place from the burthen of a perpetual moral questioning,"[17] an imaginary world with no moral restrictions. Good and evil, right and wrong, are terms foreign to this fictional space. It is our very emotional indifference, according to Lamb, that allows us to endure the artificiality of the comic whole.

Jean Paul Richter carries the argument to its logical conclusion when he claims that just as greatness evokes our admiration, so the insignificant evokes the opposite feeling.[18] The ridiculous belongs to the realm of the amoral, for in the moral realm nothing is insignificant and contempt or esteem is a necessary consequence of moral evaluation. Jean Paul thus suggests a lack of ethical substance in comedy.

Schlegel insists that mirth appeals to our animal instincts, tragedy to our moral conscience. He discerns in humans a dichotomy between the animal shell and the ethical substance. Comedy affords freedom from all restraints, for all laws are temporarily suspended, even those of probability and necessary cause and effect. In order to insure the appropriate audience response, it is imperative for the spectator to be diverted from any form of moral consideration. Schlegel contends that even the most biting satire provides little moral instruction:

> As then comedy must place the spectator in a point of view altogether different from that of moral appreciation, with what right can moral instruction be demanded of comedy, with what ground can it be expected? When we examine more closely the moral apophthegms of the Greek comic writers, we find that they are all of them maxims of experience. It is not, however, from experience that we gain a knowledge of our duties of which conscience gives us an immediate conviction; experience can only enlighten us with respect to what is profitable or detrimental. The instruction of comedy does not turn on the dignity of the object proposed but on the sufficiency of the means employed. It is, as has already been said, the doctrine of prudence; the morality of consequences and not of motives. Morality, in its genuine acceptation, is essentially allied to the spirit of Tragedy.[19]

Hegel views the comic as the purest of all the purely aesthetic artistic experiences, for it has no natural, non-artistic counterpart.[20] He thereby banishes the previously accepted notion that the comical can be found in nature and need not be created. If Hegel's argument forms a counterpoint to Freudian theory, it may be because he believes in the ultimate indestructibility of real substantive values. Thus, there exist certain natural ethical values, and the amorality of the comic, which is essentially void of ethical content, is not a natural state, but one which must be created.

Comedy's antididactic nature, on the other hand, does not negate what Hegel sees as its vital social function as an active force that clears the historical stage of outworn conventions and prejudices. In both tragedy and comedy he sees an opposition between individual and social claims which are one-sided and absolute. In the former, the individual is sacrificed for the benefit of the collective unit, whereas in comedy the individual's claim is sanctioned and the old order is destroyed. Like many theoreticians, Hegel has limited himself to those cases that substantiate his argument, one that is strongly tainted by his theory of history. For Hegel, there exists a dialectical movement from tragedy (which upholds the status quo and in which the main characters are necessarily from the ruling class) to comedy, which destroys in symbolical fashion the old order and prepares the audience for the coming of a new society. The new order will in time become the established order and be abolished in turn. He thus sees comedy as a revolutionary, tragedy as a conservative force.

According to Hegel, the conflict at the heart of a tragedy inspires the viewer because substantive and ethical values are being threatened, whereas in comedy any opposition is absurd because its excesses and contradictions have rendered the ethical content inoperative. Comedy is essentially the dramatization of the destruction or negation of social values that are inherently null from the outset, but that had been viewed initially as reliable principles within the context of the older order. Because comedy is the negation of a negation in Hegel's view, it can clear the way for the restoration of essential values in a new social structure within and without the fictitious context of the play.

What can be gleaned from the previous observations is that comedy has nearly always been studied in relation to tragedy and that by comparison it has always been treated as a subordinate genre, one less worthy of serious consideration. Certain critics have indeed been perceptive enough to discern fundamental differences that go beyond formal oppositions, between the two genres, but they have not gone so far as to advocate an entirely different critical approach to the study of comedy. Since literary scholars have all too often sought a substantive message in comedy, their resultant studies have often been less than conclusive.

As Schlegel has pointed out, comedy offers primarily a moral of experience. Failure to find "transcendent" value has led many critics in search of ethical content to posit an alternative: comedy as a social corrective. However, even such attempts at rehabilitating comedy are concessions to the "superficiality" of comedy, which corrects behavior rather than attitudes and which teaches pragmatism rather then ethics. Those who praise, as well as those who scorn comedy precisely for this lack of ethical content would often advocate abandoning any attempt to analyze an art form whose primary function is to delight.

When Lamb describes comedy as "that happy breathing-place from the burthen of perpetual moral questioning" he defines it as a locus, a space in which ethical values are temporarily suspended and replaced by ludic activity. This locus constitutes a play world and serves to heighten audience response to the comic by creating a comic contextual dimension that elicits fore-pleasure. This means that it allows a saving of cathetic energy on a durative basis by promoting the audience's awareness of a temporary sheltered circle of non-seriousness and of freedom from ordinary concerns. The comic perception is indeed a liberating experience.

In *Homo Ludens,* Huizinga sums up the formal characteristics of play and uncovers in the process the notion of boundaries enclosing a hermetic space that serves as a shelter from real life, a place of reassurance and reprieve:

> we might call (play) a *free* activity standing quite *consciously outside* "ordinary" life as being *"not serious"*, but at the same time absorbing the player intensely and utterly. It is an activity connected with no material interest, and no profit can be gained by it. It proceeds within its own *boundaries* of space and time according to fixed rules and in an orderly manner. It promotes the formation of formal *groupings* which tend to surround themselves with secrecy and to stress their *difference* from the common world by disguise or other means.[21] (The italics are mine.)

In comedy the play world can be defined as a magic circle of playful illusion, a retreat from reality, which is both gratuitous and exclusive. It is a hermetic locus present within the dramatic structure, separating characters into groups of insiders and outsiders, players and non-players, and intruders. Often, more than one circle of play is present. In-play now becomes inter-play as play worlds interact and occasionally intersect and collide.

It has been stressed that the comic perception is founded upon the interaction between the perceiver and the object perceived, in other words between the audience (us), and the comic object (him/her/them). If we return now to Freud's definition of the joke-work, we will remember that he posits both the complicity of the joke-maker/author and his or her audience/witness, or insiders, and their adversarial position toward the fool(s), or outsiders. Insofar as comedy resembles the joke-work, it must also incorporate the mitigating role of the joke-maker. Essentially three separate relationships must be examined: that between the author and his or her audience, that between the audience and the object of ridicule, and that between the object of ridicule and the author.

Once again, these relationships occur within and without the dramatic structure, providing additional complexity to spectator response. We have seen that inclusion and exclusion are intrinsic to comedy. Ludic space is created by sharply delineating the fictional locus into zones of participation and nonparticipation. If by definition the play world is exclusive, it depends for its very existence on the alienation of the other to mark its boundaries from normal activity. A type of social bonding occurs that strongly differentiates between "us" and "the others." It is this bonding that provides the reassurance necessary for comic fore-pleasure.

At this point, we must turn to the third group of comic theorists, the formalists, to examine their comments on comic character and plot. It is occasionally difficult to determine whether their remarks are descriptive or prescriptive, but Aristotle's influence is their primary common denominator: comedy imitates characters of a lower type but does not include the full range of villainy, only the ridiculous, which is a subdivision of the ugly; not the painful or destructive.[22] The general consensus among Aristotelian disciples—such as Donatus, Robortello, and Castelvetro—has been that comic characters are of mediocre fortune and lower social status than their tragic counterparts and that the action is a harmless and painless arrangement of private and civil deeds, in which comic reversal produces a pleasant outcome.

A number of objections can be raised to such formal categorizations. First of all, their validity is limited to a specific historical era. Unlike its predecessors, for instance, modern-day comedy has no compunction about mocking upper-class characters. Secondly, the description applies only to one type of comic figure: the fool. Other comic types, such as pranksters and laughers, are absent from this definition. Northrop Frye has attempted to remedy this situation by redefining comic characterization and distinguishing between a number of different character types: the *eiron*, the buffoon, etc. Unfortunately, his subdivisions, which would otherwise allow for a number of plausible applications, only add to the confusion because of their complexity. The problem, once again, is that formalists tend to neglect an understanding of the relationship between the onlooker and the object. How is comic response generated, when there is no such thing as an *inherently funny* object? This is why a descriptive analysis is in and of itself insufficient and why formalist criticism falls short of its target. It is true that these critics have given some consideration to comic response. They have patterned their ideas on Aristotle's concept of tragic catharsis, but once again they have examined what it is and not how it is elicited: "In tragedy, pity and fear, the emotions of moral attraction and repulsion, are raised and cast out. Comedy seems to make a more functional use of the social, even the moral judgement, than tragedy, yet comedy seems to raise the corresponding emotions, which are sympathy and ridicule, and cast them out in the same way."[23] One can protest, first of all, that sympathy and ridicule do not belong to the same order: the former is a feeling, the latter is a perceived attribute, the result of an opinion. Furthermore, it remains unclear in what way Frye's comic character types or for that matter his archetypal comic plot pattern would predispose the spectator to a comic response, for there is no binding relationship between the two.[24] Finally, it remains questionable how this cathartic process operates on the psychic level and in what way it would be desirable to cast out sympathy and possible to cast out ridicule.

Such considerations lead to the fundamental question of spectator bias: on what basis does the audience take allegiance? If indeed critics are right to view the comic sphere as standing outside the domain of morality, then which judgmental criteria are applicable to the play world? Although Huizinga concludes, like others before him, that play is outside the realm of ethical values, he is subtle enough to discover a different type of judgmental process applicable to play. "Though play as such is outside the range of good and bad, the element of tension imparts to it a certain ethical value in so far as it means a testing of the player's prowess."[25] In the earlier quote by Frye, this issue is alluded to, but never fully developed. Although he never eliminates the notion of moral judgment in comedy, Frye does feel that, unlike tragedy, this genre makes a more "functional use of it." Huizinga touches upon what is perhaps the single most important attribute that any participant in the play world can have: the ability to win. In comedy the winner has our sympathy because in the play world moral judgment is suspended and replaced by a far more objective, albeit superficial form of evaluation based on functional criteria. The complexity, the ambiguity, and the subjectivity of serious judgment give way to the more easily identifiable criteria of winning and losing. In Freudian terms, economy of expenditure of cathetic energy or "cathexis" is favored in such a context. Enclosure within the play world's boundaries is thus a form of retreat from reality, in which playful judgment replaces moral judgment. Players are judged according to whether they win or lose and not according to their relative moral worth. The spectator's absorption in the comic illusion may be intense, but it is always accompanied by the awareness that the characters are "only playing," that the covenant is a fragile one, and that their escape is always possible. This allows for the reassurance so necessary to comic fore-pleasure.

Thus, the characters of comedy can be divided very roughly into two categories: winners and losers. However, a number of subcategories that intersect with these should now be mentioned. The prankster is the onstage equivalent of the joke-maker. This character plays gratuitously, for the sake of playing, and enlists the support of any number of accomplices, forming with them a playful bond or circle. These accomplices are the principal laughers on stage, yet their role is primarily passive in contrast to that of the prankster. Another character may intrude upon their collaboration: the cheat. The cheat breaks the rules of the game, yet acknowledges their existence. As Huizinga points out: "It is curious to note how much more lenient society is to the cheat than to the spoil-sport. This is because the spoil-sport shatters the play-world itself. By withdrawing from the game he reveals the relativity and fragility of the play-world . . . He robs play of its 'illusion'— a pregnant word which means literally 'in-play'."[26] The spoil-sport's presence is disruptive because s/he refuses to accept the covenant between players and stands as a constant reminder of the unescapable reality outside the shelter of play. Within a comedy, the prankster and the spoil-sport are diametrically opposed. Finally, the object of ridicule is the ultimate loser, the character whose presence is undesirable within the ludic circle, yet who is essential to the formation of the play world. S/he is the other whose presence marks the boundaries of the ludic sphere. Thus, the essential comic types are: the prankster, the laugher, the cheat, the spoil-sport and the fool. They are defined by their relationship to the inner circle of playful activity.

Comic plot, on the other hand, which is much more varied than the formalists would have it, depends primarily upon the interaction or interplay between the diverse spheres of ludic activity. Bearing in mind that the play world depends for its very existence on the presence of non-participants to mark its boundaries, anyone outside the magic circle will be regarded as "other." This does not mean, however, that these "others" cannot create their own play world with rules and boundaries of its own. Thus any character can be insider and outsider at the same time, depending on one's position in relation to the locus of play.

Summing up the formal characteristics of comedy, one might say that it is a dramatic art form that elicits a comic response in its audience. This response can be a feeling of pleasurable amusement or outright laughter. In order to heighten the spectator's appreciation (cathexis) of the comic, the author creates a comic facade, a play world, in which serious judgment based on ethical considerations is temporarily suspended in favor of playful judgment founded on the functional criteria of winning and losing. This play world can be seen as a separate and exclusive locus, a shelter from reality, which affords reassurance through bonding among on and off-stage participants and through the awareness of the temporary nature of the players' covenant. A comic play is both an artifact in which the tripartite relationship between author/audience and fool comes to the fore, and a series of events witnessed "as if" they were accidental comical occurrences. The characters of comedy can be defined according to their relationship to the play world and judged according to their functional worth or their skill at playing. In accordance with these observations, the following categories of character types emerge: the prankster, the laugher, the fool, the spoil-sport and the cheat. The dynamics of comedy depend primarily on the interaction between these character types and between the various circles of play.

The preceding observations would be of little value were they not to facilitate our understanding of comedy in a very practical way. The following chapters have been devoted to an analysis of Molière's major comedies: an analysis that should prove the fruitfulness of a methodology that takes into account the uniqueness of the comic genre and that does not attempt to impose criteria foreign to it. Molière criticism has been shifting away from traditionally thematic interpretations focusing on moralistic concerns (Lanson, Eustis, Cairncross) to an overriding emphasis on the theatrical and spectacular dimension of his plays (Gossman, Moore, Defaux, Bray). Although I have taken somewhat the same direction as these latter critics, toward the study of "play for play's sake," the theoretical basis of this project is also a praxis that may prove useful for the study of comedy generally and the analytical considerations on gender-based delineation should provide a much needed feminist perspective on Molière.

In establishing circles of ludic activity, Molière draws a clear line of opposition between men and women. Although comic heroines abound, these matrons, servant girls, and ingenues often seem strangely alien to the magic circle of playful activity created by the male protagonists within his works. A type of brotherhood is formed which strongly differentiates between "us" and the "others": those within and without the ludic realm. In *Le Deuxième sexe,* Simone de Beauvoir discusses the proclivity of man to view woman as "Other": "Il est le Sujet, il est l'Absolu: elle est l'Autre. La catégorie de *l'Autre* est aussi originelle que la conscience elle-même. Aucune collectivité ne se définit jamais comme Une sans immédiatement poser l'Autre en face de soi."[27] [He is the Subject, he is the Absolute, she is the other. The category of the Other is as primordial as consciousness itself. Thus it is that no group ever sets itself up as the One without at once setting up the other over against itself.] If by definition the play world is exclusive, it depends for its very existence on the alienation of the Other to mark its boundaries from normal activity.

In an article entitled "How to Read Freud on Jokes,"[28] Jeffrey Mehlman exposes the Oedipal nature of the comic triangle, in which the presence of another enabling *man* can become a means to an indirect form of sexual aggression voiced in the presence or the absence of a targeted *woman* and can contribute to the strengthening of the male bond between joke-maker and witness. Jane Gallop further elaborates on this aspect of Freud's thought in the following terms: "Mehlman's Freud writes the myth (that is the fantasy) of heterosexuality in an economy of homology, analogy. Men exchange women for heterosexual purposes, but the real intercourse is that exchange between men. The heterosexual object is irretrievably lost in the circuits, and the man is consoled by the homology. But the pleasure in the joke, in the homology, the temptation of the analogy points to the homosexual, the anal."[29] Gallop then goes on to distinguish between the homosocial, which she considers to be the realm of identification with the father and patriarchal power, and the homosexual, which she defines as the realm of desire for the father and the subsequent humiliation of the son. Her definition also exposes the homosexual desire hidden behind the homological identification. What is important to this study is the virtual disappearance of the woman, the joke's target, from the Freudian paradigm. According to Freud, the joke's success is predicated upon the fellowship and the convergence of opinion subtending the relationship between joke-maker and witness. The optimal circumstance favoring the joke's reception would therefore be identification, sameness, homology. Woman's otherness makes her automatically appear more resistant to this exchange and it is therefore not at all surprising that she is frequently excluded from the ludic circle.

Most frequently, women are portrayed as outsiders, outcasts and spoil-sports in Molière's comedies. In the following chapters, I propose to examine the critical implications of the nonparticipation of women in the play world. By articulating their otherness, Molière's female characters inevitably articulate the powers attempting to marginalize that otherness, opening up, albeit momentarily, the possibility for modification of the societal structure, only to be ultimately reappropriated by the reigning political order.

What this study will attempt to prove is that the neutral questions previous comic theorists have attempted to resolve are in fact gendered questions. Comic theory has hitherto, under pretext of neutrality, subsumed the Other into the Same. According to Joan Kelly: "We [feminists] have made of sex a category as fundamental to our analysis of the social order as other classifications, such as class and race . . . Embedded in and shaped by the social order, the relation of the sexes must be integral to any study of it."[30] My goal, however, is not to study Molière's female characters in isolation, rather I am compelled to examine the interplay between the sexes, the sexual dynamics of inclusion, exclusion, and intrusion within the comic framework in order to better understand the significance of gender groups and the range in sex roles— how they functioned to maintain the social order and to promote its change.

Although such a reading promises to enrich our understanding of Molière's works, Gail Schwab identifies and warns against the danger of accepting the essentialist vision of woman inherent in the texts, of falling prey to what Luce Irigaray has termed "the blind spot of an old dream of symmetry"[31]: "I agree . . . that essentialism, no matter how utopian, is dangerous for feminism. We cannot risk being trapped in our own Imaginary, since the Symbolic Order, since Political Reality, are too threatening to be ignored, even temporarily."[32] I have found myself constantly torn between the need to expose the prevailing binary oppositions based on gender, such as nature/culture, form/matter, in the subtext of Molière's works and the desire to refute generalizations that lead to a limited and atrophied definition of woman. The fact that these symmetries do exist (not because they are natural and physically determined, but because they are socially imposed) allows me to hope that by exposing them I might reveal the under-

lying fragility of the symbolic order that depends on this imaginary to perpetuate its own myth and perhaps in so doing I may
allude to the moments where the text itself provides its own
models of fissures through which change can occur. As though
afraid of this gap, this hole they create, Molière's texts generally
close in upon themselves, suturing the open wound caused by a
female presence. They harden themselves to intrusion, yet not
without having offered a glimpse of what might be, what might
have been.

2

L'Avare: A Game of Give-and-Take

Il n'est rien de plus sec et de plus aride que ses bonnes grâces;
et donner est un mot pour qui il a tant d'aversion qu'il ne dit
jamais: *je vous donne,* mais *je vous prête* le bonjour.
                                                    —*L'Avare* II, 4

The tragic overtones of *L'Avare* infringe upon its comic content to
such a degree that numerous critics have labeled it as one of
Molière's darkest comedies.[1] I wish to propose a reading of *L'Avare*
that attempts to establish the basis of its unsettling ambivalence
in the bitter struggle for survival subtending the entire plot. The
play's comic element derives from the strategic interplay of the
characters within the parameters of economic bartering: a game
of give-and-take. If *L'Avare* occasionally borders upon the tragic,
this can be ascribed in part to the seriousness of the stakes involved. Harpagon's monolithic presence makes him a dangerous
destructive force intent upon consuming his own offspring for
the sake of survival. The play examines the many facets of possession and dispossession, generosity and greed, and places them
within a specifically gender-defined context. Within this context I
intend to examine feminine and masculine modes of giving and
taking, as well as their connection to matters of life and death.

The opening scene of *L'Avare* exposes the plight of two star-
crossed young lovers: Elise and Valère. In the course of their
discussion, the young man reproaches his beloved for her melancholia: "Hé quoi! charmante Elise, vous devenez mélancolique,
après les obligeantes assurances que vous avez eu la bonté de me
donner de votre foi!" (I,1)[2] [What, charming Elise, you are growing melancholy, after the obliging assurances you were good
enough to give me of your faith?] In an article on *Suréna,* Mitchell
Greenberg proposes an interesting definition of melancholia:

At the center of all melancholia is a loss, an essential void as elusive
as it is pervasive. It is the inscrutability of this void that renders melan-

33

cholia all the more opaque. It might be reasonably easy to ascertain
what "object" the melancholic thinks he has lost. Much more difficult
would be the task of finding what in this object (an object which is
always a metaphor for a more "archaic" object, for an object that is
always a fantasy for an object) has been given up. How, in other words,
has the melancholic been abandoned by the object? In melancholia
the *who* one has lost is always camouflaging the more pernicious
enigma of what has been lost in that loss.[3]

Closer scrutiny of the text reveals the true cause of Elise's sad-
ness. She has lost, or rather has given away, her heart, and in so
doing she does not regret the loss of her heart, but the forfeiture
of her will: her lost autonomy, her ability to resist or even to *want*
to resist. Elise is portrayed as an inexperienced novice overwhelmed by a situation in which she is frozen, passive, and incapable of any form of personal initiative. This creates an overriding
impression of stasis and inertia. She represents the zero degree
of resistance. Incapable of taking charge of her thoughts or her
actions, she becomes the perfect receptacle: an empty space to be
filled by masculine projections and definitions: "Non, Valère, je
ne puis pas me repentir de tout ce que je fais pour vous. Je m'y
sens entraîner par une trop douce puissance, et je n'ai pas même
la force de souhaiter que les choses ne fussent pas" (I,1). [No,
Valère, I cannot repent of anything I do for you. I feel myself
drawn to it by too sweet a power, and I haven't even the strength
to wish that these things were not so.]

Within the context of *L'Avare*, woman's giving is marked by generosity in the absolute, which implies not merely the divestiture
of an object, but of the self as well. Total self-denial implies a loss
of control and the transformation of the loving subject into love
object. Since within the context of this play, woman's empowerment operates through her desirability—that is, man's projected
desire for her—it is always a subsidiary of masculine empowerment and destines her to remain the reflection of man.[4] Elise
is acutely aware that her generosity toward Valère has already
diminished her hold on him: "Mais, à vous dire vrai, le succès me
donne de l'inquiétude; et je crains fort de vous aimer un peu plus
que je ne devrais . . . mais plus que tout, Valère, le changement
de votre coeur, et cette froideur criminelle dont ceux de votre
sexe paient le plus souvent les témoignages d'une innocente
amour" (I,1). [But to tell you the truth, the outcome gives me
some uneasiness; and I am very much afraid that I may love you
a little more than I ought. . . . but more than anything, Valère, a

change in your heart, and that criminal coolness with which those of your sex most often repay any too ardent proof of an innocent love.] Elise is apt to retain control only insofar as she remains miserly in the bestowing of her affection. J.-M. Apostolidès argues that "she does not want to tap the sentimental capital [love] represents. Like her father, but in the domain of libidinal economy, Elise fears loss, the deterioration of feeling and death."[5]

The ingenue, however, is incapable of acting in a calculated manner, strategically planning a form of negative empowerment. Lost autonomy is the very consequence of coupling for the woman whose wishes are subsumed by those of her spouse. As Hélène Cixous indicates: "To pose the question 'What do women want?' is to pose it already as answer, as from a man who isn't expecting any answer, because the answer is 'She wants nothing.' . . . 'What does she want? . . . Nothing!' Nothing because she is passive. The only thing man can do is offer the question 'What could she want, she who wants nothing?' Or in other words: 'Without me, what could she want?'"[6]

Without her lover, Elise would remain in a state of undifferentiation—chaotic, unorganized, and ungoverned. She represents a void that can now be filled by Valère as he teaches her the laws of patriarchy and imposes order on feminine chaos. One is led to wonder whether Elise really exists, whether there is a place for her: a feminine space. This interpretation is corroborated during the final scene of the first act, when Harpagon endows Valère with the status of surrogate father, granting him absolute paternal authority over his daughter, thereby reinforcing the authority the latter has already acquired on his own: "Je veux que tu prennes sur elle un pouvoir absolu. *(A Elise)* Oui, tu as beau fuir, je lui donne l'autorité que le ciel me donne sur toi, et j'entends que tu fasses tout ce qu'il te dira" (I,5). [What? I'm delighted, and I want you to assume absolute power over her. (To Elise) Yes, it's no use trying to run away. I give him the authority that Heaven gives me over you, and I mean to have you do whatever he tells you.] Greenberg defines the husband/father relationship within a patriarchal order in the following terms: "In the actual deflowering of woman, the symbolically invested taking of the hymen, the controlling of sexuality, what is functioning is the Law of the Father, the ideal of all Patriarchy, as it is invested in the containment of another it fears. In this sense, the man to whom is entrusted the task of defloration is always a surrogate for the entire patriarchal order; the husband is always also the Father."[7]

The symbolic nature of this relationship manifests itself in the vivid images of Elise's rebirth through Valère, to whom she now owes her life: "Mon coeur, pour sa défense, a tout votre mérite, appuyé du secours d'une reconnaissance où le ciel m'engage envers vous. Je me représente à toute heure, ce péril étonnant qui commença de nous offrir aux regards d'un de l'autre; cette générosité surprenante qui vous fit risquer votre vie, pour dérober la mienne à la fureur des ondes; ces soins pleins de tendresse que vous me fîtes éclater après m'avoir tirée de l'eau, et les hommages assidus de cet ardent amour que ni le temps, ni les difficultés n'ont rébuté . . ." (I,1). [For its defense, my heart has all your merit, supported by the aid of a gratitude by which Heaven binds me to you. At every moment I recall the astounding peril that first brought us to each other's sight; that surprising generosity that made you risk your life to steal mine from the fury of the waves; those most tender cares that you showed me after having drawn me out of the water, and the assiduous homage of that ardent love which neither time nor difficulties have discouraged . . .] Elise's infatuation with Valère is grounded in her perception of his "surprising generosity." Although the term "généreux" encompasses several meanings for the seventeenth-century audience, it is the word's most common denotation that carries the greatest weight in this play. It is apparent that Valère's generosity is not totally disinterested, and the depiction of the scene is highly charged with eroticism ("ces soins pleins de tendresse que vous me fîtes éclater après m'avoir tirée de l'eau; les hommages assidus de cet ardent amour") [those most tender cares that you showed me after having drawn me out of the water; and the assiduous homage of that ardent love . . .]. In economic terms, Valère's gift of life is merely a loan, to be returned with interest. Elise owes him a debt of gratitude and recognition that lies heavily on her conscience, because acceptance of the gift implies a form of dependency and subordination until restitution is complete: "Obligation is submission to the enormous weight of the other's generosity, is being threatened by a blessing . . . and a blessing is always an evil when it comes from someone else. For the moment you receive something you are effectively 'open' to the other, and if you are a man, you have only one wish, and that is to return the gift, to break the circuit of an exchange that could have no end . . . to be nobody's child, to owe no one a thing."[8]

Elise's "surprise" as she puts it, her vulnerability and her openness to the advances of the first suitor to have offered her something of value, is easily understandable in the context of this play. By standing in for the father at Elise's rebirth, Valère becomes

once again a father surrogate, not for the miserly Harpagon—
who is not a giver, but a taker of life—but for the ideal generous
pater familias: Elise's dream father.

Elise is a prime representative of the ingenue in Molière's theater. Her presence in relation to the play world remains at best
peripheral. Her deep-seated alienation derives primarily from
her status as an object whose possession is solicited as prize or
reward. Not having reached individual awareness, her character
remains largely undifferentiated from her state or status. Valère's
appropriation of Elise is followed by an attempt to enlist her
brother as an accomplice. However, when he enjoins Elise to confide in Cléante and to tell him of their mutual love, she responds
characteristically: "Je ne sais si j'aurai la force de lui faire cette
confidence" (I,1). [I don't know whether I'll have the strength to
confide this to him.] Once again, Elise's inertia qualifies her as a
non-participant in playful strategies. Playing and playacting can
be seen here as strictly masculine prerogatives. Even marginal
involvement becomes impossible as she retreats into silence and
submissiveness. Through her silence, Elise stands outside the
realms of knowledge, play and desire. When Cléante reveals his
own love for Mariane to his sister, Elise will remain reticent in
spite of the obvious opportunity at hand. Beauvoir views such
a flight from autonomy and responsibility as the temptation of
feminine complacency: "En effet, à côté de la prétention de tout
individu à s'affirmer comme sujet, qui est une prétention éthique,
il y a aussi en lui la tentation de fuir sa liberté et de se constituer
en chose: c'est un chemin néfaste car passif, aliéné, perdu, il est
alors la proie de volontés étrangères, coupé de sa transcendance,
frustré de toute valeur. Mais c'est un chemin facile: on évite ainsi
l'angoisse et la tension de l'existence authentiquement assumée.
L'homme qui constitue la femme comme une *Autre* rencontrera
donc en elle de profondes complicités."[9] [When a man makes of
woman the other, he may, then, expect her to manifest deep-
seated tendencies toward complicity. Thus, woman may fail to lay
claim to the status of subject because she lacks definite resources,
because she feels the necessary bond that ties her to man regardless of reciprocity, and because she is often very well pleased with
her role as the other.]

Cléante compensates for his sister's reticence as he waxes eloquent about his beloved Mariane. His description of her is revealing: "Une jeune personne qui loge depuis peu en ces quartiers
et qui semble être faite pour *donner* de l'amour à tous ceux qui la
voient" (I,2). [A young person who has lived in this neighborhood

only a short time, and who seems to be made to inspire love in all who see her.] Mariane has been created for the sole purpose of giving. The ambiguity of the phrasing points to the dual function of Mariane's presence. She both loves and imparts the love that others feel for her. Within the parameters of a loving relationship between Cléante and Mariane, the giving seems singularly one-sided, as the object of desire gives unremittingly of herself. Her generosity is not actively willed, but the result of a form of passive nonresistance and self-denial. Cléante's fantasies include a horizontal vision of the ingenue, or as Cixous would argue: "Woman, if you look for her, has a strong chance of always being found in one position: in bed. In bed and asleep—'laid [out]' . . . And so her trajectory is from bed to bed: one bed to another, where she can dream all the more. There are some extraordinary analyses by Kierkegaard on woman's 'existence'—or that part of it set aside for her by culture—in which he says he sees her as a sleeper. She sleeps, he says, and first love dreams her and then she dreams of love."[10]

Deprived of his father's affection and material wealth, it is not in the least surprising that Cléante, like his sister before him, is fascinated by the spectacle of generosity. Furthermore, Mariane's generous nature can be perceived as entirely disinterested, as the example of her tireless devotion to her ailing mother would tend to prove: "Elle se nomme Mariane, et vit sous la conduite d'une bonne femme de mère qui est presque toujours malade, et pour qui cette aimable fille a des sentiments d'amitié qui ne sont pas imaginables. Elle la sert, la plaint et la console, avec une tendresse qui vous toucherait l'âme" (I,2). [Her name is Mariane, and she lives under the guidance of an old mother who is nearly always sick, and for whom his lovable girl has such affection as cannot be imagined. She serves her, sympathizes with her, and consoles her, with a tenderness that would touch your soul.] If Mariane's virtuous giving is unimaginable to Cléante, it is precisely because he has never before witnessed such selflessness, to which notions of obligation and recognition do not apply. From the vantage point of self-interest, efforts bestowed on an elderly and indigent invalid are entirely wasted, for they carry no return. In his admiration for Mariane, Cléante aspires to emulate her generosity. Ironically, his concept of giving is diametrically opposed to that of the young woman: "Figurez-vous, ma soeur, quelle joie ce peut être que de relever la fortune d'une personne que l'on aime; que de donner adroitement quelques petits secours aux modestes nécessités d'une vertueuse famille; et concevez quel déplaisir ce m'est

de voir que, par l'avarice d'un père, je sois dans l'impuissance de
faire éclater à cette belle aucun témoignage de mon amour" (I,2).
[Just imagine, sister, what a joy it can be to restore the fortunes
of a person we love; to give some little help, adroitly, to the modest
needs of a virtuous family; and think how frustrating it is for me
to see that because of a father's avarice I am powerless to taste
this joy and to display to this beauty any token of my love.] The
joy of giving described by Cléante is primarily that of creating a
bond of obligation whereby Mariane will owe him gratitude and
recognition. The expression "faire éclater" reveals the spectacular
nature of Cléante's desire to impress, which must be witnessed to
have any value. Mariane's recognition would give him the autonomy and the manhood he vitally needs. Thus, the granting and
the withholding of recognition could be a vital form of feminine
power, but the ingenue is inept at manipulation or any form of
self-assertion.

Mariane's first appearance occurs very late in the play, toward
the end of the third act. Her attitude is identical to that of Elise
in the first act, for she is overwhelmed by fear and melancholy.
Her apprehension is due to an overriding feeling of powerlessness
and to her frustrating inability to determine her own destiny: "Ne
vous figurez-vous point les alarmes d'une personne toute prête à
voir le supplice où l'on veut l'attacher?" (III,4) [And can't you
imagine the alarm of a person just about to see the torture that's
in store for her?] To which Frosine replies: "Je vois bien que, pour
mourir agréablement, Harpagon n'est pas le supplice que vous
voudriez embrasser . . ." (III,4). [I see well enough that to die
pleasantly, Harpagon isn't the torture that you'd like to embrace . . .] Frosine's repartee makes rather obvious reference to
"la petite mort," that is to say sexual orgasm. Female arousal here
is associated with bondage and death, the loss of identity through
sexual pleasure, which is seen as inherently masochistic. Embrac-
ing the phallus/*supplice* (instrument of torture) is simultaneously
painful and pleasurable, but most of all terrifying in its implications. The ingenue becomes the sacrificial victim, losing her vir-
ginity/identity when she receives the patriarchal law. Is there life
after death? Frosine, who has herself overcome the limitations of
gender, hints at the resurrection of individual desire in widowhood: the freedom to choose in a form of posthumous adultery:
"Il vaut mieux, pour vous, de prendre un vieux mari qui vous
donne beaucoup de bien. Je vous avoue que les sens ne trouvent
pas si bien leur compte du côté que je dis, et il y a quelques petits
dégoûts à essuyer avec un tel époux; mais cela n'est pas pour

durer; et sa mort, croyez-moi, vous mettra bientôt en état d'en prendre un plus aimable, qui réparera toutes choses" (III,3). The game of give-and-take thus proposed by Frosine is a possible alternative only for the male protagonists or the widow. Dispossessed of her identity, the ingenue cannot take, but can only be taken. Mariane's silence upon meeting Harpagon is reminiscent of Elise's earlier reticence. The ingenue has lost even the desire for self-affirmation through language, as she has been reduced to a mere receptacle-recipient, an ear for the male voice.

Admittedly, there is one occasion in the play when Elise does give voice to an objection.[11] Upon hearing of her betrothal to an older man, she vows that she will not be reduced to such a marriage. Her resistance, however, is limited to a verbal rebuke. Feminine discourse is ineffectual and dismissed as talk or chatter, sound without meaning, an annoying but harmless disturbance. Her threat to commit suicide is ignored as an improbable alternative for a passive object of desire. Such a "masculine" act would imply the will to self-determination through self-destruction and the taking rather than the giving of life. Furthermore, Elise's statement of intent places her squarely outside the parameters of play. Her attitude is that of a misplaced tragic heroine. When Valère attempts a second time to enlist her support and approval as witness and accomplice, Elise again shows herself to be nonsupportive and totally alien to the spirit of comedy as she voices her objection—with three "mais"—to the following strategy: "Faites semblant de consentir à ce qu'il veut, vous en viendrez mieux à vos fins, et . . ." (I,5). [Pretend to give your consent to what he wants, you'll get your way better, and . . .] Elise's hesitation and state of inertia are the consequences of a general feeling of powerlessness and a steadfast adherence to the realm of moral norms, accompanied by an underlying fear of entering the forbidden (to women) realm of play.

Several analogies can be drawn between the two couples and their relationships. Like Valère in the first act, Cléante attempts to enlist Mariane's complicity in his game. When he asks her about her intentions, she responds in a manner reminiscent of Elise: "Hélas! suis-je en pouvoir de faire des résolutions? Et, dans la dépendance où je me vois, puis-je former que des souhaits?" (IV,1) [Alas! Am I in a position to decide anything? And in my dependent situation, can I do anything but wish?] To which Cléante answers reproachfully: "Point de secourable bonté? Point d'affection agissante?" (IV,1) [No other support for me in your heart than mere wishes? No well-intentioned pity? No helpful kindness? No active affection?] Mariane declines any responsibility for her fate, retreating to a rather safe dependency and abdicating an active will in favor of passive wishes. The use of the term "souhaits" in stead of "désirs" is in itself indicative of the meekness and subordination of the ingenue's will. Cléante's reproach is powerful, primarily because his wording is an implicit accusation of non-giving. In her situation of extreme alienation, the ingenue, by nature generous and giving, can supply only sentiment and tenderness, but she is unable to back these up with concrete action because her will was the first thing to be given away.

It is not surprising that at their first encounter, Elise and Mariane reach an immediate understanding based on mutual empathy. Although they qualify their sentiments as a generous friendship, it is clear that they have only moral support to offer each other. Elise exclaims: "Je sais les chagrins et les déplaisirs que sont capables de causer de pareilles traverses; et c'est, je vous assure, avec une tendresse extrême que je m'intéresse à votre aventure" (IV,1). [I know the chagrins and vexations that such crossings can cause; and, I assure you, it is with extreme tenderness that I take an interest in your adventure.] To which Mariane responds: "C'est une douce consolation que de voir dans ses intérêts une personne comme vous; et je vous conjure, madame, de me garder toujours cette généreuse amitié, si capable de m'adoucir les cruautés de la fortune" (IV,1). [It's a sweet consolation to see a person like you espousing one's interests; and I conjure you, Madame, always to keep this generous friendship for me, so capable of softening the cruelties of fortune.] It seems that here we touch upon the problematics of feminine giving. Because it is a generosity oblivious of any return on its investment, it implies self-sacrifice and self-denial. The ingenue gives *of* herself as she gives *herself* and the first step in her giving seems to be the abdication of will and power. This first step, however, curtails any future giving because it reduces her to a state of inertia, which allows her to form only generous and altruistic wishes. Her moral support may console, but it entails no enactment, no project, and no change.

The exclusion of the ingenue from the comic sphere is further heightened by her own awareness of moral obligation. When Mariane reminds Cléante of ethical principles and honorable duty, the young man rejects her code of values as too confining: "Hélas! où me réduisez-vous, que de me renvoyer à ce que voudront me permettre les fâcheux sentiments d'un rigoureux honneur et d'une scrupuleuse bienséance?" (IV,1) [Alas! To what straits you reduce me, by confining me to what is allowed by the frustrating feelings of rigorous honor and scrupulous propriety,] In the realm of play, any such reminder is viewed as "fâcheux," for it spoils the fun by denying the value of the fundamental judgmental criteria of the play world—success or failure—and by reintroducing the moral-ethical limitations and restrictions of the "real" world (see Introduction). Mariane and Elise will remain peripheral to the parameters of this comedy because female participation in playful activity is not condoned: "Mais que voulez-vous que je fasse? Quand je pourrais passer sur quantité d'égards où notre sexe est obligé, j'ai de la considération pour ma mère" (IV,1). [But what would you have me do? Even if I could override a quantity of considerations to which our sex is obliged, I have some consideration for my mother.] As she explains, the behavioral norms she adheres to are both external ("égards où notre sexe est obligé") and internalized ("considération pour ma mère"). It is interesting to note once again that this internalization passes through the image of the mother. The general paralysis characteristic of the ingenue in this play condemns her to confinement within societal norms and to complicity in her own fate. So deep is her alienation that she does not break the rules because she lacks any desire to do so. It is the previously described inertia that allows for such a complete neutralization of the female character in L'Avare.

Mariane's mention of her mother as the ultimate barrier to unorthodox behavior reminds us of the flagrant absence of the mother figure in this play. Cléante and Elise's deceased mother is referred to only once in passing. However, according to Derrida, the voice of the mother remains a disembodied presence, an admonitory force calling on her daughters to assume and internalize their subservience and reminding them of their place within the structures of patriarchy: "For the Mother is the faceless, unfigurable figure of the 'figurante'. She creates a place for all the figures by losing herself in the background like an anonymous persona. All returns to her—and, in the first place—all addresses and destines itself to her. She survives—in the condition of remaining in the background."[12] She represents the voice of moral orthodoxy, reminding her daughter of her place as Other, "outside" the realm of play.

While patriarchal tyranny causes a state of inertia and melancholy in Elise and Mariane, transforming them into women-objects, it produces a desire for survival and rebellion in the young male protagonists. This dichotomous effect is caused by the inherent difference between masculine and feminine modes of giving that imparts the underlying tension to *L'Avare.* The ingenue gives unreservedly and her generosity is a form of self-denial, whereas man's giving is governed by strategy and reckoning: it is a form of calculated generosity of which the miser-usurer is the extreme embodiment in this play and the example that the younger men unwittingly emulate. In the sexual arena, Cixous cites Don Juan as the prime example of male investment: "Take Don Juan and you have the whole masculine economy getting together to 'give women just what it takes to keep them in bed,' then swiftly taking back the investment, then reinvesting, etc., so that nothing ever gets given, everything gets taken back, while in the process the greatest possible dividend of pleasure is taken. Consumption without payment, of course."[13] Calculated generosity never loses sight of self-interest. It is spectacular in nature, a visible reminder of the debtor's obligation, demanding his recognition, and as such it insures the giver's autonomy.

By retaining complete control of his material possessions, Harpagon deprives his son of his autonomy and robs him symbolically of his masculinity. When Cléante feels faint upon hearing of his father's intention of marrying Mariane, Harpagon belittles his prowess: "Voilà de mes demoiseaux fluets, qui n'ont plus de vigueur que des poules" (I,4). [There's one of your dainty young men for you, with no more vigor than a chicken.] The father's derision reveals his desire to retain phallic power for himself, while emasculating his son. Harpagon so closely identifies with his possessions that divestiture in any form is equated with self-mutilation and castration.[14] The power conferred by money (and lack thereof) is unequivocally linked to male sexual prowess within the context of this play. As La Flèche points out, giving is so foreign to the Miser that even the act of fathering a child can be viewed as a reduction of, or an abdication from patriarchal power. Having reluctantly *given* life to his children, he now attempts to reduce his children to nonentities or at the very least to capitalize on their existence: "Si la désaffection et la souffrance des enfants se ramènent pour l'essentiel à leur manque d'argent, le pouvoir du père se fonde sur sa volonté d'agrandir le patrimoine qu'il veut *intransmissible.*"[15] [If the children's lack of affection and suffering can be attributed essentially to their lack of money, the father's power is founded on his desire to increase the patrimony that he wants to remain intransmissable.] (Translation by author) Cléante's machinations are carried out with grim desperation because his game is in reality a fight for survival and autonomy, a struggle to overthrow his father's relentless power: "Peut-on rien voir de si cruel que cette rigoureuse épargne qu'on exerce sur nous, que cette sécheresse étrange où l'on nous fait languir? Hé! que nous servira d'avoir du bien, s'il ne nous vient que dans le temps que nous ne serons plus dans le bel âge d'en jouir; et si, pour m'entretenir même, il faut que maintenant je m'engage de tous côtés; si je suis réduit avec vous à chercher tous les jours les secours des marchands, pour avoir moyen de porter des habits raisonnables" (I,2). [For after all, can anything be more cruel than this rigorous economy that is inflicted on us, this extraordinary parsimony in which we are made to languish? And what good will it do us to have money if it comes to us only when we are no longer at a good age to enjoy it, and if, even to maintain myself, I now have to go into debt on all sides, if like you I am reduced to seeking help every day from tradesmen to have enough to wear decent clothes?] Instead of providing spiritual and material nourishment for his children, Harpagon bleeds them dry, saps their strength. It is interesting to note how often the verb "réduire" is used in this context. Like the mythological father Chronos, Harpagon's ultimate intent is to consume his offspring in the absence of a protective mother, his purpose being to deny the effects of natural succession on his hegemony. The generous life-giving mother is notoriously absent and the father is determined to feed off the younger generation. The play evokes the preternatural fear of paternal destruction and infanticide.

Of all of Molière's blocking figures, Harpagon is perhaps the most menacing and the most "unnatural." The nature of his obsession is neither playful nor harmless. The Miser's presence threatens others with starvation, desiccation, and ultimately the possibility of annihilation. Although Harpagon admires Valère's admonishment—"il faut manger pour vivre et non pas vivre pour manger" (III,1) [we must eat to live and not live to eat]—he refuses sustenance to all, literally starving his children, his domestic servants, and even his horses. In spite of his infatuation with Mariane, Harpagon insists that she bring a dowry into the marriage in the following terms: "Lui as-tu dit qu'il fallait qu'elle s'aidât un peu, qu'elle fît quelque effort, qu'elle se saignât pour une occasion comme celle-ci?" (II,5) [Did you tell her that she had to bestir herself, make some effort, and bleed herself, for an occasion like this one?] Harpagon wants others to bleed themselves, to drain themselves of life-sustaining fluids, to dry up and wither away while he flourishes. His vitality is inversely proportional to that of his entourage. Like the vampire of lore, Harpagon feeds off the living in his quest for eternal rejuvenation.

Harpagon draws his formidable strength from his monolithic nature. Isolation is a necessary and desirable condition to him. The verbs "renfermer" ("to enclose") and "cacher" ("to hide") are repeatedly used to reinforce this impression of closure. His suspicious attitude causes him to stand apart, to withdraw from the sphere of public activity. He is an impenetrable block consisting of the One, the watchful eye: a seamless whole with no loopholes or cracks. Accordingly, his relationships are unilaterally adversarial. Paradoxically, his privacy invites penetration, disclosure, and exposure. However, as his opponents are drawn to him, forced to confront him on his grounds, the Miser retains the strategic territorial advantage. This becomes apparent when Valère explains his tactics to Elise: "Vous voyez comme je m'y prends, et les adroites complaisances qu'il m'a fallu mettre en usage pour m'introduire à son service; sous quel masque de sympathie et de rapports de sentiments je me déguise pour lui plaire, et quel personnage je joue tous les jours avec lui, afin d'acquérir sa tendresse. J'y fais des progrès admirables; et j'éprouve que, pour gagner les hommes, il n'est point de meilleure voie que de se parer à leurs yeux de leurs inclinations, que de donner dans leurs maximes, encenser leurs défauts, et applaudir à ce qu'ils font . . ." (I,1). [You see how I am going about it, and the adroit complaisance I have had to employ to make my way into his service; what a mask of sympathy and conformity of feelings I disguise myself under to please him, and what a part I play with him every day so as to win his affection. I am making admirable progress in this; and I find that to win men, there is no better way than to adorn oneself before their eyes with their inclinations, fall in with their maxims, praise their defects, and applaud whatever they do.] Valère's boasting conceals the essential fact that someone else is calling the shots. Harpagon is a redoubtable opponent precisely because the rules of the game are determined by his whims and to his advantage.

The game of give-and-take is primarily a man's game that pits Harpagon against a younger generation fighting quite literally for its survival. This factor accounts for the audience's ambivalent reaction to *L'Avare*. On the one hand we find a playful construct in which the criterion of success has replaced ethical qualms: a transition legitimized by Harpagon's inhumanity. On the other, we find a struggle between father and son motivated by the genuine fear of reduction and absorption into the One who "takes back." The bitterness of the conflict is illustrated by a bilateral death wish: Cléante assures his moneylender that his father will be dead within a matter of months, while Harpagon is flattered by Frosine's assurances that he will surely outlive his progeny. Having arrived at old age, the father refuses to abdicate and turn power and wealth over to his rightful heir. Instead he jealously guards the source of his hegemony. If Valère and Cléante's pranks seem so ineffective, it is because their playful ruses are inappropriate and inadequate defenses against the very real threat of annihilation represented by the Miser.

Harpagon's fascination with material wealth is at once comparable to the obsession of a fetishist, for whom objects take on a life of their own,[16] and inversely an infatuation with the power such wealth confers to him by allowing him to reduce other living beings to the status of material possessions: "This inversion of values that dehumanizes human beings likewise humanizes things, at least the most essential thing: money."[17] Although Harpagon has drawn his strength from the deprivation of others, the process has drained him of any human emotions. Frosine may know "l'art de traire les hommes" [the art of milking men], but there is no life-sustaining substance, no sap to be drawn out of Harpagon: "Le Seigneur Harpagon est de tous les humains l'humain le moins humain, le mortel de tous les mortels le plus dur et le plus serré. Il n'est point de service qui pousse sa reconnaissance jusqu'à lui faire ouvrir les mains . . . Il n'est rien de plus sec et aride que ses bonnes grâces et ses caresses, et donner est un mot pour qui il a tant d'aversion, qu'il ne dit jamais 'je vous donne', mais 'je vous prête le bonjour'" (II,4). [Seigneur Harpagon is of all humans the least human human; the mortal of all mortals who is hardest and most close-fisted. There is no service that drives his gratitude to the point of making him open his hands. Praise, esteem, and good will in words, friendliness—all you like; but money—nothing doing. There is nothing more dry and arid than his good graces and his compliments; and *give* is a word for which he has such an aversion that he never says *I give you*, but *I lend you good day*.] Once again, images of dryness and desiccation abound, as a comparison is drawn between Harpagon and an object, an empty shell. Significantly, one should remember here that Elise's "rebirth" took place in the water. La Flèche's allusion to the disparity between the gift and the loan exposes the fundamentally masculine economy governing the play world.

The introduction of the woman (Mariane) as object of desire serves both as a guarantor of sexual potency and as the reward validating the superiority of the dominant male. Within the realm of play, she maintains the status of token to be desired, bartered, and possessed. The reification of woman is best expressed by Harpagon when Frosine extols the merits of a thrifty wife: "mais ce compte-là n'est rien de réel ... et il faut bien que je touche à quelque chose" (II,5). [but there's nothing real in that accounting ... and I've got to get some money out of this.] What concerns Harpagon is not the intangible "being" or essence, not the inner self, but the palpable and controllable object. The Miser views the object as the ultimate reality. Although the process of reification described above allows him to retain control over his entourage, material goods seem inversely endowed with a life of their own. Harpagon lives in terror of things getting away from him ("s'écarter") or being worn out ("s'user") by virtue of their perishable nature. In fact, Harpagon's suspicious mind endows inanimate objects with willful insubordination.[18] The critic Montbertrand attributes the personification of money to Harpagon's subconscious efforts to infuse the object of possession (form) with his own governing ideology (substance). But inversely, the subject becomes possessed by the object, having emptied himself into its form. This, Montbertrand argues, is certainly the case of Arnolphe, in *L'Ecole des Femmes*, who becomes a slave to his own creation.[19]

Harpagon's attempt to suppress his successor by retaining phallic power expresses a desire to be without rival and to triumph over death by becoming his son's sexual surrogate. Ultimately, it is a denial of his own mortality and an affirmation of his irreplaceability. Harpagon's greed for life is reflected in a parallel manner by his choice of a husband for his daughter. Anselme, who is twice Elise's age, can be seen as another father surrogate, a means for Harpagon to symbolically retain possession of his daughter. Harpagon desires his daughter only insofar as she retains the status of an object with the potential for investment and capitalization.

Valère stands in marked contrast to Elise's submissiveness. He is an initiator who has absolved himself of any moral qualms, arguing that Harpagon's miserly behavior necessitates and legitimizes revolt: "et la manière austère dont il vit avec ses enfants, pourrai[en]t authoriser des choses plus étranges" (I,1). [and the excess of his avarice and the austere way he lives with his children could authorize even stranger things.] Valère is also a comedian who has entered the miser's household on false pretenses and under an assumed identity, sure of his ability to win Elise as his bride. There is a disturbing element of dishonesty and sheer callousness in Valère's character, reminiscent of Tartuffe: "La sincérité souffre un peu au métier que je fais; mais, quand on a besoin des hommes, il faut bien s'ajuster à eux; et, puisqu'on ne saurait les gagner que par [la flatterie], ce n'est pas la faute de ceux qui flattent, mais de ceux qui veulent être flattés" (I,1). [Sincerity suffers a bit in the trade I am plying; but when you need men, you simply have to adjust to them; and since that's the only way to win them over, it's not the fault of those who flatter, but of those who want to be flattered.] His self-exoneration might be extended to include another, more pernicious meaning: the victim of deceit is more to blame than the cheat or the joker. Valère is simply proposing the substitution of playful judgmental criteria (for instance, winner takes all) for notions of right and wrong. As a comedian, Valère glories in his freedom from ethical concerns, in his liberating and legitimized amorality, his weightlessness. Harpagon's extreme selfishness, which impoverishes and imperils the lives of his children, authorizes the creation of a play world of fantasy and disguise.

Act 2 finds Cléante setting up a strategy of his own. The weakening of Cléante's autonomy, already threatened by his father's invasiveness, is further perpetuated by his indebtedness to all and sundry. Ironically, he has unwittingly called upon his father to be his creditor, thus representing his impotence and dependency symbolically. The son's aborted attempt at borrowing from his father has a major thematic ramification. It discloses Harpagon's activities as a usurer—the epitomized embodiment of the previously discussed male economy: investment with return interest. Although any lender wields power, Harpagon's authority rests mainly on his material possessions. The very foundation of his dominance is immanent rather than transcendent. The miser's vulnerability lies in his dependency on the tangible source of his hegemony: material wealth. Cléante himself can neither understand nor imagine any system other than the one perpetuated by his father. Even more than Valère before him, he is forced to play by his father's rules.

In the course of his introduction to Mariane, Cléante succeeds, at least temporarily, in assuming his father's voice, in usurping his identity and in giving tokens of his affection to his beloved: "Souffrez, madame, que je me mette ici à la place de mon père . . ." (III,7). [Allow me, Madame, to put myself in my father's place . . .] This is an act of appropriation, not only of the father's goods, but of the ingenue as well. Cléante expresses very clearly his desire to take his father's place, rather than to define a space of his own or to invent himself. Rebellion against paternal authority does not necessarily exclude identification with paternal values.

Like the father he condemns, Cléante's gift-giving is motivated by his desire to create a bond of obligation between himself and Mariane, who is viewed as a possession to be transferred from father to son: "Le bonheur de vous posséder est, à mes regards, la plus belle de toutes les fortunes; c'est où j'attache toute mon ambition. Il n'y a rien que je ne sois capable de faire pour une conquête si précieuse" (III,7). [Yes, Madame, the happiness of possessing you is in my eyes the fairest of all fortunes; I set my whole ambition on that; there is nothing I am incapable of doing to make so precious a conquest;] Consistent with her attitude of self-denial, Mariane remains the reluctant and passive recipient of these gifts.

Sensing foul play, Harpagon devises a counterruse to learn of his son's true feelings for Mariane. In the course of the dialogue between father and son, the Miser reveals himself to be a masterful and shrewd strategist, a formidable opponent who can easily outwit the less experienced Cléante. Once again, Mariane is referred to as a prize object, whose own desires are never taken into consideration. "Je te l'aurais donnée, sans l'aversion que tu témoignes" (IV,3). [I would have given her to you, but for the aversion you show.] The difference between Harpagon and his son is one of degree and not nature. According to William Kennedy: "The play's problematic laughter stems from the idea that Harpagon's children are no more capable of justifying the proprieties than their father is. Their language of love turns out to be as abusive as his language of money, and so do their mores."[20] This statement is in direct contradiction to Pineau's contention that: "Tout un monde varié de gens qui aiment et qui s'aiment forme une couronne radieuse autour de la sinistre forteresse rebelle à tous les assauts de l'humanité [Harpagon]."[21] [A diversified world of lovers forms a radiant crown around the sinister fortress resistant to all of the assaults of humanity (Harpagon).] (Translation by author)

Harpagon ends the dispute by playing his trump card and disinheriting his son. Cléante had quite naturally been banking on his father's death and on the subsequent inheritance for his survival. This gesture ensures the refusal of autonomy posthumously:

Harpagon: Je te donne ma malédiction.
Cléante: Je n'ai que faire de tes dons.

(IV,5)

Harpagon: And I give you my curse.
Cléante: I have no use for your gifts.

The interchange contains an inherent contradiction which stresses the negative value of every one of Harpagon's gifts in the equation: giving = taking. In a sudden reversal of his previous attitude, Cléante indicates his desire for autonomy by declaring his attempt at self-reliance and his freedom from paternal purse strings. But his newfound courage will never be put to the test.

Cléante will attempt to compensate for his inadequacy by enlisting the support of La Flèche and Frosine. Frosine, the go-between, is an experienced schemer from the seamy underworld, who is forced to play in order to survive: "Tu sais que, dans le monde, il faut vivre d'adresse, et qu'aux personnes comme moi, le ciel n'a donné d'autres rentes que l'intrigue et l'industrie" (II,4). [You know that in this world you have to live by your wits, and that Heaven has given people like me no other revenue than intrigue and ingenuity.] It has by now become apparent that most of the interplay is adversarial because almost every character involved has his or her survival at stake. Frosine is the one woman to become at least marginally involved in what might otherwise be seen as a man's game. She can do so because her age has de-erotized her, unsexed her. Her presence does carry with it a certain unsavory reminder of a lubricous past, but her present neutered-neutral status affords her access into the parameters of play.

La Flèche reveals himself to be a skillful and cautious player: "Je sais tirer adroitement mon épingle du jeu, et me démêler prudemment de toutes les galanteries qui sentent tant soit peu l'échelle" (II,1). [I know how to steer clear, and keep prudently out of all those gallantries that smell the least bit of the gallows.] The valet's presence only helps to underline Cléante's general ineptitude as a trickster. It is ultimately La Flèche who most clearly understands that paternal power depends on the money box and that by stealing it he both literally and symbolically robs the Miser of his legitimacy.

Harpagon's identification with his money is so intense as to provoke a delirium that reveals his own profound alienation: "Hélas! mon pauvre argent! mon pauvre argent! mon cher ami! on m'a privé de toi; et, puisque tu m'es enlevé, j'ai perdu mon support, ma consolation, ma joie; tout est fini pour moi et je n'ai plus que faire au monde. Sans toi, il m'est impossible de vivre" (IV,7). [Alas! My poor money, my poor money, my dear friend! They've deprived me of you; and since you are taken from me, I've lost my support, my consolation, my joy; all is finished for me, and there's nothing more for me to do in this world; without

you, it's impossible for me to live.] Harpagon *is* his money. The
monolithic composure breaks under tension to reveal the Miser's
dependency:

"Le vol de la cassette aboutit chez [Harpagon] à un voeu d'anéantisse-
ment de soi, car il s'avère enfin prêt à se pendre s'il ne retrouve pas
son argent. Conformément à la déconfiture totale subie par Arnolphe
dans l'expérience du cocuage, cette obsession du vol débouche chez
Harpagon sur le sentiment aigu de sa propre désagrégation, la média-
tion de l'argent lui permettant seule d'exister dans le monde. Ainsi, à
la formule 'je possède, donc je suis,' qui pourrait s'appliquer aussi bien
au 'fanatique de la corne' qu'à l'avare, correspond la formule qui illustre au mieux leur ignominie finale: 'Je suis dépossédé, donc je ne suis
plus.'"[22] [The theft of his money-box results in Harpagon's wish for
self-annihilation, for he demonstrates his readiness to hang himself
if he does not regain his money. Similar to the total collapse suffered
by Arnolphe in his experience of cuckoldry, this obsession with theft
ends with Harpagon's painful awareness of his own disintegration,
since money is the only mediating factor allowing him to survive in
the world. Thus, corresponding to the formula 'I own, therefore I
am,' which could apply equally well to the 'one obsessed by cuckoldry'
as to the miser, is the formula that best illustrates their final ignominy
'I am dispossessed, therefore I no longer am.'] (Translation by author)

Harpagon's paranoia causes him to suspect everyone, including
himself. He is, in fact, the prime culprit, because his closure, far
from concealing his wealth, has invited the intrusion of others.
He has proven to be his own worst enemy.

Accused by Maître Jacques of stealing the money, Valère misun-
derstands the nature of the accusation, believing that Harpagon
has learned about his seduction of Elise. The ambiguity of the
dialogue between Harpagon and Valère is the most striking illus-
tration of the ingenue's object status. If the quid pro quo is so
effective, it is precisely because words like "trésor," "biens," and
"don" can be credibly applied to the ingenue. Valère's argument
implies an acute understanding of the patriarch's problem with
divestiture. He tries to reassure Harpagon by persuading him
that you can give without incurring a loss: "C'est un trésor, il est
vrai, et le plus précieux que vous ayez, sans doute; mais ce ne sera
pas le perdre que de me le laisser. Je vous le demande à genoux,
ce trésor plein de charmes; et pour bien faire, il faut que vous me
l'accordiez" (V,3). [It's a treasure, that's true, and beyond a doubt
the most precious that you have; but you won't be losing it by
leaving it to me. On my knees I ask you for it, this most charming

treasure; and to do right, you must grant it to me.] In fact, the refusal of expenditure in any form amounts to sterility and absolute loss, that is, death.[23] This is confirmed by Harpagon's death wish for his daughter. When Valère fails in his attempt to win her hand, Elise intervenes to apprise her father of his indebtedness to Valère for having saved her life. Harpagon's inhumanity is revealed by his total indifference to his daughter's well-being. If her existence stands as a sign of indebtedness, he would as soon eradicate one proof of obligation in order to avoid recognition of another: "Tout cela n'est rien; et il valait bien mieux pour moi qu'il te laissât noyer que de faire ce qu'il a fait" (V,4).

By stealing the money-box, La Flèche has enabled Cléante for the first time to have bargaining power. The players can finally match wits and confront each other with a series of give and take moves, trading money for Mariane, reducing her even further to the status of token. Cléante warns his father: "Tout ne dépend que de moi. C'est à vous de me dire à quoi vous vous déterminez; et vous pouvez choisir, ou de me donner Mariane, ou de perdre votre cassette" (V,6). [All of this depends on me alone. It is up to you to tell me what you determined and you can choose either to give me Mariane, or to lose your money-box.] Surprisingly, however, the play does not end on this note. Nor does a clever stratagem, previously conceived by Frosine, materialize. The ineffectiveness of the multiple but uncoordinated efforts by Valère, Cléante, Frosine, and La Flèche to unseat and destabilize Harpagon convincingly reveals the tenacity of his power. The importance of economics in insuring autonomy and power is all the more evident, as only the men handle or control the money, whereas the ingenue's presence can only permit the transmission of wealth from one man to another.

The ineptitude of the various pranksters in this play may have as ultimate cause a more serious obstacle: deep-seated societal consecration of the patriarchal order, as embodied in Harpagon. It will take another father, the dream father—the ideal patriarch—to supersede Harpagon. Anselme represents the father who gives as opposed to the father who takes, and fortunately for him, he has been able to preserve his riches, as he quickly points out to his children: "Oui, ma fille; oui, mon fils; je suis dom Thomas d'Alburcy, que le ciel garantit des ondes avec tout l'argent qu'il portait . . ." (V,5). [Yes, my daughter, yes, my son, I am Don Thomas d'Alburcy, whom Heaven saved from the waves with all the money he had on him . . .] As Elise's fantasies of a generous father come to life, Anselme's coincidental appearance allows for the unification of the diverse spheres of playful activity. The pranksters' separate attempts are now assumed by the generous father as the play closes on a general note of clemency for all. The unrepentant Miser abdicates his power by retiring to anonymity with his "sterile" mistress, the money box.[24]

The pernicious message inherent in the ending is that it takes one patriarch to defeat another. Anselme's overthrow of Harpagon has simply consolidated the paternal hegemony. No significant change has taken place within the structures of power. Anselme, a late entrant in the game, becomes the winner. It is through magnanimity that he usurps power and will maintain it, for Cléante and Valère have become his debtors. Unlike Harpagon, Anselme allows his currency to circulate, thereby permitting it once again to be exchanged and to "reproduce." The same holds true for the ingenues who can now be transferred to their lovers as possessions that will bear fruit.[25] The return on Anselme's invested generosity will be the subservient gratitude of his sons, which will allow him to rule unchallenged and thus preserve the status quo; a status quo that perpetuates the reification of women and hinders their direct participation in playful challenge. It is significant in this regard that Anselme's long-lost wife and the mother of his children remains offstage and invisible in this final scene of joyous reunification.

Ultimately, Cléante and Valère's failure can be blamed upon their lack of imagination and inventiveness in playing the game. Throughout they rely on rules of economic dependency established by the Father. Thus, the younger men are always playing into his hand. Their own ideas on give and take, unlike those of the ingenues, are patterned after those of the Miser they detest. Their only salvation would have been in inventing an economy of their own, where a person's value is essential and internalized. By doing so, however, they would transgress the comic sphere and enter the realm of serious drama.

3

Dom Juan: Of Myth and Men

C'est une affaire entre le Ciel et moi.
—*Dom Juan* I, 2

In her recent work on *Dom Juan,* Shoshana Felman argues that: "The lack of structure of Molière's play has often been criticized, along with the absence of connection between scenes. But such criticism fails to see that in this play breaks constitute, paradoxically, the connecting principle itself."[1] To view the play as an arbitrary sum of disorderly displacements does not take into account the consistency of Dom Juan's inconsistency. Inconstancy becomes so much a matter of principle that Dom Juan becomes a prisoner of his own evasiveness. It is the oxymoronic nature of this inverted logic subtending the dramatic structure of *Dom Juan* that fascinates the modern critic. Dom Juan is governed by a fixation similar to that of Molière's other monomaniacs, and that fixation is movement itself. According to Larry Riggs, it is this very transience that causes the hero's final "evaporation" from the play: "He tries to avoid the network of mutual obligations and expectations that gives society its cohesiveness and gives the individual both identity and ethical limitations. Indeed, he fails to recognize that identity requires limitations—it cannot exist without delimitation, or form."[2]

Lack of essence, however, determines the spectator's perception of Dom Juan as a comic figure, not to be judged according to ethical criteria, but according to his ability to win the game. David Shaw argues that: "The sympathy we feel, in varying degrees, for Elvire, Don Carlos and Don Louis is always contaminated by admiration of the way in which Don Juan outwits them."[3] Felman adds that: "Language, for Don Juan, is performative and not informative; it is a field of enjoyment, not of knowledge. As such, it cannot be qualified as true or false, but rather as *felicitous* or *infelicitous,* successful or unsuccessful."[4]

Dom Juan is presented as a ruthless tactician, a skillful gambler, and an eloquent persuader: a winner in short, whose play world contains the seeds of its own destruction, however. Although he acknowledges the rules of social interaction on the surface (i.e., the aristocratic code of honor, the laws of matrimony, the institution of charity), he breaks them for his own profit and substitutes counterfeit rewards for real ones. Dom Juan is perhaps the most flagrant example in Molière's opus of the cheat, and the cheat is by definition a solitary player who gives the outward appearance of sociable participation and adherence to the rules of the game. Although on the most basic level the play's dynamics derive from male-female adversity, *Dom Juan*'s propelling forces and dramatic tension ultimately reside in the confrontation between ethics and aesthetics, between comic and tragic vision, between the sacred realm of monumental space and time and the profane world of disconnected and fragmented moments that are associated with the play's hero.

Sganarelle opens the play by extolling the virtues of tobacco. His seemingly innocuous banter, while placing us squarely in the comic world of instant gratification, provides us nonetheless with a parody of moral *sententia*. The spectator learns from Dom Juan's valet that generosity is one of the primary attributes of the "honnête homme" and that the act of disinterested giving is synonymous with virtue: "Non seulement [le tabac] réjouit et purge les cerveaux humains, mais encore il instruit les âmes à la vertu, et l'on apprend avec lui à devenir honnête homme. Ne voyez-vous pas bien, dès qu'on en prend, de quelle manière obligeante on en use avec tout le monde, et comme on est ravi d'en donner à droite et à gauche, partout où l'on se trouve? On n'attend pas même qu'on en demande, et l'on court au-devant du souhait des gens: tant il est vrai que le tabac inspire des sentiments d'honneur et de vertu à tous ceux qui en prennent" (I,1). [Snuff not only cheers and clears your brain, but also improves your soul. You become high-minded; you learn to act like a gentleman. Watch someone take a pinch: he immediately turns friendly, loves to pass the box around, right and left, no matter where he is. He doesn't even wait for the others to ask him; he's ahead of their wishes. That proves how snuff inspires people who take it, makes them kind and honest.][5] It remains to be seen, however, what is really meant by the term "honnête homme." In the seventeenth century this human ideal is considered not so much a moral but a social prototype illustrating the values of politeness, civility and urbanity. The "honnête homme" has above all a winning disposition, which allows him to ingratiate himself with others and attain thereby a high degree of sociability. In this context, the very word "vertu" loses its moral connotation and acquires synonymy with a type of social generosity. The art of pleasing is equated with true communication and sharing between equals as opposed to affectation and vainglorious ostentation. It is doubtful, therefore, whether Sganarelle's opinion is representative of a moral perspective in the true sense of the word. In any event, Sganarelle's discourse is fraught with illogicalities and nonsequiturs. The normative language to which he gives voice is thus thoroughly discredited by its lack of coherence. Furthermore, as Riggs points out: "Sganarelle illustrates the benefits of generous gestures by distributing imaginary pinches of *someone else's* snuff. Indeed, the social consequences of gestures intended to create an impressive appearance of generosity without actually giving anything of substance are a principal preoccupation of this play."[6]

The same critic contends that Dom Juan, who tries to evade or repay real debts with empty gestures, resembles Molière's other protagonists in that he destroys his own substance by destroying that of his relationships. Sganarelle's rhetorical stance should prepare the spectator to favor Dom Juan's cynical amorality over his servant's superstitious credulity and mindless adherence to social conventions. Still, it will become increasingly apparent that the nobleman is a short-term investor strongly lacking in disinterested generosity. The protagonist's shortcomings will become increasingly apparent from an ethical as well as from a social perspective.

As Sganarelle goes on to explain, Done Elvire, the last in a long line of conquests, has come to town to confront Dom Juan with his unexplained departure: "Si bien donc, cher Gusman, que Done Elvire, ta maîtresse, surprise de notre départ, s'est mise en campagne après nous, et son coeur, que mon maître a su toucher trop fortement, n'a pu vivre, dis-tu, sans le venir chercher ici. Veux-tu qu'entre nous je te dise ma pensée? J'ai peur qu'elle ne soit mal payée de son amour, que son voyage en cette ville produise peu de fruit, et que vous eussiez autant gagné à ne bouger de là" (I,1). [You say the mistress was shocked when we took off? She came chasing after us because she loves the master so much she can't go on without him? You know what I think? Between us, I'm afraid her love's an investment with a rotten return. There's no real point in Doña Elvire's trip here. You might as well have stayed put.] The military metaphors used in this expository statement reveal from the play's inception the tenor of the male-female relationship. It is, by its very nature, conflictual. Interestingly enough, however, it is the woman, not the man, who is viewed as the aggressor. By actively pursuing the hero, Elvire has stepped out of line. She has transgressed the boundaries of "proper" feminine behavior and has entered into male territory by usurping the masculine prerogative of positive initiative. It is obvious that Dom Juan's strategy is based upon a conventional knowledge of the restrictions affecting feminine behavior, which give him the upper hand in any negotiation. Elvire's uncharacteristic aggressiveness, however, leaves the hero disarmed, since he did not anticipate such an offensive adversarial move on her part.

Sganarelle's allusion to Elvire as "mal payée" leaves no doubt as to her intention. She has come to Dom Juan, fully prepared to collect upon her investment. Having had to give up her religious vocation in exchange for marital bliss, she intends to recover her philandering husband. Characterized throughout the play by his indebtedness, the hero has no intention of honoring his obligation. As his manservant warns, "Un mariage ne lui coûte rien à contracter; il ne se sert point d'autres pièges pour attraper les belles, et c'est un épouseur à toutes mains" (I,1). [A marriage costs him nothing; it's his usual way of trapping beauties. He'll marry them all.] In the preceding chapter on *L'Avare,* I allude to Hélène Cixous' pertinent observation on the issue of Dom Juan as the embodiment of the masculine economy: "Take Don Juan and you have the whole masculine economy getting together to 'give women just what it takes to keep them in bed' then swiftly taking back the investment, then reinvesting, etc., so that nothing ever gets given, everything gets taken back, while in the process the greatest possible dividend of pleasure is taken."[7] Whereas in *L'Avare* the economic investments discussed were hard currency, here the investment is one's entire being.

Dom Juan's counterfeit commitment, his moral weightlessness endanger not only the female of the species, for whom marriage represents far more than a formal contract, but the entire social structure as well. The security of the marital relationship is the primary compensation for the ensuing loss of identity within that institution. By obliterating the value of marriage, the protagonist jeopardizes the value of the proffered word, the oath, which thereby loses its social function. It is upon such oaths that relationships of trust, interdependency, and solidarity can be built. Dom Juan's perfect disregard for any form of commitment—be it religious, filial, marital, or financial—is an assertion of an individual freedom that infringes on the freedom of others. He barely acknowledges his indebtedness to Pierrot for having saved him from

drowning. Like Elvire, the peasant is "mal payé," for not only does
Dom Juan dismiss the bond of obligation, which would by its very
nature place him in a relationship of inferiority with Pierrot, but
he repays the latter's generosity by courting his fiancée Charlotte.

As a player and tactician Dom Juan can be seen as a counter-
feiter, whose false currency endangers and nearly causes the collapse of the entire economic structure of the community in which
he operates. According to Jacques Cellard, Dom Juan's sexual
strategy might be more aptly termed a political strategy: "Don
Juan lui-même, et les femmes auxquelles il s'adresse, se disent:
'Oh, mon Dieu, notre plaisir va être dans la symbolique même
de la parole?' C'est-à-dire qu'il suffira à Don Juan d'obtenir la
transgression ou la certitude qu'il a cette transgression de la part
d'une femme. Parce que, là, il y a un acte politique, une volonté
politique de bousculer, de subvertir l'ordre de la société. Est-ce
que, fondamentalement, la sexualité de Don Juan ne serait pas
une sexualité uniquement politique, à laquelle répondrait effec-
tivement une autre forme de sexualité politique de la part des
femmes . . . ?"[8] [Don Juan himself and his female interlocutors
say to themselves: "Oh, my God, will our pleasure thus consist in
the symbolic nature of the word itself?" In other words, it will
suffice for Don Juan to obtain the transgression or the certitude
he has of that transgression by a woman. Because, if that is the
case, there is a political act, a political will to trample, to subvert
the societal order. Could it not be that fundamentally Don Juan's
sexuality is an exclusively political sexuality, to which another form
of feminine political sexuality would effectively correspond . . . ?]
(Translation by author)

Ironically, Dom Juan's moral weightlessness, his refusal to allow
for any form of infringement on his freedom, is contingent upon
perpetual movement. One might say that, paradoxically, the hero
is condemned to continuous motion in order to assert his freedom
from the societal order. The minute he stands still, he finds himself beleaguered and besieged by a host of creditors. Marcel Gutwirth points out that: "Une fois arrêté Dom Juan s'écroule. Le
branle universel de tous ceux qu'il a lésés se convertit en siège. Il
repousse tous leurs assauts jusqu'à ce que l'immobilité de la pierre
enfin l'étreigne, par cette fatalité qui veut que quiconque se fie à
un principe unique—la Force, ici, qui est pur mouvement—s'expose à périr par l'opération de son contraire—l'entropie, en qui
toute force vive a sa fin."[9]

By the same token, Dom Juan also demonstrates his lack of
commitment to Sganarelle's professed ideal of egalitarian sharing,

as his megalomania engenders an ambition that falls nothing short of conquering the entire female species. From society's point of view, Dom Juan is a public enemy, a miser of sorts, unwilling as he is to share his booty (the women) with his male equals. Max Vernet points out that "On voit combien il est important que Dom Juan meure: il est celui qui monnaye le passage du qualitatif au quantitatif, qui, travaillant à l'indifférentiation des femmes dans la séduction et des discours dans l'économique, ruine de l'intérieur le système qui lui a pourtant attribué la différence de naissance dont il se sert pour le miner."[10] [One understands how important it is that Dom Juan should die: it is he who subsidizes the passage from the qualitative to the quantitative, and who, working towards the levelling of women in the realm of seduction and of discourse in the realm of economics, destroys from within the very system that has given him the birthright which he employs to undermine it.] (Translation by author)

Like Harpagon, Dom Juan plays a solitary game, refusing any form of social bonding. His circle of ludic activity is limited to himself and Sganarelle, who is unwillingly bound to his master for reasons of economic necessity. This is why Dom Juan's tactics are ultimately doomed to failure the moment he stops to rest. This point is mirrored by the structure of the play itself: the hero spends the first three acts moving about and the final two at home, cornered by a series of adversaries.[11]

The hero's fear of stagnation is motivated by an underlying fear of death: "La belle chose de vouloir se piquer d'un faux honneur d'être fidèle, de s'ensevelir pour toujours dans une passion, et d'être mort dès sa jeunesse à toutes les autres beautés qui nous peuvent frapper les yeux!" (I,2) [Do you expect a man to remain the property of the first object that catches him? To give up the world for it? Never to look at anything again? A great idea—to take pride in false mortality, to remain forever faithful, shrouded in one passion, with our eyes dead from youth onwards to all those beauties elsewhere. No, no: constancy is for corpses.] His constant agitation and his elusiveness are a means for Dom Juan to continuously assert to himself that he is indeed alive: "In the Donjuanian perspective, faithfulness is tantamount to an acceptance of the end, of death, whereas 'falling in love' constitutes precisely a new birth. The passage from one woman to another, from Elvira to the fiancée whom Don Juan proposes to carry off by sea, is thus explained as the necessity of transcending death by the experience of rebirth."[12] Subtending the desire to penetrate is the will to appropriate both the mystery of the womb where he has been conceived and the secret of his origin. The life he leads, however, has no depth, no essence: it is a chronological continuum of disconnected moments and sexual encounters rather than a fusion of enriching and passionate experiences. Dom Juan's concept of temporality is one of multiple departures devoid of any notion of project, progression, or arrival, any one of which becomes synonymous with death. The hero's assertion of freedom, which is intimately linked to his ability to forget history, is the very cause of his lack of substance and consequently his status as comic hero. The tragic dimension of this play will ultimately stem from the encounter between the hero's play world and the locus of serious, even sacred values: the realm of eternity. According to Julia Kristeva, the concept of monumental time is more akin to space than to temporality and is closely linked to female subjectivity:

> As for time, female subjectivity would seem to provide a specific measure that essentially retains *repetition* and *eternity* from among the multiple modalities of time known through the history of civilizations. On the one hand, there are cycles, gestations, the eternal recurrence of a biological rhythm which conforms to that of nature and imposes a temporality whose stereotyping may shock, but whose regularity and unison with what is experienced as extrasubjective time, cosmic time, occasion vertiginous visions and unnameable *jouissance*. On the other hand, and perhaps as a consequence, there is the massive presence of a monumental temporality, without cleavage or escape, which has so little to do with linear time (which passes) that the very word 'temporality' hardly fits.[13]

The fact that there is no escape from "women's time," from this spacial temporality, merely serves to make Dom Juan's desperate attempts to break free from its hold appear ludicrous.

It is interesting, but perhaps not too surprising, that in a play dealing with the theme of seduction, individual women should have such a low profile.[14] Their collective presence (that of all women, of the feminine principle) is manifest in the fear of eternity subtending Dom Juan's inconstancy. The hero attempts to minimize the feminine presence by denying female specificity. This seemingly "egalitarian" treatment relegates women to the status of nonessential beings who are no more than mere trophies authenticating his position as society's dominant male—vouchers of his sexual vigor. Women are viewed as essentially interchangeable according to Dom Juan's principle of infinite substitutability. Unsuccessful in his attempt to abduct a young beauty during a

boating expedition, the hero finds quick consolation with the peasant girl Charlotte: "La jeune paysanne que je viens de quitter
répare ce malheur; celle-ci vaut bien l'autre" (II,2). [Still, meeting
that peasant girl—and what a charmer she is!—offsets our bad
luck.] As in *L'Avare,* women are regarded as merchandise and inventory, while relationships are considered in terms of economic
barter and exchange.[15] Dom Juan literally takes inventory of
Charlotte's various attributes while asking her to strike various
poses for his inspection: "Sganarelle, qu'en dis-tu? Peut-on rien
voir de plus agréable? Tournez-vous un peu, s'il vous plaît. Ah!
que cette taille est jolie! Haussez un peu la tête, de grâce. Ah! que
ce visage est mignon! Ouvrez vos yeux entièrement. Ah! qu'ils
sont beaux! Que je voie un peu vos dents, je vous prie. Ah! qu'elles
sont amoureuses, et ces lèvres appétissantes!" (II,2)[16] [Sganarelle,
what do you say? Have you ever come across anything more ravishing? Please, turn around slowly. Ah, a superb figure! Kindly
lift your head a bit. Ah, a bewitching face! Open your eyes wide.
Magnificent! And just a glimpse of your teeth? Adorable! So are
those appetizing lips.] The fact, however, that Dom Juan seeks to
establish his supremacy over his male rivals exclusively within the
space of desire excludes him from the possibility of sublimating
and transcending his role of conqueror. By limiting his activity to
the victimization of women, he refuses direct confrontation with
masculine adversaries, thus aborting any attempt at true heroism,
which generally rests on the sacrifice and transcendence of the
divisive lure of immediate gratification and which leads to the
metaphorization of human activity.

In order to conceal his lack of heroic stature, Dom Juan attempts to glorify the enemy. It has been noted that he does not
differentiate between individual women, rather he tends to view
the opposite sex as an army with a collective face and himself as
the sexual equivalent of Alexander the Great, who triumphs over
feminine resistance and enjoys the spoils of violent conflict: "Enfin, il n'est rien de si doux que de triompher de la résistance d'une
belle personne, et j'ai sur ce sujet l'ambition des conquérants, qui
volent perpétuellement de victoire en victoire, et ne peuvent se
résoudre à borner leurs souhaits" (I,2). [In the end, nothing is
more exhilarating than wearing down the resistance of a beautiful
woman. In this respect I'm like those empire-builders who flit
from victory to victory: the only thing they can't conquer is their
ambition.] For Dom Juan, sex is never an end in itself, but a
weapon, or perhaps more accurately a brand that allows him to
establish his ownership of the hymen before moving on to the

next conquest. This may account for the hero's ability to be satisfied with so very little physical contact and for his casual attitude
toward the object of his desire. This megalomaniac frenzy can be
associated with an underlying fear of women, who represent the
chaotic forces of nature unleashed and ultimately of death itself.
Woman's sexuality is often protrayed, and feared, as an insatiable
hunger, a voracity (a hole) that will swallow the man whole. According to Monique Schneider: "On pourrait voir tout le mouvement de Don Juan passant de femme en femme, non pas comme
une quête du féminin mais comme une fuite du féminin. Rester
auprès d'une femme, ce serait rester à l'intérieur de sa matrice,
qui est vue comme un lieu de mort."[17] [One could view Don Juan's
movement, passing from woman to woman, not as a quest for the
feminine, but as a flight from the feminine. To remain in the
presence of a woman would be to stay inside the womb, which is
considered to be a place of death.] (Translation by author) This
army of women represents a threatening feminine disorder that
is uncontrollable and incomprehensible. Their passion and the
emotional excess they inspire are associated with mortality and
are recalcitrant to political accommodations, whereas the phallus
is seen as a way to subdue these harbingers of death by branding,
ordering, appropriating, and subsuming them to patriarchal Law.

There is, however, an inherent contradiction in Dom Juan's portrayal of women. Although in one breath he depicts them as victims who try but are ultimately unable to resist his advances, in
another he refers to them as aggressors who lay claim to him. He
portrays himself as a *généreux* who would consider it an injustice
to deprive any deserving beauty of her just reward. "[T]outes les
belles ont droit de nous charmer, et l'avantage d'être rencontrée
la première ne doit point dérober aux autres les justes prétentions
qu'elles ont toutes sur nos coeurs . . . Quoi qu'il en soit, je ne puis
refuser mon coeur à tout ce que je vois d'aimable; et dès qu'un
beau visage me le demande, si j'en avais dix mille, je les donnerais
tous" (I,2). [All lovely women deserve the chance to charm us.
Because one of them was lucky enough to be the first we met, she
has no right to rob the rest of their share of love . . . I can't
withhold my love from everything I find lovable. What happens
later—happens. A beautiful face has only to ask for my heart. If
I had ten thousand hearts, I'd give them all.] The hero's redefinition of reality allows him, and not the object of his quest, to become the valuable object of desire, whereas the desiring woman
is indebted to him for his favors. Dom Juan portrays himself as
the center toward whom all eyes are turned, but in spite of his

claim of passive surrender to the female seductress, he retains control of the distribution of his favors, thus reaffirming his authority and supremacy in a complete reversal of the male-female relationship. By subverting definitions of taking and giving, the protagonist is able to insinuate female indebtedness to him, thereby eradicating his own indebtedness and characterizing women as supplicants. On the face of it, Dom Juan is able to retain his stature as *honnête homme* whose generosity is truly egalitarian. As a strategy, Dom Juan's parsimonious distribution of sexual favors divides the female contingent. The women's downfall is in the final analysis their lack of solidarity when vying for the same prize.

To be without rival in matters of seduction is the supreme wish of Dom Juan. To achieve this, he must always be ready to mark his difference from others, his territorial boundaries, with a convincing show of power. Like Arnolphe, who is in many ways his opposite, Dom Juan's fear of women derives from his dependency on them to certify his dominion over others. Like Arnolphe, Dom Juan equates honor with renown and spectacular ostentation. Therefore, the slightest rejection is terrifying because it means instant and complete negation. The hero's frantic activity is the result of an incessant need to be the unique center of all desire and the focal point of the feminine gaze. According to Jean-Pierre Dens: "le désir de Dom Juan est circulaire, concentrique, car il en est à chaque instant le point de mire et l'aboutissement. On ne saurait trop insister sur ce narcissisme; incapable d'une affection véritable, Dom Juan n'aime en fin de compte que lui-même."[18] [Dom Juan's desire is circular, concentric, for it is at all times its own aim and its own result. One cannot insist enough on this narcissism; incapable of true affection, Dom Juan loves only himself in the end.] (Translation by author) In order to achieve this, he must be everywhere at once, commanding several intrigues simultaneously. This is why his own "desire" is most typically engendered by jealousy and can be most accurately described as a desire to be desired: "La tendresse visible de leurs mutuelles ardeurs me donna de l'émotion; j'en fus frappé au coeur et mon amour commença par la jalousie. Oui, je ne pus souffrir d'abord de les voir si bien ensemble; le dépit alarma mes désirs, et je me figurai un plaisir extrême à pouvoir troubler leur intelligence, et rompre cet attachement, dont la délicatesse de mon coeur se tenait offensée" (I,2). [Never have I seen two people so happy with each other. They radiated love. And aroused the same emotion in me. I was struck to the heart: it all began with jealousy. I couldn't stand seeing them so much in love. My desire was multiplied by spite. I thought about the joy it would give me to break up this tender arrangement, which jarred my sensibilities.]

Once Dom Juan has taken possession of a woman, her physical presence becomes dispensable and even oppressive. She is now branded, as the act of coupling transforms her into a pale projection of her male partner. In the realm of patriarchal hegemony, the female is expendable and easily replaced; she is dismissed as the mere receptacle of the male. In matriarchal society the reverse is true: the male is expendable once the reproductive act is complete. Upon encountering Elvire, Dom Juan greets her with a "rencontre fâcheuse," (annoying encounter) thus identifying her from the outset as a spoil-sport seeking to invade his private sphere of ludic activity. The hero's obvious embarrassment at his wife's informal attire ("Est-elle folle, de n'avoir pas changé d'habit, et de venir en ce lieu-ci avec son équipage de campagne?" [I,2]) [Is she mad to travel to the city without changing her country clothes?] reveals his tendency to view her as a reflection or extension of himself. Although he no longer has any desire for her, she will remain out there with the countless others he has seduced and abandoned, a testimony to his prowess and a projection of his image over which he will always attempt to retain a modicum of control. The impossibility of such a project is the basis of the hero's vulnerability.

Elvire's desperate departure from passive acceptance allows her to impose her presence as an individual in direct confrontation with Dom Juan. The latter is in the habit of overlooking feminine individuality in order to plan seductive strategies based upon a collective image of woman. His silence is an insolent affront to his wife's urgent plea. Although initially one might assume, as does Elvire, that the hero's silence is the result of his perplexity and embarrassment, it soon becomes apparent, especially in the light of the persuasive eloquence he displays in the next act, that any attempt at defending himself is simply not worth the effort it would demand. In fact, Dom Juan attaches so little value to feminine discourse and to the appeasement of Elvire's anger, that he assigns his own replies to his valet Sganarelle.

Yet beneath the humiliation, Elvire's very real emotions for Dom Juan are quite transparent. She not only most generously blames herself for his abandonment of her, but actually attempts to coax her husband into lying to her and telling her what she really wants to hear:

Ah! que vous savez mal vous défendre pour un homme de cour, et qui doit être accoutumé à ces sortes de choses. J'ai pitié de vous voir la confusion que vous avez. Que ne vous armez-vous le front d'une noble effronterie? Que ne me jurez-vous que vous êtes toujours dans les mêmes sentiments pour moi, que vous m'aimez toujours avec une ardeur sans égale, et que rien n'est capable de vous détacher de moi que la mort? Que ne me dites-vous que des affaires de la dernière conséquence vous ont obligé à partir sans m'en donner avis; qu'il faut que, malgré vous, vous demeuriez ici quelque temps, et que je n'ai qu'à m'en retourner d'où je viens, assurée que vous suivrez mes pas le plus tôt qu'il vous sera possible; qu'il est certain que vous brûlez de me rejoindre, et qu'éloigné de moi, vous souffrez ce que souffre un corps qui est séparé de son âme? Voilà comme il faut vous défendre, et non pas être interdit comme vous êtes. (I,3) [Well, what a weak defense you offer for a courtier, a man to whom this must be a routine matter! You're all confused. I pity you. Why not brazen it out? Put on a lofty front. Swear your feelings for me haven't changed. You still love me with unequaled warmth. Only death can separate us. Say the most urgent business compelled you to leave without letting me know. If you are detained here for a while, against your own wishes, all I have to do is to return home and you'll follow me as soon as you can. You ache to be back with me because as long as we're apart, you suffer the torture of a body deprived of its soul. Defending yourself like that is much better than stumbling over your words.]

As she readily admits, Elvire is "trop bonne" [too good]. Her willingness to assume the guilt for a failed marriage, her pathetic eagerness to be deceived by lame excuses of her own invention show how easily Dom Juan could win her back. Elvire has already laid the groundwork for a reconciliation by generously preparing ready-made replies for her husband. In order to do so, she has had to intuitively penetrate the mind of a male seducer in order to formulate his disculpation and in doing so she has had to become fully cognizant of the humiliation of her own victimization. Elvire uses seductive language to produce a self-referential illusion: the reflection of her own narcissistic desire. Felman explains the paradoxical position of women in Dom Juan's play world: "Est-ce que les femmes sont simplement victimes ou est-que les femmes sont actives? . . . Tout d'abord, dans la version de Molière, il est évident que les femmes sont complices: la rupture des promesses ne vient pas seulement de la part de Don Juan mais aussi de la part des femmes. C'est-à-dire que Don Juan fait quelque chose de très astucieux: il force toutes les femmes qu'il séduit à rompre d'abord une promesse à elles. Ainsi, les femmes participent, activement, de l'infidélité même dont elles vont devenir les victimes."[19] [Are the women simply victims or active participants? . . . First of all, in Moliere's version, it is obvious that the women are accomplices: the breaking of promises does not only come from Don Juan, but also from the women. That is to say that Don Juan does something quite clever: he forces all of the women he seduces to first break one of their own promises. Thus, the women participate actively in the very same infidelity of which they will become the victims.] (Translation by author)

Dom Juan takes no heed of Elvire's conciliatory advances. He counters her attempts to interpret and imitate the discourse of seduction with a counterimitation of Elvire's own normally moralistic tone. He perniciously blames himself for having caused his wife to forsake her religious vows and in so doing attempts to assert his moral superiority over Elvire by implying that the blame is mostly hers. In other words, whereas Elvire tries to disculpate her philandering husband, Dom Juan counters by morally stigmatizing his wife. His discourse is nothing short of blasphemous, foreshadowing his later attempts to resort to hypocrisy, and it causes Elvire to righteously invoke the heavens as witness to this outrage. It is thus initially a woman who invokes divine justice.

Constant references to the heavens ("le ciel") throughout the play are reminders of the active participation of the supernatural in Dom Juan's game. Behind the multitude of desirable women lies the real adversary: the heavens. Women are merely the means for the protagonist to flaunt his disregard for ethical principles. Dom Juan himself is aware that the ultimate conflict will take place on a higher plane: "C'est une affaire entre le Ciel et moi" (I,2). [That's between God and me.] Dom Juan's real ambition is immense: the establishment of his supremacy over divinity itself. His rivalry with the heavens is a filial rebellion against the ultimate form of patriarchal law: the Scriptures. Dom Juan attempts to replace the old order and its superstitious beliefs with newfangled rationalism. As will be seen, the beginning of act 3 sheds further light on his personal credo.

One is forced to concur with the accuracy of Dom Juan's judgment of medicine. He is not one to be fooled by false appearances and illusion. Sganarelle, however, equates his master's lack of reverence toward the medical profession with religious impiety. By extension, the protagonist's ability to penetrate beneath the mask and beyond false appearances in both the domain of religion and of medicine can be associated with sound common sense and the renunciation of superstitious credulity. Dom Juan believes, as he says, that two and two are four, whereas Sganarelle's beliefs are fraught with superstition. The master's sound pragmatism is highly cost-effective. He refuses to take into consideration anything that does not serve his immediate interests. However, as a tactician his field of vision is too limited and this causes him to make a major tactical error in underestimating the power of his adversary.

The difficulty, however, in coming to grips with such an elusive character as Dom Juan is his constant refusal to be categorized. Movement, surprise, and unpredictable behavior are his primary strategic weapons. Every time one chances to anticipate his behavior he foils expectations. Act 3 constitutes a major interpretive problem in this respect. Forced to flee the revenge of Elvire's clansmen, the master and his valet have continued their journey under assumed identities. In the forest, they come across a hermit who warns them of the dangers they might encounter. It turns out, however, that the poor man's advice is not entirely disinterested. This seems to confirm Dom Juan's cynical view of human nature. He can also relate to such behavior, as gratuitous generosity is foreign to his own way of thinking. The hermit attempts to reassure the nobleman that a return on his generous donation can be expected from the heavens. Dom Juan, however, sees the hermit's own poverty as visible proof that no such heavenly benefit would be forthcoming. By offering the hermit money on condition that the latter renounce his moral principles, Dom Juan attempts to substitute his own immediate tangible reward for that of eternal bliss. Apostolides interprets Dom Juan' gesture in the following terms: "As a figure of gold, Dom Juan plays in the economic universe the same role the devil plays in the theological universe. He is a transforming force, wearing the *minus* sign in one world, the *plus* sign in the other. He is a counter-God who frees beings from the weight of tradition, he is the very principle of movement."[20] When the poor man refuses the temptation, Dom Juan tosses him a louis d'or with the contemptuous comment: "Va, va, je te le donne pour l'amour de l'humanité" (III,2). [All right, I give it to you—for the love of humanity.] Having failed in his attempt to pervert a devoutly religious man and to substitute his own satanic reward for that of the heavens, Dom Juan can save face only in this manner. Those who have interpreted his behavior as a sudden and surprising display of genuine generosity have missed the mark. To give contemptuously is equivalent to stripping a person of his or her dignity. It allows the protagonist to reassert his superiority over the hermit who will finally accept the tainted gift. Dom Juan's unpredictable generosity can be interpreted as a strategic move—a gesture of aristocratic magnanimity that displays his own freedom from conventional behavior. Paradoxically, this generous gesture is unavoidable and therefore far from gratuitous. Nathan Gross's analysis of this scene is pertinent in this regard, for it stresses the hero's limitless ambition in imitating the disinterested giving of divinity: "Giving disinterestedly 'pour l'amour de l'humanité' constitutes an imitation of God who gives and restores life, in creation and salvation, without expecting the creature ever could match in return such gifts . . . He unwittingly parodies God's loving relationship to man, and does not understand how close he has come to escaping the dialectic of obligation with a free, disinterested act of charity. What should be a profound, religious, humanizing experience, the imitation of divine love, is a grandiose mocking gesture meant to save face."[21]

More puzzling than this, however, is the noble behavior he displays in the following scene. Witnessing an armed attack of one man by three bandits, Dom Juan does not hesitate to endanger his own life for the sake of a stranger. Ironically, he justifies his behavior in the following terms: "Notre propre honneur est intéressé dans de pareilles aventures" (III,3). [Under these circumstances it was a matter of honor.] With the clear-sightedness of La Rochefoucauld, he understands the self-interest governing honorable behavior. The hero is not so much interested in honor per se as in a strategic advantage that honorable conduct can give him over his peers. At the end of the third act, Dom Juan makes a very nonheroic suggestion to his servant Sganarelle. The two should exchange clothing so that the servant might have the honor of dying for his master should they encounter any hostilities during their journey. Although the protagonist is certainly no coward, he is a pragmatist who understands the shortcomings of misplaced idealism and who seeks the strategic advantage in every situation. This point is further illustrated when Sganarelle, seeking to defend the unfortunate Pierrot, receives a blow instead of him. Dom Juan's cynical reprimand—"Te voilà bien payé de ta charité" (II,3)—seems in direct contrast to his own charitable intervention in favor of Dom Carlos. The apparent contradiction between discourse and action here is explained by Dom Juan's previously mentioned comment. It is not charity, but self-interest that governs his actions, for he firmly believes that divine retribution does not intervene in human activity and that virtue is nothing more than a sort of moral elegance. Instead, rewards and penalties are the result of able or poor gamesmanship. It remains necessary to determine, however, in what manner Dom Juan might expect to benefit from his assistance to Dom Carlos.

If Dom Juan's generosity is indeed selective, it is because any benefits he might hope to reap from his social inferiors, the oppressed, and from women in particular, are considered to be a god-given right. Self-sacrifice has long been an attribute of womanhood and woman's generosity is therefore seamless and invisible, an a priori function of the feminine condition. Dom Carlos and Dom Alonse are, however, his social equals and therefore his rivals. If the protagonist accepts, on the face of it, his adversaries' code of conduct, it is primarily in order to rise above it to assert his superiority over his peers. Dom Juan's courageous intervention forces the recognition of his enemy and postpones the latter's desire for immediate revenge. Dom Carlos is fully cognizant of the bond of subservience that now links him to his sister's husband. It is precisely in order to rectify the imbalance that he must at all costs protect Dom Juan from harm. The latter's familiarity with the honor code allows him to gain the strategic upper hand over Dom Carlos by anticipating his behavior. The ideologue is in the unfortunate tactical position of being entirely predictable and he is thereby prey to the imaginative and unpredictable moves of his adversary.

It is interesting to note that Dom Carlos' adherence to his code of honor is quite halfhearted. He has not enthusiastically espoused the ideology he champions. When referring to his sister Elvire's unfortunate circumstances, he bemoans the necessity to intervene on her behalf. "[N]ous nous voyons obligés, mon frère et moi, à tenir la campagne pour une de ces fâcheuses affaires qui réduisent les gentilshommes à se sacrifier, eux et leur famille, à la sévérité de leur honneur, puisqu'enfin le plus doux succès en est toujours funeste, et que, si l'on ne quitte pas la vie, on est contraint à quitter le Royaume" (III,3). [My brother and I must keep to the countryside, thanks to one of those miserable affairs that turn noblemen and their families into self-sacrificing slaves of honor. At best, when we're successful, we can only come to a sad end. If we don't say good-bye to life, we must flee into exile and say good-bye to our homeland.] Having been greeted by her husband's "rencontre fâcheuse" [annoying encounter], Elvire is now referred to as the cause of "une de ces fâcheuses affaires" [miserable affairs]. Her presence is clearly felt as an intrusion and a constraint in male society and male bonding. Moreover, Dom Carlos justly perceives his sister as the key to his vulnerability while he demonstrates very little real sympathy for her plight. His family's honor directly depends upon Elvire's virtue and her brother's ability to safeguard her reputation. The honor code, he observes, leaves the nobleman prey to the unpredictable strategies of a predator such as Dom Juan. The latter's repudiation of any behavioral code affords him the strategic advantage.

Dom Carlos' social commentary is a just appraisal of the problematics of the reification of woman. Considered as an object of possession, she is not only transferable, but eminently stealable. Elvire's own desire to break her vows and follow Dom Juan is never mentioned. From the family's point of view she was seduced and kidnapped, remaining entirely passive during the whole ordeal. Although Elvire's own assertiveness belies such a portrayal, it remains a fact that any such image of woman (as devoid of will) leaves the responsibility for her protection entirely up to her kinsmen. This does not imply, however, that the victim is considered to be blameless. One of the strange quirks in the portrayal of women as victims of rape, seduction, or violence is the inference of guilt, which she ultimately shares with her disparager. It is assumed that the woman has most often, be it unconsciously or subliminally, incited the violence that was perpetuated against her. Dom Carlos' strict adherence to a code of honor makes him feel acutely his own dependency on a female "other" whose behavior eludes his control, even if this behavior is characterized as passive incitation. Such frustration is a constant among Molière's male protagonists, from Alceste to Arnolphe. From such a perspective woman becomes both a guarantor of male superiority and the key to his downfall. Dom Juan's ambitions as conqueror of womankind have his male rivals as their ultimate target.

As fate would have it, however, Dom Carlos discovers himself to be in an oxymoronic situation because of Dom Juan's act of courage. Bound by two contrary obligations, he must first rid himself of his burden of gratitude toward Dom Juan before he can act on Elvire's behalf. Dom Juan's magnanimous gesture is a double-edged sword for his brother-in-law, a satanic gift. It forces the latter to swear allegiance to the devil and to recognize his own indebtedness to him. In this scene Dom Juan fully achieves what he had sought to accomplish with the beggar: substitute himself for the sacred principle in one man's life.

Dom Juan's rivalry with divinity may ultimately account for his final gesture in act 3, which will eventually lead to his demise. Having chanced upon the tomb of the Commander, a man Dom Juan has killed, the latter seizes the opportunity at hand to challenge the supernatural itself by issuing a dinner invitation to his former enemy's statue. Here, once again, the generous act is coupled with hostility and bravado. As with the earlier instances, the act of giving for Dom Juan is always an aggression and a vehicle for dominance. Giving is always paradoxically equated to taking, as generosity is to self-interest. Dom Juan's invitation serves as an explanatory model for his previously baffling behavior toward the beggar, toward Dom Carlos, and toward women as well. The gift that he so eagerly wishes to bestow upon his female victims is a form of sexual aggression. This accounts for the ambiguity of his language in describing his relationship to women. In inviting the Commander to dinner on his own terms, Dom Juan, understandably believing the stone statue to be inert, makes a major strategic error. His inability to comprehend the supernatural leads him to dismiss its powers. The stone statue's coming to life, its passage from inertia to motion, is paralleled dramatically by the hero's passage from movement to stasis.

The invitation to supper is the turning point of the entire play. It is at this point that the hero loses control of the game. This loss of control is paralleled by his sudden stationary posture. Having returned home, he must now play host to a series of visitors who have come to beleaguer him with requests for repayment in one form or another. No longer an aggressor, he must now beat a defensive retreat to a more vulnerable position: "From this moment on, Don Juan is no longer master of the direction or meaning of his movement: heading toward the future, he moves toward the past ... Don Juan, a figure of flight and of displacement between death behind and death ahead, is finally cornered by the statue, the figure of immobility that calls a halt to Don Juan's own movement: 'Stop, Don Juan (V,6)!'"[22]

Significantly, the first in this long line of intruders is his creditor, M. Dimanche. The latter's name conjures up images of the day of reckoning, for his presence places notions of economic repayment and divine judgment in ironic contiguity. Dom Juan's strategy for dealing with the financier is reminiscent of his earlier behavior toward the commander: he will once again issue an invitation to dinner. M. Dimanche is justifiably baffled by such an unseemly gesture, as he is quite aware of his unworthiness in terms of social rank. It is here that Dom Juan most clearly expresses the tactic that governs his conduct throughout the play: "Il est bon de les payer de quelque chose et j'ai le secret de les renvoyer satisfaits sans leur donner un double" (IV,2). [It's better to make some payment. I know a way to send them off satisfied without giving them a penny.] Dom Juan's generosity is always illusory and is generally an aggressive form of appropriation. By insisting that his creditor sit down, the protagonist effectively obligates and confounds the latter with his magnanimous egalitarianism. However, his politeness is ambiguous, for it can be interpreted as disdainful paternalism as well as gracious consideration for his guest. M. Dimanche finds himself obligated to thank his debtor, thereby recognizing the latter's superiority. According to Vernet: "Le contrat est en fait un échange différé et c'est de cette dimension temporelle que joue le grand seigneur méchant homme. Le contrat se trouve assimilé au jeu et à la promesse . . . En ceci Dom Juan est loin d'être unique, c'est une vieille habitude noble, qui repose sur le déni de l'égalité entre contractants."[23] [The contract is in fact a delayed exchange and the wicked nobleman plays upon this temporal dimension. The contract becomes assimilated to the game and to the promise . . . In this matter, Dom Juan is far from unique, it is an old aristocratic custom that is based upon the denial of equality among contracting parties.] (Translation by author)

M. Dimanche's departure is closely followed by the arrival of Dom Juan's father. Once again, the topic of indebtedness is broached. This time, however, the tenor of the confrontation is more serious. Dom Juan owes his life to his father. It is precisely this debt that Dom Juan most pressingly wants to eradicate. In his quest for divine stature, the protagonist wishes to achieve truly mythical proportions, owing his life to no one but himself. This wish is made explicit in the following comment, which points to the hero's obsessive drive to eliminate his origins: "Eh! mourez le plus tôt que vous pourrez, c'est le mieux que vous puissiez faire. Il faut que chacun ait son tour, et j'enrage de voir des pères qui vivent autant que leurs fils" (IV,4). [The sooner you drop dead the better. You had your turn. It infuriates me when fathers live as long as their sons.] Dom Juan's greatest sin against the patriarchal order is his refusal of genealogy, of linear descent from man to man. Never having outgrown the Oedipal phase, he wishes for the death of his father, so that he might appropriate not only his mother, but all women, all possible objects of masculine desire. He wants not only to replace his father without acknowledging the man's role in his creation, but he desires to demonstrate his superiority in the patriarchal order, becoming its central focal point: the Father, the Law, the Absolute. Dom Juan refuses to take his natural place in the hierarchical, evolutionary chain of successive generations of men. He is therefore a menace to the patriarchal order, as it is his intention to become the lawgiver himself and redefine the rules. For Dom Louis, the son must prove his worth by adhering to family values and by making every effort to resemble his ancestors: "Aussi nous n'avons part à la gloire de nos ancêtres qu'autant que nous nous efforçons de leur ressembler; et cet éclat de leurs actions qu'ils répandent sur nous, nous impose un engagement de leur faire le même honneur, de suivre les pas qu'ils nous tracent, et de ne point dégénérer de leurs vertus, si nous voulons être estimés leurs véritables descendants" (IV,4). [We share in our ancestors' glory only as long as we do our utmost to resemble them. The reflections of their greatness, falling on us, are a commitment: we will reciprocate by following their example; we will not fall away from their high standards if we wish to be judged their true heirs.]

Subservient emulation is anathema to Dom Juan, whose sole purpose is to make a name for himself and to distinguish himself from all who have come before. However, in his attempt at differentiating himself from all others and his father in particular, Dom Juan both challenges the patriarchal order and affirms it. His response to his father's sermon is brief and insolent. He asks his father to sit down. This not only emphasizes the son's disregard for the father's discourse and his authority, but demonstrates how he seeks to establish his dominance over the latter. According to Felman: "The Donjuanian deconstruction of the value of the 'first,' of the principle of an ordinal series, implies at the same time a general deconstruction of the very concept of beginning as a basis for identities. In this way Don Juan subverts the principle of genetic reasoning and the institution of paternity. [He] deconstructs this paternal logic of identity, this promise of metaphor, by the very figure of his own life, which is that of the anaphora, of the act of beginning ceaselessly renewed through the repetition of promises not carried out, not kept."[24]

The father ends his diatribe by self-righteously invoking the heavens. It is interesting to note how the father's own past experience seems to confirm Dom Juan's disbelief in the value of prayer or in the principle of divine justice. Having prayed for an arduous son, Dom Louis has found himself repaid by a cruel hoax. The father is "mal payé" [poorly compensated] not only by his male heir but it seems by the heavens as well.

The next visit is that of Done Elvire. Her appearance and her demeanor have changed noticeably. She is no longer the individual wife who has come to claim her stray husband, she has become Woman. She appears veiled, already an emissary of the heavens. Her love for Dom Juan has become truly altruistic. Woman, once again, is portrayed as a disinterested giver:

"Je ne viens point ici pleine de ce courroux que j'ai tantôt fait éclater, et vous me voyez bien changée de ce que j'étais ce matin. Ce n'est plus cette Done Elvire qui faisait des voeux contre vous, et dont l'âme irritée ne jetait que menaces et ne respirait que vengeance. Le Ciel a banni de mon âme toutes ces indignes ardeurs que je sentais pour vous, tous ces transports tumultueux d'un attachement criminel, tous ces honteux emportements d'un amour terrestre et grossier; et il n'a laissé dans mon coeur pour vous qu'une flamme épurée de tout le commerce des sens, une tendresse toute sainte, un amour détaché de tout, qui n'agit point pour soi, et ne se met en peine que de votre intérêt" (V,5). [I had to come and speak to you without delay. I am no longer incensed, as I was this morning, no longer the Dona Elvire who railed against you, threatened you, and swore vengeance. God has lifted from my heart all traces of my unseemly passion for you, all those excesses of a sinful infatuation, that demeaning exhibition of crude, worldly love. He has purified my love for you, cleansed it of its sensuality, left it sacred, detached, unselfish, intending only what is best for you.]

The voice of the heavens is thus initially portrayed as a feminine voice, a harmonious appeal for generosity and forgiveness. Elvire has assumed the role of Mary, intervening for the sinner, supplicating and warning him before it is too late (though Dom Juan refuses her even the satisfaction of his own salvation). Elvire's charitable love has enabled her to communicate with the above and to become the heavens' spokeswoman. In order to do this and to be subsumed by the Christian patriarchal religious order where woman is generally perceived as dangerous, she has had to repress her own desire, unsex herself, and transform herself from fury-mistress to the redeeming mother. She escapes Dom Juan's hold, becomes inaccessible to him at the moment she gives of herself the most. This leads unavoidably to a brief rekindling of the hero's passion. Elvire survives and becomes idealized as a character on condition that she lose her individuality and her sexuality. In exchange she assumes the role of the Mother. Her glory is in her passivity, in her total abdication of individual will and desire in favor of her surrender to the will of the Father-God—her total abnegation of self, which is qualified as divine.

In light of this development, Dom Juan's response seems highly ironic: "Oui, ma foi! il faut s'amender; encore vingt ou trente ans de cette vie-ci, et puis nous songerons à nous" (IV,7). [That *is* it! How to reform. Another twenty or thirty years of living this way, and then we'll consider that we should do.] (A more literal translation would end with "we'll think about ourselves.") The implication is that he is presently not thinking of himself but of the welfare of others. This would corroborate his previous statements on his "generosity" toward women.

The final visitor is the Commander's statue that has at last come to the fateful dinner. It is noteworthy that the progression of intruders goes from the very mundane M. Dimanche to the indignant patriarch, followed by the otherworldly Elvire, and finally by the supernatural appearance of the statue. Although the feminine voice is one of forgiveness, behind her lurks the omnipotent avenger. In consenting to dine with the Commander's statue, Dom Juan is lured into the final entrapment.

Cornered by his adversaries, Dom Juan senses his imminent defeat. This awareness leads to his final attempt to retain a certain degree of independence through hypocrisy. What he fails to realize, however, is that this solution is a form of suicide, for it involves abdication of self-promotional tactics. Dom Juan has built his entire persona on his notoriety, without which he is a nonentity. Hypocrisy is a constraint that indicates the hero's ultimate dependency on his father and the values he represents. In an attempt to safeguard his pleasure, Dom Juan envisions the possibility of forsaking his reputation. It becomes increasingly apparent, however, that his reputation is dearer to him than life itself. When called upon one final time by the specter of death to repent, Dom Juan defiantly cries: "Il ne sera pas dit, quoi qu'il arrive, que je sois capable de me repentir" (V,5). [No. Whatever happens, it shall never be said that I could repent.] This statement directly contradicts his earlier intention of playing the zealot. Dom Juan's defeat is ultimately linked to his blind and steadfast adherence to rationalism in a world in which the supernatural has been proven to exist. There is inconsistency in his own behavior, for while refusing to recognize the existence of supernatural forces, he has acknowledged them all the same by inviting the Commander's statue to dinner. This gesture of acknowledgment has left him vulnerable to forces that now materialize within him and that are generated by his own mind.

Behind the loving, giving, self-sacrificing mother lurks the other face of Woman: the image of death. From the play's inception, Dom Juan seems driven by a desire to dominate and subjugate the chaotic forces of feminine desire by means of the phallus. This desire is linked very early on to an obsessive fear of death. It becomes increasingly apparent in this play that Dom Juan has been playing a dangerous game: in courting women he has been courting and flirting with death itself. In the patriarchal order, as Dom Louis points out to his son, different generations of men fuse to create one eternal masculine essence. Together, the successive generations form a unity that points to a progressive evolution in time—to decay and death, but also to the negation of death through one's descendants, one's history. In seeking to impose his own hegemony by rejecting the patriarchal linear model of his forefathers, Dom Juan leaves himself prey to an attack by the darker forces embodied by women in this play, forces that had remained a dormant threat subtending the patriarchal system. The association between women and death is forcefully represented in scene 5 of act 5, when a sinister specter in women's garb and vaguely reminiscent of Elvire suddenly changes into the allegorical figure of Time with its scythe. The ambivalence of the feminine principle is thus clearly stated. Elvire's celestial voice masks woman's embodiment of the chaotic and unharnassable forces of nature: the phallic mother. She is the symbol of both life and death.

The androgynous nature of the final spectral apparition is of great significance. It is noteworthy that the divine principle so often invoked in the course of the play is always referred to as the heavens ("le ciel"). Neither the wrath of god the father, nor the mercy of the son are ever mentioned. These are not the patriarchal heavens of Christian belief—ruled by the holy trinity of male divinities—but rather the supernatural forces of mythology, predating the imposition of sexual difference. The heavens as they are portrayed in Dom Juan are therefore representative neither of a feminine essence of materiality nor of a masculine ideality, but rather of a primary bisexuality.

Limited by a narrowly rationalistic vision of the world, Dom Juan is able neither to measure the strength of his adversary nor to comprehend its irrational cruelty. There is an immense disparity in this play between the victim (Dom Juan) and the executioner (nature-matter). This disparity is reflected by the structural paradigms of the play. The hero's initially seemingly boundless freedom is gradually replaced by opposition from all sides, which eventually immobilizes and annihilates him. Felman makes a pertinent observation about Don Juan's disappearance into a bottomless pit. In her view, the gap is emblematic of the mouth, organ of pleasure and seduction: the place of mediation between language and the body.[25] It can also, however, be assimilated to another, entirely different dimension, the matrix space, anterior to the One, to God and, consequently, defying metaphysics, thus allowing for what Viviane Forestier has termed a "naissance invertie ou à l'envers"[26] [inverted birth]. In view of the crushing odds, Dom Juan gains a certain amount of heroic stature in the final act of the play through his unrepentant defiance, which is simultaneously tragic and comic.

4

L'Ecole des femmes: Marriage and the Laws of Chance

Mon Dieu, ne gagez pas: vous perdriez vraiment.
—*L'Ecole des femmes* II, 5

It would be difficult to undertake a study of the dialectics of inclusion, exclusion, and intrusion of the female character in relation to the parameters of the comic circle without examining *L'Ecole des femmes*. The theatrical motif is immediately apparent and leads to an early division of the characters into three groups: director, spectator, and object of ridicule. These roles, however, do not remain static but are in constant mutation throughout the play. Not only can the real-life spectator easily identify the shifting parameters of play, but s/he can thereby examine the dynamics of participation and nonparticipation in the game. Within the context of *L'Ecole des femmes*, it is matrimony that is defined as a game of chance in which the relationship between men and women is intrinsically adversarial.

The play begins with an altercation between two friends, Chrysalde and Alceste, concerning the perils of wedlock. An interesting definition of marriage can be reconstructed by scrutinizing the dialectics of their argument. Alceste views it as a game of deception and trickery in which the adversaries are by the very nature of the institution, gender delineated:[1]

> Je sais les tours rusés et les subtiles trames
> Dont, pour nous en planter, savent user les femmes.
>
> (I,1)

> [I know each cunning trick that women use
> Upon their docile men, each subtle ruse,
> And how they exercise their slight-of-hand.]

77

According to Huizinga, every game includes a set of rules or a
code of conduct to be accepted by all participants, while cheating,
a frequent occurrence within the ludic framework, implies the
outward acknowledgment of these rules.[2] From Arnolphe's perspective, marital rules are the foundation of patriarchal hegemony and serve to subjugate the recalcitrant other who is
continually striving to break free. Since ludic activity implies willing acceptance of the rules, woman's role in relationship to conjugal play is at best problematic. She must either internalize her
own subservience in order to participate "freely," passively accept
her alienation, or, failing that, resort to deception.

Although rules are an important component in any game, the
element of chance can be an equally pivotal concept. When Arnolphe later makes a mockery of cuckolded husbands, Chrysalde
reminds him of the role of fate, thus establishing the tone for the
rest of the play, which will bear witness to his reply:

> Ce sont coups du hasard, dont on n'est point garant,
> Et bien sot, ce me semble, est le soin qu'on en prend.
>
> (I,1)

> [Against these blows of chance there's no defense;
> To me our vain precautions make no sense.]

Thus, participation in the game, which is always voluntary, implies
the player's acceptance not only of the rules and restrictions but
also of the risks involved. Arnolphe shows a keen awareness of
the rules and of the ways in which they are circumvented through
deceit, but his persistent blindness to the role of chance leaves
him prey to a reversal of fortune. His desire to participate in
the game without anticipating the risks dramatically increases his
chances of disillusionment and loss.

More accurately yet, one might define marriage according to
L'Ecole des femmes as a spectator sport:

> Enfin, ce sont partout sujets de satire;
> Et comme spectateur, ne puis-je pas en rire?
>
> (I,1)

> [In short, when all around lies comedy,
> May I not laugh at all these things I see?]

As an outsider to the institution of matrimony, Arnolphe has hitherto distanced himself from the participants, thereby incurring

no risks. Serge Doubrovsky reminds us that: "Le rire est ici un isolant. Arnolphe est séparé de ses contemporains, il se pose en s'opposant à eux. Ce spectacle, qu'il voit et juge du dehors, sans y participer, souligne son individualité irréductible. Il se *singularise* au sens profond du terme."[3] [Laughter here is an insulator. Arnolphe is separated from his contemporaries, he assumes his pose, by opposing them. This spectacle, which he sees and judges from outside, without participating in it, emphasizes his irreducible individuality. He makes himself conspicuous in the most profound sense of the term.] (Translation by author) Not content to privately witness the husbands' misfortunes, he discloses private scandals to the public eye, thereby enlisting the support of witnesses. Thus, he is not merely a spectator, but director, producer, and master of ceremonies as well. Arnolphe's indiscretion is an ostentatious means of displaying his superiority to others, though this superiority is predicated on a fundamentally negative principle: Arnolphe considers himself a hero of his times not because he *is* an object of admiration, but because he *is not* an object of public ridicule.[4] Accordingly, the comic manifestation of the heroic project is defined in the negative:

> On est homme d'honneur quand on n'est point cocu,
> A le bien prendre au fond, pourquoi voulez-vous croire
> Que de ce cas fortuit dépende notre gloire,
> Et qu'une âme bien née ait à se reprocher
> L'injustice d'un mal qu'on ne peut empêcher?
>
> (IV,8)

> [His honor's safe, no matter what his life,
> Provided he enjoys a faithful wife.
> Come now, how can you make our reputation
> Depend on such a chance consideration?
> Why should a well-born soul have to repent
> Brooking a wrong that no one can prevent?]

Because the husband's honor is predicated in this instance upon his wife's fidelity, a relationship of dependency is established in which empowerment essentially belongs to his wife, even though it is ostensibly the man who enforces the rules. Nowhere is the paradox so clearly stated as in scene 2 of act 3:

> Votre sexe n'est là que pour la dépendance:
> Du côté de la barbe est la toute-puissance.
> Bien qu'on soit deux moitiés de la société,

> Ces deux moitiés pourtant n'ont point d'égalité:
> L'une est moitié suprême et l'autre subalterne;
> L'une en tout est soumise à l'autre qui gouverne . . .
> Songez qu'en vous faisant moitié de ma personne,
> C'est mon honneur, Agnès, que je vous *abandonne*.

(III.2)

> [For frailty your sex is made and reared;
> Authority is vested in the beard.
> Although you form half of the society,
> Between our halves is no equality;
> One is supreme, the other one abject;
> One must submit, the other one direct; . . .
> Note that in giving you my life to share,
> Agnès, I place my honor in your care;]

The continual repetition of the word "moitié" demonstrates Arnolphe's underlying obsession with the notion of codependency and reliance on the unpredictable behavior of the woman who is to become his Other (half). Arnolphe wants to be without rival, thereby marking his difference from other husbands in a compelling manner. Arnolphe's honor, which is continually on display, has become pure spectacle. Therefore any slight, imagined or real, is tantamount to instant and total humiliation.

Arnolphe sets out to guarantee his marital rights by limiting the knowledge of his future wife, Agnès, who has been raised according to his personal specifications. The ingenue's inexperience is, however, an ideal breeding ground for vice as well as virtue:

> Une femme d'esprit peut trahir son devoir,
> Mais il faut, pour le moins, qu'elle ose le vouloir;
> Et la stupide au sien peut manquer d'ordinaire
> Sans en avoir l'envie et sans vouloir le faire.

(I,1)

> [Now when a clever woman goes astray,
> At least she knows, and means it just that way;
> A stupid one may fall in the same snare
> Not wishing to and wholly unaware.]

Chrysalde reminds his friend here that virtue and ignorance are incompatible concepts. True moral character is always a function of willful and rational freedom of choice. When decisions are not arrived at through conscious self-determination, chance predominates over reason.

Unbeknownst to Arnolphe, fate has already claimed its first victory. During his absence, a fortuitous encounter has taken place between the ingenue Agnès and the *blondin* Horace. Upon learning of the imminent threat to his plans, Arnolphe counters by establishing a rigid code of conduct. Fate, however, can only be circumvented through versatility and adaptability, it cannot be avoided by traditional means of empowerment. As Chrysalde reminds his friend:

> Mais comme c'est le sort qui nous donne une femme,
> Je dis que l'on doit faire ainsi qu'au jeu de dés
> Où, s'il ne vous vient pas ce que vous demandez,
> Il faut jouer d'adresse et, d'une âme réduite,
> Corriger le hasard par la bonne conduite
>
> (IV,8)

> [But since we owe our choice of wives to chance,
> As in a game of dice we should behave,
> Where, when you do not get the roll you crave,
> You must reduce your stakes, control your play,
> and change your luck by caution and delay.]

Arnolphe's foolhardy self-assurance is founded on Agnès' ignorance. In choosing a four-year-old child as his bride-elect, he has sought to establish his ascendancy from the earliest stages of critical reason. He seeks to become the very source of her being, to mould her and in-form her:

> En femme, comme en tout je veux suivre ma mode.
> Je me vois riche assez pour pouvoir, que je croi,
> Choisir une moitié qui tienne tout de moi . . .
>
> (I,1)

> [Right. Every man his way.
> I have my own to choose a fiancée.
> I'm rich enough, I think, to have felt free
> To have my wife owe everything to me . . .]

In the realm of the masculine political order the female is expendable, except as a receptacle of the male. By directing Agnès' every action and thought, Arnolphe believes it possible to make her a mirror image of himself. It is this narcissism that reflects the subject's complete self-absorption and enclosure within himself. It is the tantalizing image of a perfect, self-sufficient whole rather than Agnès herself that becomes the object of his obsession. She enables him to project his own presence into an empty receptacle, for the only "other" one can depend upon unequivocally and whose desires are the unadulterated reflection of one's own is one's double (albeit an intellectually inferior copy of the original).

The first phase in Arnolphe's strategy is to make Agnès aware of her unworthiness and her lack. Subtending his admonition is the message that without him she is nothing, a nonentity, and that she needs her tutor to create and shape her:

> Je vous épouse, Agnès; et cent fois la journée
> Vous devez bénir l'heure de votre destinée,
> Contempler la bassesse où vous avez été,
> Et dans le même temps, admirer ma bonté,
> Qui de ce vil état de pauvre villageoise
> Vous fait monter au rang d'honorable bourgeoise.

(III,2)

> [Agnès, I'm marrying you; and you ought
> A hundred times a day to bless your lot,
> To keep your former low estate in mind
> and marvel that a man can be so kind
> As I, who found you just a country lass,
> And raise you to the honored middle class,]

In Arnolphe's view, Agnès' value is not intrinsic, but is derivative of his own identity. Patrick Dandrey confirms this in the following terms: "Agnès n'aura aucune des qualités que la nature et l'histoire prêtent aux femmes, parce qu'elle sera sans qualité aucune: définie par soustraction sans reste, par négation interne. Ombre obscure et fidèle de la seule positivité du monde selon Arnolphe: lui-même."[5] [Agnès will have none of the qualities that nature and history bestow upon women, because she will be without any attribute whatsoever: defined by subtraction without a remainder, by internal negation. Dim and faithful shadow of the only positivity in the world, according to Arnolphe: himself.] (Translation by author) According to Irigaray, "The rejection, the exclusion of a female imaginary certainly puts woman in the position of experiencing herself only fragmentarily, in the little-structured margins of a dominant ideology, as waste, or excess, what is left of a mirror invested by the (masculine) 'subject' to reflect himself, to copy himself."[6]

Not only does Arnolphe assume the role of patriarchal lawgiver when he supplies his pupil with a document entitled *Les Maximes du Mariage ou Les Devoirs de la Femme Mariée*, but he also teaches her to be aware of her own ignorance by mocking her outrageous naïveté. Agnès can become his wife on condition that she accept the 'void' that masculinity needs to find in a woman. She must remain a nonperson in order to reflect her husband's image: her moon to his sun. What goes almost without saying is that from this perspective, the ideal wife is also the perfect child: the child bride, the woman-child, the sex kitten. Man is both husband and father to this creature (the word implies both the idea of creation and receptivity), whose presence allows him to supplant the mother by usurping the role of life giver and creator. Once again, within patriarchy the mother's presence represents the barely disguised chaotic forces of nature, ever threatening to invade the phallic order. By replacing the mother with the father as embodiment of reason and structure, the harmony of the patriarchal order is maintained. However, the paternal figure's attraction to the woman-child is troubling to say the least, for it borders on incestuous desire.

One of the advantages of a marital relationship in which the wife is a true reflection of her husband is that attention is always drawn to the dominant male figure, to the original, not the copy. The problem with an educated and independent woman is that the husband's presence becomes peripheral and incidental:

> Moi, j'irais me charger d'une spirituelle
> Qui ne parlerait rien que cercle et que ruelle,
> Qui de prose et de vers ferait de doux écrits,
> Et que visiteraient marquis et beaux esprits,
> Tandis que sous le nom du mari de Madame,
> Je serais comme un Saint que pas un ne réclame?
>
> (I,1)

> [*I* should take on some lady of *esprit*,
> Full of her literary coterie,
> Dashing off prose and verse in tender bits,
> Attended by the marquises and wits,
> While I, known as the husband of Madame,
> Play the unworshiped saint *ad nauseam*?]

What Arnolphe has failed to realize, however, is that ingenuousness and idiocy are not synonymous, though he uses the terms interchangeably.[7] Initially at least, Agnès is situated at an ambiguous moment that predates the onset of her sexual awareness. Her enlightenment will coincide with her encounter with Horace. In other words, there seems to be, at least in popular credence, a coalescence between nascent sexual awareness and intellectual awakening in women. What is interesting about such a concept, is that it is once again the more experienced male counterpart who becomes the vehicle for this enlightenment. As Agnès readily admits:

> C'est de lui [Horace] que je sais ce que je puis savoir,
> Et beaucoup plus qu'à vous je pense lui devoir.
>
> (V,4)

> [It is from him I know all that I know:
> Much more than you, he is the one I owe.]

Despite her growing awareness, Agnès will never bypass the stage of obligation and recognition to achieve full autonomy. Her indebtedness will mark her dependency throughout the play. Furthermore, the bond of recognition effectively demonstrates a correspondence between the sexual and the intellectual identity of woman. The play conveys the impression that unlike men, women cannot separate their ability to reason from their emotional state or their reproductive function and that their thinking is implicitly muddled and confused by sensations, in other words, by their materiality: "Agnès libère sa parole comme se libère le désir, la sexualité: dans la relation; elle parle à, pour apprendre à parler; l'ambiguïté grossière des vers 1560/1562 (Vous fuyez l'ignorance, et voulez, quoi qu'il coûte, / Apprendre du blondin quelque chose?) suggère que la bouche et le sexe, le savoir et le désir sont solidaires."[8] [Agnès liberates her speech much in the same manner that sexual desire is unleashed: in the relationship; she speaks *to* in order to learn to speak; the crude ambiguity of lines 1560/ 1562 (you flee ignorance and want to learn something from the young man at all costs?) suggests that language and sex, desire and knowledge are solidary.] (Translation by author) Most of the laughter Arnolphe derives from Agnès' lack of knowledge stems from her inexperience in sexual matters:

> Et parfois elle en dit dont je pâme de rire.
> L'autre jour (pourrait-on se le persuader?),
> Elle était fort en peine et me vint demander,
> Avec une innocence à nulle autre pareille,
> Si les enfants qu'on fait se faisaient par l'oreille.
>
> (I,1)

[I simply marvel at her naivetes,
And could die laughing at the things she says.
Just fancy that, a day or two ago,
She came to me distraught, wanting to know—
So innocent, so candid and sincere—
If children are begotten through the ear.]

Arnolphe's dual role as spectator and stage director has already been discussed. In calling upon an audience of fellow laughers to witness the humiliation of others, he distances himself from the common masses, thus establishing his superiority. However, in recounting his personal adventures, he opens himself up to attack. In other words, once he switches from third- to first-person narrative, he becomes a vulnerable target of criticism. His need to inform others of his project is similar to that of Horace in act 1, scene 3. In mocking his younger rival, however, Arnolphe unwittingly targets his own shortcomings:

Enfin, mon étourdi n'aura pas lieu d'en rire;
Par son trop de caquet il a ce qu'il lui faut.
Voilà de nos Français l'ordinaire défaut:
Dans la possession d'une bonne fortune,
Le secret est toujours ce qui les opportune;
Et la vanité sotte a pour eux tant d'appas,
Qu'ils se pendraient plutôt que de ne causer pas.

(III,3)

[Well, my young fool will have no cause to beam.
He talked too much, and now he pays the price.
That is our Frenchmen's ordinary vice:
When they are lucky in a love affair,
Secrecy is a thing they cannot bear;
And vanity holds them so much in thrall,
They'd rather hang themselves than not tell all.]

And since no narration is complete without the *narratee*, no spectacle without an audience, Horace himself admits:

Et goûtat-on cent fois un bonheur trop parfait,
On n'en est point content si quelqu'un ne le sait.

(IV,6)

[And perfect happiness, if it's unknown,
Tastes flat; we cannot savor it alone.]

thereby offering a variation of his mentor's attitude. Horace's statement leads one to speculate on the intimate link between love and self-esteem. Once again, the object of desire is merely a reflection of personal worth and a validation of dominance in the sexual sphere. Arnolphe's project is essentially a theatrical one that requires the display of his ill-conceived sense of superiority.

The presence of the servants Alain and Georgette does more than merely add an element of farce. Their primary function throughout the play is to serve as guards who protect Agnès from contact with the outside world. The fact that they are utterly inept at this function merely leads one to draw certain inferences as to the futility of imposing external constraints on a person's behavior. The very idea that Arnolphe would need a backup system to his foolproof plan is an outward manifestation of his lack of control. Upon his return home, he questions Georgette as to whether or not Agnès missed him during his absence. The question itself suggests emotional involvement on his part and provides the servant woman with an effective means of targeting his vulnerable ego:

> Elle vous croyait voir de retour à toute heure;
> Et nous n'oyions jamais passer devant chez nous
> Cheval, âne ou mulet, qu'elle ne prît pour vous.
>
> (I,2)

> [She kept thinking she saw you coming back;
> Each time a horse or mule or donkey passed
> She was quite sure that it was you at last.]

When in the next scene Arnolphe's sexual desire for Agnès becomes apparent through innuendo, she responds that she has spent much of her time during his absence making "cornettes." Such an answer should resonate in the mind of someone utterly obsessed with "cornes," but it obviously eludes Arnolphe as he praises his pupil's pudicity. He is blind to the fact that his sense of honor is irrevocably tied to and dependent upon a young woman with no worldly experience, very little common sense, and no moral conscience.

Arnolphe's dependency on others becomes increasingly manifest in the following scene. His aforementioned need for an audience is echoed by that of Horace, who finds in his old friend Arnolphe a captive one. The latter actually encourages him to recount his adventures:

Je me donne souvent la comédie à moi.
Peut-être en avez-vous déjà féru quelqu'une.
Vous est-il point encore arrivé de fortune?

(I,4)

[It is sport for a prince; and what I see
Is an unfailing source of comedy.
Already you have smitten one, I'll bet.
Haven't you had some such adventure yet?]

To continue the theatrical metaphor, the younger man, who fancies himself to have staged a comedy of seduction, is desperately in need of a producer. He appeals to Arnolphe to lend him the funds to finance his endeavor. Much to Arnolphe's chagrin, however, he finds himself in the unusual position of being both producer and spectator of a play in which he is the object of ridicule, thus becoming his own enemy: not a deceiver deceived, but a laugher mocked. To add insult to injury, Horace expects his rival's active complicity through supportive laughter:

Horace: Riez-en donc un peu . . .
Je ne puis y songer sans de bon coeur en rire;
Et vous ne riez pas assez, à mon avis.
Arnolphe: (avec un ris forcé)
Pardonnez-moi, j'en ris tout autant que je puis.

(III,4)

[Horace: Then how about a laugh? . . .
I never heard of anything so funny;
I can't help laughing, not for love or money.
But you're not laughing very hard, I'd say.
Arnolphe: [*forcing a laugh*] I'm laughing—pardon me—as best I
  may.]

This is the direct result of Arnolphe's new identity as Monsieur de la Souche. Unbeknownst to Horace, he has taken on a nobleman's title. Ironically, however, the protagonist's double identity is reflected not only in the dual roles he plays, but in the contradictory and paradoxical nature of a double desire. As spectator, he feels compelled to learn the truth. As participant, he is driven by jealousy to know what he might otherwise prefer to ignore. He attempts to make use of this double identity to gain his rival's confidence, thereby transforming his passive observance into active resistance, his role of spectator into that of stage director. These constantly shifting parameters within the borders of the

comic circle are a direct reflection of the struggle for power between the two male rivals. What remains enigmatic is the extent
to which the feminine presence can emerge as a positive or negative force within this context.

Initially at least, Agnès' means to empowerment can only be
defined negatively as the unconscious failure to meet Arnolphe's
expectations:

> Elle n'a pu faillir sans me couvrir de honte,
> Et tout ce qu'elle a fait enfin est sur mon compte.
> Eloignement fatal! voyage malheureux!
>
> (II,1)

> [A lapse of hers would cover me with shame;
> Her acts may be imputed to my name.
> Why was I absent? Why did I go away?]

The desire to create's one's mirror image in another would seem
at first to permit the creation of a perfectly symmetrical coincidence of will, thereby ensuring total control over the object of
desire. However, the smallest flaw in the creation will inevitably
reflect back upon the creator, tying his destiny to hers and revers-
ing the order of empowerment. Once again, Arnolphe's loss of
control is echoed by his recognition of the need to remain continually vigilant. His own personal freedom is limited by the necessity to limit that of Agnès.

It seems interesting that in this play, jealousy appears to be
an emotion reserved exclusively for men. The female characters
neither feel it, nor comprehend it. Georgette cannot understand
Arnolphe's possessive rage and must rely on Alain for an explanation. Jealousy is more intimately connected to self-esteem than
to love. Women are defined throughout the play as redoubtable
adversaries primarily because they lack the self-esteem necessary
to feel jealous. Since their sense of personal honor is not tied to
their husbands' moral conduct, they are free of the emotional
turmoil such an enslavement would imply. Alain, of course,
stresses the consumerism as well as the process of reification implicit in Arnolphe's definition of marriage in act 3, scene 2:

> La femme est en effet le potage de l'homme;
> Et quand un homme voit d'autres hommes parfois
> Qui veulent dans sa soupe aller tremper leurs doigts,
> Il en montre aussitôt une colère extrême.
>
> (II,3)

[Well, woman is in effect the soup of man.
When one man sees others ready to swoop
And try to dip his fingers in his soup
He flies into a fury right away.]

But, as we have seen from the beginning, a woman's passivity can
never be counted on. It is, paradoxically, man's desire to transform
woman into a passive object devoid of ethical values of her own,
that affords her the moral freedom to subvert his carefully constructed plans. In Arnolphe's mind, women are empowered by
their disregard for moral principles and their absence of an honor
code. They are viewed as the ultimate winners in marriage.

Woman's identity seems so closely connected to her sexuality in
this play that it is not surprising that adultery becomes her principal weapon in opposing the patriarchal order. Unlike Célimène,
in *Le Misanthrope*, however, the wives (who remain peripheral to
the action but whose ever present danger haunts Arnolphe's
imagination) do not remain evasive in order to increase their desirability while eschewing entrapment but rather they seek pleasure for its own sake. Their empowerment stems not from
withholding but from their self-fulfillment through sexual gratification. The act of granting sexual favors is in itself an act of
empowerment for it implies the freedom to bestow rather than
to be taken. Within the confines of the patriarchal order, however,
giving and taking are the prerogatives of men. The only form of
"giving" permissible to woman is the art of self-sacrifice, in which
personal pleasure is entirely sublimated and subsumed by the
political order. Thus, it is necessary to establish behavioral constraints intended to limit personal freedom. The concept of sin,
with its implicit consequence of punishment, now comes to the
fore.

Religion and sin are invoked in this play primarily as negative
constraints designed to enforce law and order. Agnès' naive commentary points out the arbitrary nature of heaven's decrees,
which Arnolphe is unable to justify in rational terms. If virtue is
indeed, as was implied earlier, incompatible with ignorance, then
by the same token so must be sin. The truly ignorant person,
unaware of the margins between good and evil, is by definition
amoral. In such a character, impulse is translated directly into
action without passing first through the channels of moral scrutiny or critical reasoning: Agnès' discourse is that of "la pure
nature," according to her lover Horace, and she herself admits
that she can exert no control over her impulses: "Peut-être qu'il

y a du mal à dire cela; mais enfin je ne puis m'empêcher de le dire" (III,4). [Perhaps it's a bad thing to say that; but anyway I can't help saying it, and I wish it could be done without its being wrong.]

The sexual opposition serves as a metaphor for the conflictual relationship between nature and culture.[9] In these camps the natural is associated with a feminine essence, whose history in metaphysics is associated with matter, and culture is associated with the masculine, a concept essentialized as "form" or "ideal." And as Arnolphe obviously believes, the ideal can shape matter:

> Ainsi que je voudrai, je tournerai cette âme:
> Comme un morceau de cire entre mes mains elle est,
> Et je puis lui donner la forme qui me plaît.
>
> (III,3)

> [I'll shape her soul at will, and mold her life.
> Between my hands she's like a piece of clay,
> And I can fashion her in any way.]

The spectator's first impression of Agnès coincides with that of her master: she is pure negativity, a void to be filled and shaped by imposition of the strictures of patriarchy. Through her sexual awakening, however, feminine nature reasserts its prerogatives, all the more forcefully as Agnès lacks the intellectual tools necessary to truly comprehend and internalize social conventions. Agnès' essence was essentially dormant, waiting to be awakened by Prince Charming's kiss. Thus, when Will G. Moore contends that L'Ecole des femmes portrays a struggle between Arnolphe and the forces of nature,[10] he is right on the mark, for Arnolphe's frustration lies in his continual attempts to impose the strictures of symmetry on an object of both fear and desire: feminine "nature" whose chaotic forces cannot be harnessed by patriarchal law. The inevitability of the reaffirmation of nature is structurally parallel to the inescapability of fate. By Arnolphe's own definition of Agnès, she is incapable of sinful intent and therefore beyond the Law. The protagonist's attempts to threaten her with moral retribution fall on deaf ears. However, Agnès' growing awareness of her own sexuality leads one to view physical desire as an entirely innocent natural phenomenon.

It becomes increasingly apparent that within marriage (a microcosmic reflection of society itself), the sexual opposition provides a metaphor for a more essential coupling: the ultimately unresolvable conflict between the male principle, the Law, and the female principle, Chance. Fear of the feminine stems from the ungovernable nature of the forces of fate. Despite man's best attempts at elaborating the strictures of symmetry and order that are attained only through repression, a part of the game always remains unpredictable and beyond his reach. A reversal of the hegemonic order is possible at any moment. It seems appropriate that it is Agnès who indirectly hints at the impossibility of harnessing chance:

Arnolphe: Quelques voisins m'ont dit qu'un jeune homme inconnu
Etait en mon absence à la maison venu,
Que vous aviez souffert sa vue et ses harangues;
Mais je n'ai point pris foi sur ces méchantes langues,
Et j'ai voulu gager que c'était faussement . . .
Agnès: Mon Dieu, ne gagez pas, vous perdriez vraiment.

(II,5)

[Arnolphe: Just think: some neighbors came to me to say
That a young man came while I was away,
That you received, and listened to, this male.
But I would not believe this wicked tale,
And I proposed to bet them, to their cost . . .
Agnès: Good Lord, don't bet! Oh my! You would have lost.]

What is so interesting about the ingenue's presence within this comedy is that in spite of her as yet undifferentiated identity, in spite of her transferral as object of possession from one master to another, her presence alone serves to disrupt Arnolphe's carefully instrumented game plan. Furthermore, the protagonist's awareness of Horace's tactics serves no strategic purpose, for each new victory of his rival is always presented *a posteriori*, as a *fait accompli*. This is what Myrna Zwillenberg has termed the "retroactive reality" device within the play.[11] It only serves to emphasize the absurdity of man's attempts to anticipate events by applying logical rules of cause and effect and it undermines the very concept of rationality. It shows man's efforts to impose his will on events, people, and objects to be ultimately futile and meaningless. Arnolphe's parodic echoing of Pompée, the Cornelian hero's words—"Je suis maître, je parle: allez, obéissez" (II,5) [Enough, I'm master: when I speak, obey]—merely draws attention to the diminishing control he has over the events in question. When Arnolphe returns from his travels, Horace has already won Agnès' heart. Her tutor overlooks this important event, for his main concern is whether or not some *thing* has been taken from her: "Ne vous a-t-il point pris, Agnès, quelque autre chose?" (II,5) [Agnes, was there anything else he took?] The "thing" he is referring to is ostensibly her virginity. Thus, the reduction of a woman's worth to her hymen is an attempt to make the intangible tangible. Since it is virtually impossible to govern another person's emotions, Arnolphe imposes his authority externally, exerting control through physical constraints.[12] In this context, the hymen becomes symbolic of man's attempt to appropriate or possess a woman's body-as-object while disregarding her internal feelings. The hero is reduced to contenting himself with the possession of an object rather than a desiring subject:

> Si son coeur m'est volé par ce blondin funeste,
> J'empêcherai du moins qu'on s'empare du reste . . .
>
> (IV,7)

> [If I have lost her heart to this blond pest,
> At least I'll see he shall not have the rest . . .]

Although Agnès never achieves full autonomy, she emerges progressively as an assertive force and this development would seem at least initially to be causally linked to each new external constraint. Thus, a pattern of action and reaction is established in which each new law is met by its transgression. However, since the transgression frequently predates the constraint, it appears less deliberate than fated. Agnès' first mutinous act of independence occurs when she changes Arnolphe's stage directions. The latter has ordered her to cast a stone at her lover Horace. She artfully turns this spiteful gesture to her advantage by attaching a message to the missile. It is interesting to note, however, that it is only in the following scene that Arnolphe specifically forbids her to write:

> Le mari doit, dans les bonnes coutumes,
> Ecrire tout ce qui s'écrit chez lui.
>
> (III,2)

> [It is the husband's job to think,
> And what needs writing he will write.]

Thus the maxim has been transgressed before it was even issued.

Without realizing it, Arnolphe has schooled his pupil in the art of deception by requiring her to display a false image to Horace. Her own cheating is only a realistic consequence of a lesson dutifully learned. Ironically, her tutor even compliments her on her acting ability, which he attributes to his own talent as a director:

> Oui, tout a bien été, ma joie est sans pareille:
> Vous avez là suivi mes ordres à merveille,
> Confondu de tout point le blondin séducteur,
> Et voilà de quoi sert un sage directeur.
>
> (III,1)

> [Yes, all went well; I can't contain my glee:
> You all followed my orders to a tee,
> and put to rout that prince of libertines.
> Now that is what good generalship means.]

Although Arnolphe admits that the best strategy might be to let destiny play itself out, thereby allowing Agnès to fall prey to her own fate, he cannot give up his compulsive urge to control and to impose his own order on the events in question. He has by this time acknowledged the adversarial forces of fate without, however, understanding the futility of countering chance: "Il se faut garantir de toutes les surprises" (IV,2). [I must protect myself against surprises.] As proof of this, each new precaution is met with predestined failure. This backfire principle is at the very foundation of passionate love itself. Since the intensity of the feeling is predicated on the desire for an absolute possession of the ever elusive other, Arnolphe comes to the painful realization that his passionate obsession is proportional to Agnès' growing autonomy. Thus the dialectics of his relationship with Agnès demonstrate the absurdity of his heroic project. Ultimately Arnolphe will be forced to accept his inability to harness the forces of fate:

> Ciel, faites que mon front soit exempt de disgrâce;
> Ou bien, s'il est écrit qu'il faille que j'y passe,
> Donnez-moi tout au moins pour de tels accidens,
> La constance qu'on voit à de certaines gens.
>
> (III,5)

> [Heaven, keep my forefead free from any horn;
> Or, if it was for that that I was born,
> Grant me at least, to help me bear the shame,
> The fortitude of some whom I could name.]

Arnolphe uses the terms "destin," "hasard," "surprise," and "accident" interchangeably, even though the first term implies the existence of an invisible order or an organizing principle, in contrast to the others. Although the unpredictable events seem to be chance occurrences, an underlying structuring principle does seem to be at work. Arnolphe's successive tactical moves consistently result in the opposite of the desired goal. As Horace gleefully exclaims:

> Je viens vous avertir que tout a réussi,
> Et même beaucoup plus que je n'eusse osé dire,
> Et par un incident qui devait tout détruire.
>
> (V,2)

> [I came to say
> That things turned out in a delightful way,
> Both better than I could have hoped, and faster,
> Thanks to a plan that seemed to bring disaster.]

Once this cause-and-effect relationship becomes apparent, the only possible alternative is a policy of non-intervention and humble acceptance of adversity. Ironically, Arnolphe's resistance shapes his own destiny: he is the architect of his own fate. After years of observing the less fortunate husbands, he has yet to learn the lesson implicit in the following lines:

> En sage philosophe on m'a vu, vingt années,
> Contempler des maris les tristes destinées,
> Et m'instruire avec soin de tous les accidents
> Qui font dans le malheur tomber les plus prudents ...
>
> (IV,7)

> [For twenty years, a philosophic sage,
> I've watched the hapless husbands of this age,
> Studied all their disasters, tried to know,
> How even the most prudent are brought low ...]

In his own words, there is no precaution that can guarantee against accidental occurrences. Thus, his goal is indeed an indication of hubris, for it would place him beyond the reaches of fate. However, Chrysalde once again reminds him: "Si le sort l'a réglé, vos soins sont superflus ..." (IV,8). [If fate has willed it, nothing you can do can change it; it won't come consulting you.] Ultimately, this statement sheds a comic perspective on all human activity, which is seen as futile in view of man's inability to counter chance in even the most insignificant events.

The deeper one delves into the problematics of fate, the more one becomes aware of a fundamental dichotomy that the play itself is trying to resolve. The feminine concept of Fortuna, or chance, is a destabilizing principle. Because it is ultimately random and unpredictable, it rocks the very foundations of the Law. The fear it inspires is based upon man's disturbing inability to anticipate or control it. Ultimately the play strives to replace the feminine principle with the more neutral concept of *Fatum*, or destiny. Although fate is also seen as an ungovernable force, the very notion that it is preordained by some higher power is reassuring, for it eliminates the notion of absurdity and reaffirms the masculine order based upon a rational and comprehensible, if not always foreseeable, governing principle. In contrast, chance is by its very nature unreckonable and therefore disturbing because it defies anticipation. Within the play itself, there is a progressive substitution of terms such as "coups du hasard," "accidents," "surprises," and "jeu de dés" with "destin," "astre," and "fatalité." The final act is a demonstration of the rules of fate: ultimately an underlying and invisible structuring principle was in operation from the very outset—Horace's betrothal to Agnès. This structuring principle is analogous to the act of comedy writing itself. Although at first glance, Molière's play appears to lack any predictable structure, it becomes obvious retrospectively that it is kept from wandering by the retroactive operations of fate. Thus, although on one level *L'Ecole des femmes* represents the disturbing failure of one man's attempt to counter an adverse destiny, the comedy is ultimately reassuring in its reestablishment of law and order based upon a rational principle to which the protagonist was simply blind.

Within this framework, Agnès remains a symbolic representation of chance. Initially, her deep-seated alienation is the result of her lack of political, moral, or rational governing principles. Not having reached full autonomy or internalized a corpus of ethical values, she retains the status of object. Because of this lack, Agnès' actions are essentially random and unforeseeable and her presence is equivalent to that of an amoral force; she cannot control her own desire for self-gratification and pleasure: "Le moyen de chasser ce qui fait du plaisir?" (V,4) [How can you ban what sets your heart on fire?] Her inability to control through denial or repression that which exceeds the limits marks her, for the masculine, as the embodiment of a dangerous indeterminacy. Although she is therefore an unsettling commodity within the patriarchal hegemony, her status as nonperson, or object whose shape has yet to be determined, leaves her prey to victimization and abuse. On one hand, her presence in relation to the play world remains somewhat marginal because of her relative inertia and submissiveness. On the other, it seems the only way to control her as a symbolic representation of fate is to appropriate her. This idea is emphasized by the terms of economic barter employed in the following replies:

> *Arnolphe:* [. . .] est-ce qu'un si long temps
> Je vous aurai pour lui nourrie à mes dépens?
> *Agnès:* Non, il vous rendra tout jusques au dernier double.
>
> (V,4)

> [Arnolphe: . . . does it make sense
> To bring you up for him, at my expense?
> Agnes: Oh, no. He'll pay each penny back again.]

Agnès seems to recognize the inevitability of her transferability and her appropriation, which occur primarily through obligation. In order to turn this to his own advantage, Arnolphe attempts to bestow a magnanimous pardon on an unworthy object. This is a miscalculation: since Agnès is incapable of feeling guilt, she is equally unable to feel the weighty benefit of his forgiveness. Once again, the amorality Arnolphe has bred into his pupil works to his disadvantage.

Agnès' incipient autonomy seems to coincide with her recognition of indebtedness, and therefore her total liberation from a male tutor is never fully achieved. Although she demonstrates incipient playfulness and deceitfulness through the coalescence of her sexual and verbal awakening,[13] which could bring about the disintegration of the male play world through her total disregard for the rules of the game, her sense of obligation toward Horace will hold these tendencies in check. Still, the audience remains fully aware that she possesses an intrinsic means of retaliation: infidelity. She not only owes her sexual and intellectual enlightenment to Horace, but she is also obliged to him for not having taken advantage of her vulnerability. The inference here is that she has not yet learned to govern her impulses and desires. Even her desiring suitor senses the danger of excess in such behavior and sees himself compelled to control the situation, imposing those very same rules that he would otherwise attempt to break:

> Considérez un peu, par ce trait d'innocence,
> Où l'expose d'un fou la haute impertinence,
> Et quels fâcheux périls elle pourrait courir
> Si j'étais maintenant homme à la moins chérir!
>
> (V,2)

[Think how that madman's utter lack of sense
Exposes her in all her innocence,
And of the perils that she might go through
If I did not adore her as I do.]

Thus one senses a certain fear of unbridled female sexuality coupled with the titillation that it engenders. In other words, Agnès' peripheral presence alone is disruptive in that it causes both Horace and Arnolphe to react (rather than act) in ways contrary to their own interests.

The paradoxical dilemma evoked by this play becomes increasingly apparent. The male protagonist's attempts to retain exclusive control in the realm of *scientia* and reason by keeping the female character in the dark are motivated by a desire to keep the masculine play world intact. Any endeavor to gain access to self-determination and reason must be suppressed because it endangers the fragile existence of the balance of power within marriage. However, what occurs in effect is that the representative of the female principle, relegated to her status as nonperson devoid of ethics or reason, becomes an embodiment of the ungovernable amoral forces of fate, thereby disrupting the male hegemony even more effectively. This is ultimately why every strategic action undertaken by Arnolphe is followed by an adverse reaction. Paradox is the very foundation of the strictures of the play world that he has so carefully constructed.

How then can this oxymoronic situation be resolved? The first step would be to have woman become cognizant of her own passivity and to have her *consciously* internalize her submissiveness. The host of cheating wives alluded to in the beginning are empowered by their refusal to do so. On the other side of the spectrum, however, we have seen that Agnès' very ignorance transforms her into an instrument of fate. Arnolphe constantly attempts to summon her to orthodoxy by constantly reminding her not to violate the limits that circumscribe and define her. Because, however, he has provided her with no critical frame of reference, he is unable to co-opt her into internalizing her servitude as a natural condition so that she will assume her dependent position in the paternal order. It is Horace who will achieve this goal when Agnès openly recognizes him as her teacher/master.

Thus, Arnolphe's attempts to impose external constraints, be they physical or moral, upon the ingenue can be seen as totally ineffective in relation to the internal constraints that Agnès ultimately imposes upon herself. The protagonist's departure from the play world marks this failure. Having witnessed his displacement from spectator to director-producer as well as to object of ridicule, he refuses to acknowledge the new order along with its rules and thus becomes a spoil-sport whose expulsion from the play world becomes a necessity. His departure coincides with the arrival of the real father figure. His sexually equivocal role of father-lover is neutralized by splitting apart and being assumed by two characters: Horace and Enrique. Enrique, the patriarch of the new order, can symbolize paternal order and arbitration because, unlike Arnolphe, he is not swayed by the feminine. Thus, infringement of the incestuous taboo is avoided, and the destabilization implicit in such a double role, which threatens patriarchal order, is avoided.

The ending reestablishes the permanence of the Law and stresses the perfect balance or coincidence of chance and reason. As Horace tells Enrique:

> Le hasard en ces lieux avait exécuté
> Ce que votre sagesse avait prémédité.

(V,9)

> [In all this chance has managed, as you'll find,
> Exactly what your wisdom had in mind.]

Thus, the masculine and feminine principles are reconciled, but this reconciliation is founded upon the final subservience of chance to reason. "Le destin" has simply executed what the father's wisdom had premeditated. The play's final optimism—if it can be called that—rests on the reaffirmation of the preeminence of the patriarchal law whose authority is sustained by "le Ciel, qui fait tout pour le mieux" (V,9). [Heaven, which does all for the best.] Such a *dénouement* is eminently logical within the context of the play. Those critics who dismiss the ending as hastily contrived or arbitrary[14] have failed to note the determining role of fate throughout the play, which has paved the way for the final intervention of destiny.

5

Le Bourgeois gentilhomme:
The Interrupted Banquet

Je ne sais ce qui me tient, maudite, que je ne vous fende la tête
avec les pièces du repas que vous êtes venue troubler.
— *Le Bourgeois gentilhomme* IV, 2

When considered from the standpoint of causal linkage, *Le Bourgeois gentilhomme* is at variance with the classical ideal of linear
unity. The first two acts have most often been referred to as a
series of *lazzi* [gags] in the vein of the commedia dell'arte; the
third act introduces two rather unrelated plot strands that Molière
does not hesitate to interrupt most blatantly with a lengthy lovers'
quarrel; the fourth act sets the stage for the Turkish illusion,
whereas the fifth, composed of the *Ballet des Nations*, removes the
spectator even further from the prosaic reality of Jourdain, the
bourgeois gentilhomme himself. Modern critics do not find fault
with this lack of linear progression. They simply attribute the
play's underlying unity to its contextual dimension. Yet even they
do not agree: does the play's coherence stem from its recurrent
theme of illusion versus reality, from its musical dimension, from
Jourdain's unchanging obsession, from an ironic paradox, from
the operations of instinctual impulses, or from the author's psychic makeup and obsessions? There is no doubt that the resolu-
tions of the love triangle of Dorante, Dorimène, and Jourdain,
on the one hand, and of Cléonte and Lucile's dilemma on the
other would remain unsatisfactory were they not to dissolve into a
second, surrealistic dimension. Stock situations and the traditional
happy ending undergo a transfiguration through music and
dance. Festive interludes become more frequent and increasingly
lengthy as the play progresses, until in the end they take over
altogether. In *Le Bourgeois gentilhomme*, the play world slowly

merges with a festive and ceremonial dimension in which aesthetics play a predominant role. This movement is paralleled by a radical transformation from prosaic to poetic discourse. Subtending the conflictual dynamics between bourgeois ethics and aristocratic aesthetics one can find once again the dialectics of gender delineation, as Mme Jourdain, the stolid wife, and Dorante, the protean count, assume the roles of adversaries in the confrontation.

As the curtain rises for the first act of *Le Bourgeois gentilhomme*, our attention is drawn immediately to the center of the stage, where a young musician is silently composing a piece of music. This initial image of artistic creation will become a metaphor for the entire play, which should essentially be viewed as a dynamic process of creation and transformation: a work in the making. This may account somewhat for the fluidity of the play's structure and its final dissolution into pure fantasy. Jesse Dickson makes a pertinent observation, likening *Le Bourgeois gentilhomme* in some ways to a musical composition:

> Les sketches composant les actes I et II sont organisés en partie suivant une progression dramatique ... Mais leur succession s'ordonne moins par la progression que par un mouvement inutile à la progression, par exemple, la répétition. Le modèle subit certaines modifications (de légères différences de caractère entre les maîtres), concession nécessaire à la variété, mais sans échapper à la règle, et sans que le retour rhythmique soit moins entraînant. Il en résulte ainsi une impression de mouvement sur place, d'activité non-dirigée qui ne mène nulle-part et qui semble n'avoir d'autre but que son propre épuisement.[1]

> [The sketches composing acts I and II are organized in part according to a dramatic progression ... But their succession is ordered less by this progression than by a movement unnecessary to the progression, i.e. repetition. The pattern is subject to certain modifications (slight differences in character among the masters), a concession necessary for variety, but without escaping the rule, and without making the rhythmical return less captivating. Thus, the ensuing result is an impression of stasis, of non-directed activity that goes nowhere and seems to have no goal other than its own exhaustion.
> (Translation by author)

The first two acts of *Le Bourgeois gentilhomme* not only serve the purpose of a lengthy character development, but also prepare a context for later spectacular developments. They arouse the spectator's curiosity concerning future events, not through open-ended segments projecting toward a goal, but by conveying an impression of anticipation and preparation. The initial acts can be seen as a lengthy prelude, a *répétition*, or dress rehearsal, in which Jourdain assumes step-by-step the various attributes essential to his new identity. Nor is Jourdain the only character for whom such a metaphor is appropriate: the musicians' and dancers' repeated appearances show them to be preparing for some future event. The recurrence of the spectacle motif paves the way for the Turkish ceremony and the final play within a play. Gérard Defaux was one of the first to suggest such a reading of *Le Bourgeois gentilhomme*. What follows is his analysis of the first act:

L'ouverture se fait par un grand assemblage d'instruments, *une* Musicienne—Mlle Hilaire—est priée de chanter l'air que vient de composer l'Elève du Maître de musique. Qu'à ce *solo* succède un *duo*, un dialogue pour lequel entrent sur scène *un* Musicien et *deux* Violons! Que le *duo* se fait *trio* par l'intervention de l'Elève du Maître de musique. Qu'ensuite vient le tour du Maître à danser, et de *quatre* danseurs, et qu'enfin apparaît le Maître Tailleur, accompagné de *six* garçons tailleurs qui habillent Monsieur Jourdain en cadence. Ce langage arithméthique, qui naturellement ne doit rien au hasard, définit déjà, dans sa simplicité, un esprit de lecture. Tout se passe en fait comme si Molière avait voulu ménager un envahissement progressif de la scène—plus en plus de danseurs—en vue du ballet sur lequel clôt l'acte, et dans lequel se trouvent pɔur la première fois réellement mêlées la musique et la danse.[2]

[The overture consists of a large assemblage of musical instruments, *one* Musician—Mlle Hilaire—is asked to sing the melody that the Music Master's Pupil has just composed. That this *solo* should give way to a *duo*, a dialogue for which *one* Musician and *two* Violins come on stage! That this *duo* should become a *trio* due to the participation of the Music Master's Pupil. That next should come the Dance Master's turn, accompanied by *four* dancers, and that finally the Master Tailor should appear, accompanied by *six* apprentice tailors who dress Monsieur Jourdain in cadence. This arithmetical language, which naturally owes nothing to chance, defines from the outset, in its simplicity, a mode of interpretation. Everything happens in fact as if Molière had wanted to arrange a progressive invasion of the stage—more and more dancers—in view of the ballet that concludes the act, and in which for the first time music and dance are truly combined.]
(Translation by author)

The various song lyrics interspersed throughout the play become progressively incorporated into the fabric of the drama.

The first song of any length in act 1 describes the lovesick woes of shepherds and has very little to do with its immediate context. Its content may even appear strikingly out of place, for the subtleties of its casuistry seem totally lost on the insensitive Jourdain. The second song is introduced in the first scene of act 4, when two musicians raise their glasses and perform a toast in honor of Dorimène. This time the music is more fully integrated into its context, as it is appropriate to the action it accompanies. The lyrics combine the love theme with that of epicurean delights while Jourdain lavishes his attention on the beautiful marquise. The third and the fourth musical interludes continue the process of integration. The Turkish ceremony is a direct result of the father-son conflict and serves a useful purpose in terms of plot development, but it takes on a length and an importance which show it to go beyond its original goal. The ritual becomes a pretext for spectacle and virtuoso performance. The lyrics become important in their own right, as evidenced by their degeneration into nonsense syllables. The point is that now spectacle is no longer integrated by subordination to prosaic reality, but rather that prosaic reality is integrated into and subsumed by spectacle. The final ballet is the most elaborate production of all, consisting of a medley of vastly different lyrics, languages and styles of music.

The same type of progression can be discovered in the dance performances. Each of *Le Bourgeois gentilhomme*'s five acts ends with an *entrée de ballet* [dance interlude]. This device provides the play with a greater formal symmetry than one would expect at first glance. Furthermore, the importance of these dance segments increases with each act until spectacle takes over altogether in the end. These miniature productions serve a dual and somewhat paradoxical purpose. On the one hand, they hermetically close or seal off each act, interrupting plot continuity by projecting the action into a different order, marking the limits of each unit with a very formal, rigid, and stylized cadre. On the other, they provide contextual and thematic continuity in terms of the play as a whole and afford a glimpse at another, less prosaic reality. Out of the old order, a new one has been created, a play world that magically provides a way for Jourdain to fulfill his wishes and to attain an illusory but poetic nobility entirely within the realm of aestheticism, music, dance, and spectacle. It is a world governed by secret codes, mock-religious ritual, and childish utterances.

The feast in honor of Dorimène is a pivotal scene in this respect. Though it is causally linked to the rest of the play, it is also part spectacle and music: a fact that seems to lift it out of bourgeois reality and give it a life of its own. The act ends with the appearance of the dancing cooks as they bring out the feast: a striking parallel to the tailors' dance at the end of act 2. Not only does this form a structural association between the two parts of the play, but it once again halts linear progression by introducing the spectator to another level of illusion governed by rhythmic movement and harmonious sounds: a fantastic realm where dancing cooks are not only possible, but probable. As the prosaic world of the bourgeoisie dissolves evermore into the magical realm of poetry, music and dance, different laws of probability and necessity take over: aesthetic laws. Within this context, Ronald Tobin concludes that the food itself becomes an art form: "Molière has suggested from the outset of this particular set piece that eating is akin to artistic endeavor: elegance, erudition, taste, *bienséances*, rules, the 'pièces' of a meal, the science of 'bons morceaux' must be united to create the perfect object that appeals to the imagination."[3] Dancing tailors and cooks belong to the same level of reality as Jourdain and yet somehow broaden it to prepare us for the finale. For musicians to play and for dancers to dance is not unusual: it is spectacle, rehearsed and prepared. But tailors and cooks are by their very definition prosaic, and their spontaneity and joy in dancing is a magical transformation that ultimately prepares us for Jourdain's initiation and metamorphosis.[4]

The arrival of the dance master and the music professor in act 1 signals the beginning of a debate on aesthetics and ethics, which is squarely rooted in a social context. The music master's emphasis on tangible results rather than lavish praise reveals the prerequisite behind any form of idealism: the satisfaction of basic needs. In the debate, the words "lumières," "louanges," "mérite," "fierté," and "gloire" characterize aristocratic aspirations that transcend basic instincts. Yet the music master is quick to put such values in their proper place: "Des louanges toutes pures ne mettent pas un homme à son aise: il faut y mêler du solide; et la meilleure façon de louer, c'est de louer avec les mains" (I,1).[5] [But that adulation does not keep you alive; praise by itself does not make a man well off; you have to mix in something solid; and the best way to praise is to praise with the open hand.] From a bourgeois perspective, civilized ideals lose their ethical significance and become purely playful. When compared to the need for survival, they appear to be unnecessary frills. Furthermore, the dialogue suggests a clear and unsurmountable division between the activities of the aristocracy and the bourgeoisie: according to the music master Jourdain "paiera pour les autres ce que les autres loueront pour lui" (I,1). The inference here is that within the hierarchical class system, productivity and idealism do not mix.[6] While the lower and middle classes ensure their survival through productivity, the nobleman's calling is primarily aesthetic. He projects an image, creates and shapes his identity. However, within this comedy, the aristocratic substitution of socio-aesthetic conventions of politeness, decorum, and taste for the moral criteria of truth and virtue, opens the way for the erosion of class boundaries through deception and disguise.

As the play progresses, the association between civilized behavior and the superfluous or frivolous becomes ever more pronounced. Jourdain's outrageous new outfit is a prime visual example of the artificial creation of needs, of civilization gone to excess. The dress is impractical, for the relationship between form and function has been completely disrupted. A practical man, Jourdain attempts to reestablish and justify the article's usefulness: "Donnez-moi ma robe pour mieux entendre!" (I,2) The protagonist's middle-class background prevents him from understanding that from an aristocrat's point of view it is precisely the outfit's afunctional nature that gives it value.

A self-made man, Jourdain is still uncomfortable and unaccustomed to the superfluous. His lackeys' function is primarily decorative, yet Jourdain attempts somewhat futilely to "employ" them. Their presence on stage contributes to the visual representation of the artificial creation of needs in a civilized society:

> *M. Jourdain:* Laquais, holà! mes deux laquais.
> *First Lackey:* Que voulez-vous, monsieur?
> *M. Jourdain:* Rien. C'est pour voir si vous m'entendez bien.
>
> (I,2)

> [Monsieur Jourdain: Lackeys! Hey, my two lackeys!
> First Lackey: What do you wish, sir?
> Monsieur Jourdain: Nothing. It was just to see if you hear me all right. (I,2)]

Jourdain's comments unveil the ornamental, but afunctional nature of civilized aristocratic activity.

The parasites surrounding Jourdain are constantly striving to create new needs for their benefactor without considering the long-term danger of an endless proliferation of desires. Indeed, Jourdain has already taken it upon himself to hire a tailor, a fencing master, and a philosopher. Seeing their primary source of income imperiled and sensing that their benefactor evaluates the arts primarily in terms of their practical value, the music and dance instructors attempt to persuade Jourdain that their respective arts fulfill a useful function. The illogicality of their arguments, based on the literal and figurative meanings of "s'accorder ensemble" [to harmonize together, to agree] and "faire un mauvais pas" [to stumble, to blunder], points out the precise opposite: the impossibility of judging artistic achievement by anything other than aesthetic standards.

The aspirations of the aristocracy can be termed playful because of their association with the artificial, the superfluous, and the purely formal. It is not surprising, therefore, that Jourdain displays an "apparent inability to differentiate between the formal aspects of the nobility [the hired tutors] present to him and the real nature of that 'quality' he seeks to emulate."[7] The fencing lesson makes a mockery of any pretense of transcendent value subtending the aristocratic ideal. Like the other masters before him, the fencing master proclaims the importance of his art: "Je vous l'ai déjà dit, tout le secret des armes ne consiste qu'en deux choses, à donner et à ne point recevoir; et, comme je vous fis voir l'autre jour par raison démonstrative, il est impossible que vous receviez si vous savez détourner l'épée de votre ennemi de la ligne de votre corps; ce qui ne dépend seulement que d'un petit mouvement du poignet, ou en dedans ou en dehors" (II,2). [I've told you already, the whole secret of swordplay consists in just two things: in giving and in not receiving; and as I showed you the other day by demonstrative reasoning, it is impossible for you to receive if you know how to return your opponent's sword away from the line of your body; which depends simply on a tiny movement of your wrist either to the inside or to the outside.] In his infinite naïveté, Jourdain unmasks the deeper significance of such a statement: "De cette façon donc, un homme, sans avoir du coeur, est sûr de tuer son homme, et de n'être point tué?" (II,2) [Then in that way a man, without being brave, is sure of killing his man and not being killed?] Efficiency and skill replace substantive values such as courage and valor, while winning at any cost becomes the ultimate achievement. What Jourdain perceives is the discrepancy between cause and result: the denial of the primacy of moral intent and the pragmatic emphasis on the final effect. By implication, civilization is comparable to a game whose proffered purpose of ennobling mankind is ultimately fraudulent.

Jourdain's awkward and misguided attempts at becoming an aristocrat are based on his desire for acceptance in a privileged and exclusive society or circle of play. His difficulties arise from his socioeconomic background, which affords him very little real understanding of the gratuitous nature of ludic activity and certainly no appreciation for aesthetic harmony. In an excellent chapter entitled "Esthétiques et société chez Molière," Jules Brody suggests that Molière supported an aristocratic aesthetic. In his view, therefore, the main conflict is not between morality and immorality, but between *grâce* and *gaucherie*. Thus, Jourdain's fault is "une insuffisance esthétique plutôt qu'une tare morale."[8] [an aesthetic deficiency rather than a moral defect.] (Translation by author)

It is ultimately the bourgeois' lack of taste that prevents his entry into the world of nobility. This is conveyed no more forcefully than through his discourse. Jourdain's language is characteristically off-key and off-color: a literal message that passes directly from impulse to its expression without being filtered by reason, reflection, or an awareness of social norms. It strikes a note of disharmony and vulgarity as a counterpoint to an otherwise melodic and refined conversation. Jourdain's idiom is as discordant as the "trompette marine" [trumpet marine] he wishes to include in his instructor's concert. His replies are generally brief and to the point, occasionally monosyllabic ("Euh?") and frequently childishly willful ("Je veux . . ."). They reflect his inability to form a chain of coherent thought or to embellish his language with rhetorical devices. Jourdain's idiom is bourgeois prose: too direct, too colorful, and too impulsive to suit aristocratic sensitivity. The aristocratic ideal is, as evidenced by M. Jourdain's many tutors, a by-product of learning. It requires the repression of natural impulse and the restriction of spontaneous expression. In scene 5 of act 2, Jourdain's comments to the tailor on his new attire can be read as a metaphorical representation of inhibition:

M. *Jourdain:* Vous m'avez envoyé des bas si étroits que j'ai eu toutes les peines du monde à les mettre, et il y a déjà deux mailles de rompues.
Le *Maître Tailleur:* Ils ne s'élargiront que trop.
M. *Jourdain:* Oui, si je romps toujours des mailles. Vous m'avez fait faire des souliers qui me blessent aussi furieusement.

(II,5)

[Monsieur Jourdain: The silk stockings you sent me were so tight that I had all the trouble in the world getting them on, and there are already two stitches broken.
Master Tailor: They'll stretch all you need, and more.

Monsieur Jourdain: Yes, if I keep breaking stitches. Also, the shoes you made me hurt terribly.]

Unable to suffer the confinement of "aristocratic" apparel, Jourdain bursts out of his seams both literally and figuratively. The protagonist's spontaneity is set in continual contrast to the constrictions of society: the strangling of natural movement of any sort, be it emotional or physical.

Although Jourdain's obtuseness makes him a dubious candidate for scholarly activity, the philosophy lesson is not entirely lost on him. For one thing, he is taught the significant difference between poetry and prose and he makes the astonishing discovery that he has been speaking prose all his life. Prose is thus the faithful but unimaginative reflection of ordinary bourgeois reality, the plain talk of everyday life. More importantly perhaps, he rediscovers a childlike fascination with language as sound and ultimately with poetry itself: "M. Jourdain's initial apotheosis occurs early, in act two, scene four. Discovering how to emit vowels, he jubilates. This spontaneous jubilation is a structural, prehypnotic presage of Jourdain's culminating linguistic ecstasies during the famous ceremony with the Turkish potentate . . . From ludicrous linguistic childishness has spurted knowledge of creative beauty and a possible new self, to be discovered in sound."[9] Interestingly enough, Jourdain's sensitivity to the sound of language rather than to its meaning was previously manifest in his refusal to study the regular syllogisms (Barbara, Celarent, Darii, Ferio, Baralipton): "Voilà des mots qui sont trop rébarbatifs. Cette logique-là ne me revient point. Apprenons autre chose qui soit plus joli" (II,4). [Those words are too crabbed. I don't like that logic. Let's learn something that's prettier.] This important revelation will intensify as linguistic creation accompanies Jourdain's transformation from ordinary bourgeois to magical mamamouchi and as his newly discovered poetic idiom becomes the secret code of entry into the play world of his own delusions.

The first appearance of female characters occurs relatively late in the play. Jourdain summons his servant Nicole in act 3 so that she might receive his orders. Thus the initial representation of the male-female relationship is one of domination and submission. Nicole's explosive reaction—her irrepressible laughter—is a direct subversion of her master's authority. Unable to harness or control the urge, regardless of the punitive consequences, she represents the unorganizable feminine construct. Her laughter must be silenced at all costs as it eludes masculine order. Nicole's reaction is one of speechlessness. She chokes on her words, but her body talks through its laughter: "L'hilarité de Nicole est bêtifiante. Car, chose rare, le langage du corps remplace momentanément le langage des mots, et du coup réduit l'écart arbitraire qui sépare la chose de son expression."[10] [Nicole's mirth is stupefying. For a rare phenomenon occurs: the body's language momentarily replaces the language of words and instantly reduces the arbitrary gap separating the thing from its expression.] (Translation by author) In the end, her laughter disturbs and her presence is nothing but disturbance. In her examination of a Chinese tale in which an emperor's wives are decapitated for laughing and giggling in response to military orders, Cixous writes:

> It is hard to imagine a more perfect example of a particular relationship between two economies: a masculine economy and a feminine economy, in which the masculine is governed by a rule that keeps time with two beats, three beats, four beats, with pipe and drum, exactly as it should be . . . It's a question of submitting feminine disorder, its laughter, its inability to take the drumbeats seriously, to the threat of decapitation . . . Women have no choice other than to be decapitated, and in any case the moral is that if they don't actually lose their heads by the sword, *keep them on condition that they lose them—* lose them, that is, to complete silence, turned into automatons.[11]

Jourdain responds to Nicole's hilarious attack on his authoritative voice by threatening violent action, but it is ultimately his assignment of household chores that silences the servant's hilarity. Nicole's forthright belly laugh would be considered even more unseemly behavior for heroines of higher rank. To make women feel that their laughter is somehow socially inappropriate is an effective means of barring them from the play world. Their sour nature and ill humor at the men's boyish pranks reinforce their difference and alienation. Although the servant girl Nicole does have a sense of humor and vents her laughter freely, her outburst is not so much a sign of participation in the play world as a direct attack upon it. She is, in fact, not laughing *with* but *at* the male protagonist. From Jourdain's point of view, this type of laughter is simply further evidence of woman's otherness. Though Nicole's reaction is contagious, it is generally ineffective in disrupting the male hegemony.

Enter Mme Jourdain: the voice of normalcy and the chief embodiment of the bourgeoisie. As Jourdain's wife, she has certain prerogatives, most notably that of unsilenced, uninterrupted speech. Taking up the fight where Nicole has left off, Mme Jourdain stands her ground with a verbal onslaught. The power of language to disrupt and disturb is evidenced by Jourdain's repeated and frustrated attempts to silence the two women. "Taisez-vous, ma servante et ma femme . . . Taisez-vous, vous dis-je: vous êtes des ignorantes l'une et l'autre; et vous ne savez pas les prérogatives de tout cela . . . Paix; songez à ce que vous dites . . . Taisez-vous . . . Taisez-vous, vous dis-je . . . (III,3) Voilà pas le coup de langue? . . . Taisez-vous impertinente; vous vous fourrez toujours dans la conversation . . . Voilà bien du caquet! Ah! que de bruit!" (III,12) [Be quiet, my maidservant and my wife. . . . Be quiet, I tell you: you are both ignoramuses, and you don't know the prerogatives of all that . . . Peace, think what you're saying . . . Be quiet, here he is . . . Be quiet, I tell you. . . . There goes your tongue . . . Shut up, you with your impertinence. . . . You're always butting into the conversation.] Although Mme Jourdain has very little real power, her husband does fear her sharp tongue. Unable to silence her, Jourdain's only viable alternative is to dismiss her language as empty noise or chatter, for she can surely not engage in meaningful conversation as she remains outside the realm of knowledge. "Vous parlez toutes les deux comme des bêtes et j'ai honte de votre ignorance . . . J'enrage quand je parle à des femmes ignorantes" (III,3). [You're both talking like fools and I'm ashamed of your ignorance . . . It makes me mad to see ignorant women.]

From the standpoint of the masculine hegemony operative within the play, Mme Jourdain's weapon is the word because she talks incessantly, overflowing with sound, but her feminine discourse is ultimately rejected as uninformed and insignificant. Jourdain's bid to regain mastery over the situation is coupled with a characteristic attempt to teach, to in-form his two feminine adversaries. Rather than communicate true knowledge, however, Jourdain wishes to teach his wife and his servant to be aware of their own ignorance. It is interesting to note that the lesson imparted relates to the fundamental difference between poetic and prosaic discourse. Jourdain awkwardly reiterates the half-digested philosophy lesson in order to justify its usefulness. The categorical declaration that "Tout ce qui n'est point prose est vers, et tout ce qui n'est point vers est prose" infers a clear and unsurmountable distinction between two forms of expression that cannot overlap. Such a division is paralleled structurally by an earlier reference to the separation of the social classes, notably the bourgeoisie and the aristocracy. By silencing his wife's plain speech, Jourdain would effectively silence the voice of the bourgeoisie, a constant foil to his imaginary nobility and a reminder of his past. Although imbued with common sense, Mme Jourdain's prose is limited by its lack of imagination and intellectual curiosity, by its deterministic conformism and simplistic absolutism. She warns her husband that: "Tout ce monde-là est un monde qui a raison et qui est plus sage que vous" (III,3). [This everybody is people who are right, and who have more sense than you.] According to Ciccone: "For Madame Jourdain, language is a tool for expressing judgment; its importance lies in the communication of messages to be evaluated—language's referential function. For Monsieur Jourdain, however, language is essentially metalinguistic and manifests itself as an object of analysis whose definition supplants any judgment."[12] In the course of five acts, Jourdain's language evolves from bourgeois prose to metalanguage and finally dissolves into pure sound.

Mme Jourdain's straight talk is not merely that of an individual, but that of a whole social stratum as well. As a woman, she has espoused the very values that repress and subdue her. Her opinions cannot be attributed to any one person, for hers is the voice of orthodoxy and public rumor. This is the "qu'en dira-t-on" that supersedes the paternal prerogative. Refusing to allow her daughter to marry above her station, she admonishes: "S'il fallait qu'elle [ma fille] me vînt visiter en équipage de grande dame, et qu'elle manquât, par mégarde, à saluer quelqu'un du quartier, on ne manquerait pas aussitôt de dire cent sottises. Voyez-vous, dirait-on, cette madame la marquise qui fait tant la glorieuse? . . . Je ne veux point tous ces caquets" (III,12). [If she had to come and visit me decked out like a grand lady, and by mistake failed to greet someone in the neighborhood, right away people wouldn't fail to say a hundred stupid things. 'Do you see that Madame la Marquise,' they'd say, 'with her high and mighty airs?' . . . I don't want all that gossip.] Aside from her self-appointed role as guardian of the status quo, Mme Jourdain considers herself to be an advocate for women's rights: "Ce sont mes droits que je défends et j'aurai pour moi toutes les femmes" (IV,2). [It's my rights I'm defending, and all the women will be on my side.] Thus, through the presence of Mme Jourdain, bourgeois moral orthodoxy and the feminine admonitory voice are intimately linked.

As a proponent of the serious moral values and/or the sound common sense of the "real world," the good wife can be regarded primarily as a non-laugher who refuses to recognize or condone the existence of a separate male society of play. Characterized by her refusal to humor her husband or to participate in his fantasies, she is the ultimate incarnation of the spoil-sport. Although her prose threatens to destroy the fragile circle of Jourdain's playful illusions, it becomes increasingly inappropriate and discredited by the ever widening poetic dimension within the play: "[L]e monde imaginaire, artistique et poétique de Jourdain triomphe du monde prosaïque et bourgeois de son épouse . . . Plus Jourdain s'éloigne de ses origines, plus il échappe à l'empire du réel."[13] [Jourdain's imaginary, artistic and poetic world triumphs over the middle class prosaic world of his wife. . . . The more Jourdain distances himself from his roots, the more he escapes from the influence of reality.] (Translation by author) It would therefore be erroneous to view Mme Jourdain's common sense as a measuring stick for normative behavior within the play. René Bray refutes any such attempt to identify Molière's characters with the voice of reason: "Il n'y a pas de raisonneurs dans le théâtre de Molière . . . Chaque personnage est exigé par sa fonction dramatique, non par une prétendue fonction morale inventée par la critique . . . L'intention de Molière, la pensée qui donne à son oeuvre la force et l'unité, ce n'est pas une pensée de moraliste, c'est une intention d'artiste."[14] [There are no reasoners in Molière's theater. . . . Each character is required by his or her dramatic function, not by a so-called moral function invented by critics. . . . Molière's intention, the idea that gives his work its forcefulness and cohesiveness, is not that of a moralist, but of an artist.] (Translation by author)

Every time Mme Jourdain appears on stage, her presence is disruptive. During the evening's entertainment in honor of Dorimène her quarrelsome voice interrupts the festive mood, not to mention the music. This interruption is all the more blatant as the participants' anticipatory energy (or Freudian fore-pleasure) has been building up to this climactic moment in the play, thus signaling its importance. Although her husband's behavior may warrant reproach, her strident discourse is quite literally that of a *trouble-fête* [spoil-sport] whose just cause is discredited because of its untimeliness. Her vision is accustomed to the real world and she has trouble adjusting to a playful perspective. Dorante appeals to her: "Prenez, Madame Jourdain, prenez de meilleures lunettes" (IV,2). [Madame Jourdain, put on a better pair of spectacles.]

The wife's next intrusion occurs when she unceremoniously breaks the spell of the Turkish ceremony, with its ritualistic chants and cadenced movements, at the end of the fourth act. Just as the realm of fantasy threatens to take over permanently, Mme

Jourdain's sound bourgeois sense almost spoils the fun. By now, however, dementia has gained enough momentum to thwart the most assiduous attempts at halting it and Mme Jourdain in her own turn will have to become "raisonnable" (that is, according to her husband's inverted definition of the term). Once the initiation ritual has consecrated Jourdain's central role within a play world of his own creation, any form of dialogue between the two spouses becomes inoperable. The husband's discourse has become so out-landish as to bar communication entirely. His earlier fascination with language as sound has degenerated into a series of "hou la ba la"'s resembling infantile utterances. Jourdain has inverted the definitions of reason and madness, thus preventing his wife from employing logical argumentation. The two modes of expression have no common convention and Madame Jourdain's bewilder-ment is echoed by repeated queries: "Qu'est-ce que cela veut dire? Comment? Qu'est-ce à dire cela? Qu'est-ce donc que ce jargon-là? Que voulez-vous donc dire?" (V,1) [What does that mean? What? What is it you mean by that? Just what is this jargon? Just what is all this?]

Mme Jourdain's refusal to make the necessary adjustment makes her the most untiring antagonist of the world of fantasy and places her squarely outside of the locus of play. As the play progresses toward its final dementia, her voice becomes increas-ingly isolated and discordant, until she alone stands as the beacon of reason in a sea of madness. It becomes evident that those who have participated in the game are quickly losing patience with Jourdain's wife, whose blindness so nearly spoils the fun: "Il y a une heure, madame, que nous vous faisons signe: ne voyez-vous pas bien que tout ceci n'est fait que pour nous ajuster aux visions de votre mari; que nous l'abusons sous ce déguisement, et c'est Cléonte, lui-même qui est le fils du Grand Turc?" (V,6) [Madame, we've been trying to make signs to you for an hour. Don't you see that all this is being done just to fall in with your husband's visions, that we're fooling him in this disguise, and that it's Cléonte himself who's the son of the Grand Turk?] Madame Jourdain is the only character who needs to have the situation clearly and literally spelled out for her in plain prose. Upon realizing that her advo-cacy of sound bourgeois common sense has been abandoned by all, in favor of her husband's demented fantasies, Mme Jourdain remains speechless. Her total incomprehension of the new linguis-tic convention, and poetic discourse generally, robs her of any form of expression. Her silence is rightly perceived by Jourdain as a personal triumph. The patriarchal hegemony remains untouched and unaltered. By silencing the feminine voice, Jourdain has succeeded in reducing the women in the play to mere objects to be redistributed at will:

Madame Jourdain: Et Nicole?
M. Jourdain: Je la donne au truchement; et ma femme à qui la vou-
dra" (V,6).

[Madame Jourdain: What about Nicole?
Monsieur Jourdain: .I give her to the interpreter; and my wife to anyone that wants her.]

The plain speakers are proponents of the earnest normative values of the bourgeoisie. As such, Cléonte, Lucile, and the mutinous Mme Jourdain stand on the negative side of the would-be gentleman. In view of the fact that aristocratic values are associated with playful activity, it is not surprising that this comedy's principal prankster, Dorante, is a dissolute and unscrupulous nobleman. As such, he is Mme Jourdain's chief antagonist. According to Nathan Gross: "Dorante, the only nobleman in the play so far, treats [Jourdain] in the same way that Dom Juan handles his creditor, Monsieur Dimanche, keeping him off with gestures of civility, but the audience, like Mme Jourdain, perceives these as abuse . . . Since in the naive and hopeful way of thinking, aristocracy is inseparable from the loftiest values, Jourdain extrapolates ethical content from visible forms and gestures to define aristocracy."[15]
Though endowed with roguish charm and wit, Dorante is an utterly amoral character, completely devoid of heroic ideals or ethical standards. His relentless pursuit of Dorimène will eventually lead to success, but in the end, the question of Dorante's guilt or innocence in misappropriating Jourdain's funds is never resolved—indeed it appears to be completely irrelevant: "That Dorante's knavery, however cynical, is fundamentally benign in the moral world of *Le Bourgeois gentilhomme*, receives further confirmation in his roles as master of revels . . . Inasmuch as *Le Bourgeois gentilhomme* is a spectacular defense of entertainment, laced with song, dance and ceremony, Dorante's role is absolutely central to the play's purpose."[16]
What is important, however, is the perception one has of Dorante as a winner. More than any other factor, this generates a positive response to his antics. The spectator's appreciation of Dorante's abilities increases as the shift from prosaic reality to

poetic fantasy becomes more pronounced. Initially reprehensible, this character becomes more appealing as the play world takes over. Mme Jourdain and Dorante are, in fact, the principal antagonists in this play for they are the main embodiments of bourgeois and aristocratic values, respectively. The more the former's point of view is discredited, the more the nobleman gains the audience's sympathy, as well as that of the beautiful marquise. Much of the play's dramatic tension derives from this bipolarity, for Mme Jourdain and Dorante are set in constant opposition: the illusion-maker and the illusion-breaker.

Just as seriousness and moral self-righteousness are associated with a feminized bourgeoisie, playfulness is the prerogative of a masculine aristocracy. Because of her sex, Dorimène's presence will remain marginal to the circle of play. Unlike the ingenue Lucile, the marquise—by virtue of her high rank, financial independence, and widowhood—is, or appears to be, empowered with the right to self-determination. On the other hand, she is the coveted prize validating the victory of Dorante over his adversary and rival, Jourdain, who unabashedly attempts to buy her: "Une femme de qualité a pour moi des charmes ravissants; et c'est un honneur que j'achèterais au prix de toute chose" (III,6). [A woman of quality has ravishing charms for me, and it's an honor I would pay at any price.] The initial impression of female autonomy is in fact soon effaced by Dorimène's self-avowed passivity: "Je ne sais pas, Dorante; je fais ici une étrange démarche, de me laisser amener par vous dans une maison où je ne connais personne" (III,15). [I don't know, Dorante; this is another strange thing I'm doing here, letting you take me into a house where I don't know anybody.] Having gained her freedom from marital ties, the young widow's readiness to abandon it in favor of the unscrupulous Dorante is downright disconcerting. Her alienation, expressed in the following terms, can perhaps shed some light on her abdication: "Mais vous ne dites pas que je m'engage insensiblement chaque jour à recevoir de trop grands témoignages de votre passion. J'ai beau me défendre des choses, vous fatiguez ma résistance, et vous avez une civile opiniâtreté qui me fait venir tout doucement à tout ce qu'il vous plaît" (III,15). [But you don't mention that I'm becoming involved imperceptibly every day by accepting excessive tokens of your passion. I try to defend myself against these things, but you wear down my resistance; and you have a polite obstinacy which makes me come around gradually to whatever you like.] By nature generous,[17] this woman's response to the bond of obligation is not to dismiss it or tear it asunder, but to give of herself in return. Nonetheless, in her bewilderment at her alienation, she intuits the inimical presence of "things" that surround her, besiege her, and ultimately imprison her. Unable to defer to a higher power, Dorimène must claim responsibility for her own defeat or justify her decision by internalizing and assimilating her subservience to man. Unlike the ingenue, therefore, Dorimène cannot simply be bought or solicited from a father: she must be convinced to willingly sacrifice her autonomy. Although Dorimène professes to consent to marriage out of pity for Dorante, this is obviously a last attempt to save face and maintain an illusion of dominance. The marquise's role throughout seems to be that of spectator. Following her submission to Dorante's will, Dorimène will be relegated to the position of peripheral passive observer of the final comedy, whereas her husband-to-be remains an active prankster and participant in the game, exploiting Jourdain's confusion to marry Dorimène in his rival's presence.

Very much in contrast to Dorante, Cléonte is a man of honor and as such he is out of his element in the play world. Initially he belongs to the clan of plain speakers. Characterized by his utter seriousness and his literal-mindedness, he is very much a man of his class and the ideal son-in-law for Mme Jourdain. His language and his ideals are better suited to the world of melodrama than to that of comedy and his words seem strikingly out of place. Cléonte's adherence to ethical values proves to be a major liability in seeking Lucile's hand in marriage. When asked whether or not he is a *gentilhomme,* he responds: "Je trouve que toute imposture est indigne d'un honnête homme, et qu'il y a de la lâcheté à déguiser ce que le ciel nous a fait naître, à se parer aux yeux du monde d'un titre dérobé, à se vouloir donner pour ce qu'on n'est pas. . ." (III,12). [I think that any imposture is unworthy of an honorable man, and that there is cowardice in disguising what Heaven had us born to be, in adorning ourselves in the eyes of the world with a stolen title, in trying to pass ourselves off for what we are not . . .] Plain prose and straight talk rob Jourdain of his illusions, which are built primarily on a linguistic redefinition of terms rather than on actual transubstantiation. From Jourdain's own query it becomes apparent that he does not necessarily require a noble son-in-law, but simply one who calls himself noble.

Covielle admonishes his master Cléonte for his inability to temporarily disengage himself from moral self-righteousness. In the topsy-turvy world of comedy, lying becomes a virtue, hypocrisy a means of compromising and adapting. Self-righteousness leads to the intractable rigidity, the unwillingness to compromise of tragic heroes and ultimately to the refusal of life itself. Covielle realizes the necessity to playfully acknowledge the father's delusions: "Vous moquez-vous de le prendre sérieusement avec un homme comme cela? Ne voyez-vous pas qu'il est fou? et vous coûtait-il quelque chose de vous accommoder à ses chimères?" (III,13) [Are you joking, to take the matter seriously with a man like that? Don't you see he's crazy? And was it costing you anything to accommodate yourself to his fancies?]

Jourdain's madness is a locus outside of reality, playful and fantastic, a locus where prosaic language is discredited and unintelligible. Covielle will therefore obligingly redefine Jourdain's ancestry in order to flatter him. This purely linguistic redefinition recognizes the primary difference between bourgeois and aristocratic values by minimizing the necessity for survival and by emphasizing the casually gratuitous aspects of Jourdain's father's business endeavors. Thus, in the first phase of the initiatory ritual, Jourdain sheds his old skin, his past identity. Out of this symbolic form of suicide a new being must be created, whose past must be reinvented. Covielle exclaims: "Lui, marchand? C'est pure médisance, il ne l'a jamais été. Tout ce qu'il faisait, c'est qu'il était fort obligeant, fort officieux; et, comme il se connaissait fort bien en étoffes, il en allait choisir de tous les côtés, les faisait apporter chez lui, et en donnait à ses amis pour de l'argent" (IV,3). [He, a merchant? That's sheer calumny; he never was. All he did was that he was very obliging, very helpful; and since he was a real connoisseur of cloth, he went around and picked it out everywhere, had it brought to his house, and gave it to his friends for money.]

It is, of course, Covielle, not Cléonte, who is accountable for perpetrating the final hoax. Although Cléonte will be persuaded to participate in playful activity, thus abandoning momentarily the realm of normality, the Turkish ceremony is the result of his servant's machinations. As strategists, Dorante and Covielle form a mutual admiration society. Although they are conducting different games, they can readily improvise and play off of each other. Dorante's compliment to Covielle bridges the social gap that separates them: "Je ne devine point le stratagème, mais je devine qu'il ne manquera pas de faire son effet, puisque tu l'entreprends" (IV,5). [I can't guess the strategem, but I can guess that it won't fail to work, since you're undertaking it.] In act 4 their strategies merge in a final attempt to achieve victory over Jourdain. The question as to who the ultimate victor might be remains the most paradoxical point in the play.

A clash becomes inevitable when male prankster and female spoil-sport collide. As the primary representative of bourgeois values, Mme Jourdain is suspicious of any form of unproductive activity. Play is anathema to her, and her seriousness is a foil both to Dorante's weightlessness and to her husband's aspirations. During her first encounter with Dorante, literal-mindedness is pitted against figurative discourse. Mme Jourdain "decodes" or translates the nobleman's polite but vacuous banter into plain parlance. By doing so she unveils the underlying hostility of the encounter:

Dorante: Comment se porte [votre fille]?
Madame Jourdain: Elle se porte sur ses deux jambes . . .
Dorante: Je pense, madame Jourdain, que vous avez eu bien des amants dans votre jeune âge, belle et d'agréable humeur comme vous étiez.
Madame Jourdain: Trédame! monsieur, est-ce que madame Jourdain est décrépite, et la tête lui grouille-t-elle déjà?

(III,5)

[Dorante: How is [your daughter] getting along?
Madame Jourdain: She's getting along on her own two legs. . . .
Dorante: I think, Madame Jourdain, you had plenty of suitors in your younger days, pretty and good-humored as you were.
Madame Jourdain: Land's sakes, sir! Is Madame Jourdain decrepit and doddering already?]

It is interesting to note how frequently translations of terms become necessary in this play. This is due, of course, to the many different levels of language employed (ordinary prose, poetic discourse, and nonsensical vagaries) as well as to the Turkish ceremony of act 4 and the numerous dialects of act 5. The progression of Jourdain's delusions is paralleled by his ever increasing need for interpreters. Dorante finds it necessary to translate Jourdain's awkward prose into elegant discourse, so that Dorimène might "understand" its meaning. The translator is empowered with the designation of meaning. He is the one through whom all discourse must pass and thus he detains the key to the Symbolic. Dorante and the resourceful servant Covielle will employ this stratagem to their advantage, distorting the truth and assigning new meaning whenever necessary. Covielle assumes the official role of interpreter to the "fils du Grand Turc" [Son of the Grand Turk]. His translation of French into Turkish hinders rather than helps communication, thus reinforcing the general atmosphere of folly.

The delirium of the Turkish ceremony brings the madness to vertiginous heights. From the standpoint of causality, the Turkish illusion has a definite purpose: it permits the resolution of the Cléonte-Jourdain conflict without the slightest concession on either side. The lovers will thus be united and the wits will achieve their ends. Yet the ending points to its own absurdity, for the possibility of a true solution is denied by the illusory nature of the final acts. Plot continuity, so tenuous during the initial acts, now no longer depends upon rational cause-and-effect progression, but upon the propelling forces of madness. It is indeed Jourdain's madness that governs the final phases of the action and destroys the possibility of any relationship between cause and effect. Such action, which creates its own meaning outside of the real world of serious values and which seems to be movement for its own sake, can only be termed playful.

Jourdain's inability to achieve mastery of aristocratic discourse bars his access to the play world he desperately wants to join. His alternative is to create his own imaginary play world in which mastery of a fantastic, nonsensical mumbo jumbo called Turkish becomes the secret code of access. Quintessentially poetic—"La langue turque est comme cela, elle dit beaucoup en peu de paroles" (IV,4) [Yes, the Turkish language is like that, it says a lot in a few words.]—this language is easily assimilated by Jourdain: "A la maladresse a soudain succédé la grâce, Jourdain n'est vraiment chez lui, n'est vraiment lui, qu'en Turquie. Son compliment, d'abord balbutiant et pratiquement incompréhensible . . .—devient tout à coup, ô miracle, d'une élégance proprement mamamouchéenne . . . Sa nouvelle dignité a transformé Jourdain au point de lui apprendre à parler."[18] [Awkwardness has suddenly given way to charm, Jourdain is only truly at home, is only truly himself, in Turkey. His compliment, at first bumbling and practically incomprehensible, suddenly and miraculously attains the elegance befitting a mamamouchi. . . . His new dignity has transformed him to the point of teaching him how to speak.] (Translation by author)

Jourdain's new identity makes him appear more ridiculous than ever from a bourgeois point of view and yet, in the end, it is not Jourdain but the point of view that changes. Following the initiation ritual, the logical order collapses and folly reigns. In such an environment, the bourgeois' whims are quite appropriate and it is with effortless grace that he now takes over the role of master of ceremonies and leads us into the realm of festive illusion. In the final analysis, Jourdain's newfound ability to make himself understood is the direct consequence of the progressive acceptance by all other characters, including his recalcitrant wife, of his very own frame of reference: his game. It is a convention that allows for the inclusion of the fantastic, thereby liberating language from its mimetic adherence to prosaic reality.[19]

Though initially the wits seem to have gained the upper hand, they have done so at their own expense, for by trying to subdue and contain patriarchal power, they are forced to consolidate the very basis of that power: this is the reason for Jourdain's ultimate resilience. As the play progresses, his game becomes increasingly gratuitous and in the end, he plays for the sake of playing, while those around him are still bound by self-interest. This opinion is confirmed by Jourdain's largesse, which corresponds to his expansive nature. As Covielle puts it, they have adjusted themselves to the patriarch's vision. Jourdain ultimately gains control, imposes the rules, and defines the final game plan.

As prose finally gives way to poetic fantasy, feminine discourse is silenced and the "real" outcome is deferred by the superimposition of a poetic dimension where laws of probability and necessity dissolve into a play world governed by formal necessity. As it becomes increasingly difficult to distinguish reality from illusion, Lucile asks for clarification: "Est-ce une comédie que vous jouez?" [Are you acting in a play?] To which Jourdain hastily replies: "Non, non ce n'est pas une comédie; c'est une affaire fort sérieuse" (V,5). [No, no, it's a very serious matter.]

Once dementia has taken complete control, the boundaries between play and reality have been erased, and no discernible difference remains between comedy and real life. In an article entitled "*Le Bourgeois gentilhomme* en contexte," Michèle Vialet proposes one of the most thoughtful interpretations of the play's controversial ending:

Monsieur Jourdain est délibérément évolutionniste . . . En d'autres termes, il propose un nouvel ordre, utopique puisque refusant de considérer la réalité comme inévitable, nécessaire ou inchangeable. Bien que sa tentative se.solde par un échec, son rêve n'en a pas moins le pouvoir d'exprimer son refus de la réalité sociale. La pensée utopique est précisément capable de concevoir, au delà de l'état institutionalisé des choses, un processus dynamique novateur. La réalité n'est plus une donnée immuable, mais un processus ouvert, en évolution.[20]

[Monsieur Jourdain is deliberately evolutionistic. In other words, he proposes a new order, utopian in that it refuses to consider reality as inevitable, necessary or unchangeable. Although his attempt results in failure, his dream has nonetheless the power to express his refusal of social reality. Utopian thought is precisely capable of conceiving a dynamic innovative process beyond the institutionalized status quo. Reality is no longer an immutable given, but an open, evolutionary process.] (Translation by author)

Thus, if the return to reality is inevitable, the seeds of a new concept of reality have been planted through imaginary theatrical enactment. The three marriages consecrate a new order in which bourgeois values have been inalterably affected on an imaginary level by their contact with the festive realm of play. Through the process of initiatory ritual a new identity has been conferred upon the patriarch, thus allowing him to consolidate his power, at least within the realm of the imaginary, by discrediting his wife's adherence to normalcy.

6

Le Tartuffe: The Transference
of Homoerotic Desire

Il l'appelle son frère, et l'aime dans son âme
Cent fois plus qu'il ne fait mère, fils, fille et femme.
C'est de tous ses secrets l'unique confident,
Et de ses actions le directeur prudent.
Il le choie, il l'embrasse, et pour une maîtresse,
On ne saurait, je pense, avoir plus de tendresse.
—Le Tartuffe I, 2

The recurrence of the love triangle as a leitmotif subtending and informing comic plot can be attributed to its structural concomitance with the comic triangle itself, consisting of the joke-maker, the accomplice, and the object of ridicule (see the Introduction). Whereas it is traditionally the wife and her lover who subject the husband to indignities, reducing him thereby to the status of powerless bystander, *Le Tartuffe*'s plot is complicated by the subversion or perhaps more accurately the perversion of the standard tripartite relationship. The prevailing ambiguity and fluidity surrounding gender roles in Molière's masterpiece transform what initially might appear to be a classical love triangle, in which Elmire and Tartuffe deceive a credulous Orgon, into a more intricate struggle in the arena of sexual politics. Tartuffe attempts to cast himself in the role of Elmire's lover at Orgon's expense; however, the latter, enthralled by the impostor's compelling presence, seems to be adrift between the somewhat fluid boundaries of homosocial (pertaining to male bonding) and homosexual desire. Orgon's need for ever greater intimacy and communion with Tartuffe has resulted in the exclusion of his wife from his private circle. Elmire must now desperately attempt to shift the precarious balance of power within the household in order to gain readmittance into the realm of political expedience

121

by transforming the intruder into an object of derision. The indeterminacy of sexual roles is the key to understanding Elmire's
relation to the parameters of play within *Le Tartuffe*.

Mme Pernelle's presence in the expository scene is significant
in regard to understanding this indeterminacy. Elmire's mother-
in-law virtually bursts in on the stage, with six other characters in
her wake. Her energetic pace marks and defines the rhythm of
the play's first scene. Despite her advanced age, the younger rela-
tions can barely keep apace. The matriarch's ire is fueled by the
family's apparent disregard for her morally edifying principles.
She gives the initial impression of having firmly established herself as the family's lawgiver, and her discourse is reminiscent of
that of the patriarchal tyrant. It admits of no interruptions and
allows for no contradictions. As Larry Riggs points out: "As her
son will do later, she demands that others remain silent and allow
her to preach uninterrupted. *Her* interruptions of *them* underline
the close relationship between speech and power. Her desire for
discursive dominance disguises itself as devotion to impersonal
moral principles and delineates a solid, potent identity for her
by defining the Other as defective."[1] The "others" find extreme
difficulty in expressing their opposition. Mme Pernelle's language
is authoritative and aggressively direct, targeting the specific
weakness of each family member in turn. The family's concern
about placating the outraged matron would seem indeed to substantiate her claim to a position of authority within the clan.

Little by little, however, Dorine's voice manages to overpower
that of the older woman, and a verbal fencing match ensues. The
servant girl, "un peu trop forte en gueule" (I,1) [too quick to
speak her mind], does not share the reticence of her employers,
as she counters one by one Mme Pernelle's arguments, ultimately
reducing her to silence.

The debate centers on religious fervor and pious moralizing. In
Dorine's view, such practices are generally based less on altruistic
concern than upon the desire to control the behavior of others
by assuming the authoritative voice of power. The ineluctable
presence of such a motive subtending moralistic rhetoric exposes
transcendence as a delusion.

Tartuffe is initially described in the following manner:

> S'il le faut écouter et croire à ses maximes,
> On ne peut rien faire qu'on ne fasse des crimes;
> Car il contrôle tout, ce critique zélé.
>
> (I,1)[2]

[He plans to preach an ethic so sublime
That anything we do becomes a crime.
He frowns on everything and runs it down.]

—a statement that Mme Pernelle wholeheartedly endorses:

Et tout ce qu'il contrôle est fort bien contrôlé.

(I,1)

[And everything he frowns on earns his frown.]

It becomes apparent that the matriarch considers Tartuffe instrumental in her own attempts to police family activity.

Mme Pernelle sees her family's reputation as an extension of her own. This leaves her vulnerable to public opinion and neighborhood gossip. Dorine dismisses such rumors as contemptible and in particular condemns the prude Orante's exemplary life style as a hypocritical *pis-aller* [last resort]. Her comment that:

L'exemple est admirable, et cette dame est bonne!
Il est vrai qu'elle vit en austère personne;
Mais l'âge dans son âme a mis ce zèle ardent,
Et l'on sait qu'elle est prude à son corps défendant.

(I,1)

[A fine example, quite without a peer!
It's true that now her life is most austere;
Her years have brought her purity; but still
She's only virtuous against her will.]

could be interpreted as an oblique reference to Mme Pernelle's own attitude. When woman loses her desirability, when she can no longer exert control over masculine desire, this is tantamount to the loss of her sexual identity and simultaneously of her claim to power, which is seen as defined by the masculine recognition on which it depends for its very existence. Quite to the contrary, the male of the species is not solely defined by his sexual identity and in relation to woman, but constitutes the norm whereby others are measured. The older man, though unsexed, nonetheless retains political hegemony. The older woman is not only cast out into a sexual limbo but finds herself disenfranchised and disempowered by the same token. Her moral self-righteousness, be it that of Orante or Mme Pernelle herself, is merely an attempt to realign herself in accordance with political necessity, to reassume control through moral censorship within a different sphere of activity. It does not appear surprising, therefore, that the matriarchal voice in this instance bears some resemblance to authoritarian patriarchal discourse. Significantly, while Mme Pernelle makes her exit, she physically and verbally abuses her servant Flipote.

Mme Pernelle's mean-spirited despotism and her blind adherence to Tartuffe's teachings are soon set in a context of relativity. She has been characterized as a quarrelsome tyrant and as someone who, paradoxically, seeks to attain power through her devotion to Tartuffe. Riggs explains that: "She favors univocal authority, with herself and Orgon as interpreters of that one voice, and with Tartuffe as its source."[3] Traditionally, this has been considered a feminine strategy: to exert authority through a male figurehead, to operate through devious channels, ever behind the scenes of History. But whatever her shortcomings, those of her son Orgon are considerably worse. Thus, Orgon is from the very outset depicted as a deviant, both a weakling and a tyrant, who maintains control of the patriarchal seat of authority through unorthodox "feminine" means. Tartuffe's presence has a visibly stultifying effect on the *pater familias*.

> Mais il est devenu comme un homme hébété,
> Depuis que de Tartuffe on le voit entêté;
> Il l'appelle son frère, et l'aime dans son âme
> Cent fois plus qu'il ne fait mère, fils, fille, et femme.
> C'est de tous ses secrets l'unique confident,
> Et de ses actions le directeur prudent;
> Il le choie, il l'embrasse: et pour une maîtresse
> On ne saurait, je pense, avoir plus de tendresse . . .
>
> (I,2)

> [But since he's taken Tartuffe as his hero,
> His sanity has been reduced to zero;
> He calls him brother, holds him far above
> Mother, wife, son, or daughter in his love.
> There's not a secret he will not confide
> To him, as to his spiritual guide.
> He pets and spoils him with such tenderness,
> A mistress would be satisfied with less; . . .]

Orgon, who at one time, it seems, was both wise and courageous, has been quite literally mesmerized into speechless dumbfoundedness. In his attempt at exerting tyrannical power through Tartuffe's imposing presence, Orgon has virtually lost command of authoritative discourse. A transference has occurred in which the figurehead has drained the patriarch of his leadership and has become in turn the source of the Law.

As Dorine puts it:

> Certes, c'est une chose aussi qui scandalise,
> De voir qu'un inconnu céans s'im*patron*ise . . .
>
> (I,1)

> [I think it's scandalous, a real disgrace,
> To see this stranger seize the master's place.]

Orgon's view of the relationship between himself and Tartuffe is one of intimate fraternal bonding, which would imply an egalitarian sharing of power. To outside observers, however, the relationship is tainted by sexual ambiguity. Orgon's passionate obsession with Tartuffe exceeds the boundaries of propriety and although the latter is explicitly compared to a mistress and a confidante, it is the former's enthrallment and consequent disempowerment that are emphasized here.

The hypocrite has become by all accounts the older man's *directeur de conscience*. Thus, Tartuffe has gained access to power by presenting himself as an object of passion and desire, who has expropriated the role of the legitimate wife. McKenna defines Orgon's idolatry in the following terms: "For what idolatry signifies is the desire of the other's desire. This takes the form of worship of the other's desire."[4] Tartuffe's strategy of seduction is sexually ambiguous and essentially a "feminine" means to empowerment designed to subvert Orgon's hegemony. The feminine will to power is considered to flow through devious channels and is characterized by the indirectness of its manifestations. Whereas, however, with women such manifestations are the direct result of their status as political nonentities, the masculine expedients of hypocrisy, deviance, and tyrannical cowardice appear to be all the more contemptible means to exert authority as they are deemed unnecessary.

The greatness of *Tartuffe* is directly linked to its portrayal of ambivalent sexual roles and the subtle fluidity of the masculine and feminine principles. In some respects the characters find themselves grappling with a topsy-turvy reality, in which the subversion of masculine and feminine roles is the norm.

Upon his return from the country, Orgon is most anxious to inform himself of Tartuffe's well-being. In act 1, scene 2 Orgon's

lack of concern for Elmire's recent illness is repeatedly demonstrated by his impatient "Et Tartuffe?" Not only does this scene
authenticate Dorine's vivid depiction of her master's enthrallment,
but it strikingly elucidates the parasitic nature of the hypocrite's
endeavor. Indeed, Elmire's state of health seems somehow to be
directly connected but inversely proportional to that of Tartuffe, who:

> Contre tous les maux fortifiant son âme,
> Pour réparer le sang qu'avait perdu madame,
> But, à son déjeuner, quatre grands coups de vin.
>
> (I,4)

> [And, girding up his soul at any cost,
> To make up for the blood Madame has lost,
> He downed at breakfast four great drafts of wine.]

Orgon's indifference to his wife is directly related to his fascination with Tartuffe; it has critically impaired the familial power
structures.

As a woman, already subordinate to her husband's demands,
Elmire can only hope to assert her influence through her desirability. Yet even the channels of secondary empowerment have
become inaccessible to her, for Tartuffe, Orgon's "mistress," now
commands the patriarch's attention. Thus, Elmire's position is,
from the very beginning, one of total disenfranchisement. Much
of the play will be based upon her struggle to regain a position
of secondary empowerment within the confines of the immediate
family. This attempt implies the reaffirmation of her discourse as
authoritative and meaningful. She must at all costs make Orgon
listen to her words rather than summarily dismiss them. The difficulty of such an enterprise is indeed considerable, for the relationship between Orgon and Tartuffe is intimate and exclusive.
Their male bonding has given rise to a play world that delineates
their own separate space through the imposition of rigid boundaries. Or, as Orgon would have it:

> [Tartuffe] m'enseigne à n'avoir affection pour rien,
> De toutes amitiés il détache mon âme;
> Et je verrais mourir frère, enfants, mère et femme,
> Que je ne m'en soucierais autant que de cela.
>
> (I,5)

[He guides me on new paths in new directions,
Trains me to mortify all my affections,
And liberates my soul from every tie.
My brother, children, mother, wife could die,
And I would see it without *(snaps his fingers) that* much pain.]

Like most of Molière's monomaniacs, however, Orgon has lost sight of the temporary and playful nature of his detachment.

This is due, in great measure, to the theatricality of Tartuffe's presence. Orgon's mesmerization is repeatedly emphasized by the use of visual metaphor:

Ah! si vous aviez *vu* comme j'en fis rencontre,
Vous auriez pris pour lui l'amitié que je montre.
Chaque jour à l'église il venait *d'un air* doux,
Tout *vis-à-vis* de moi se mettre à deux genoux.
Il attirait *les yeux* de l'assemblée entière
Par l'ardeur dont au ciel il poussait sa prière;
Il faisait des soupirs, de grands élancements,
Et baisait humblement la terre à tous moments;
Et lorsque je sortais, il me devançait vite
Pour m'aller, à la porte, offrir de l'eau bénite . . .
Je lui faisais des dons: mais avec modestie,
Il me voulait toujours en rendre une partie.
Et quand je refusais de le vouloir reprendre,
Aux pauvres, *à mes yeux*, il allait le répandre.

(I,5)

[Ah, if that day we met, you'd been on hand,
You'd feel as I do now—you'd understand.
Each day he came to church, meek as you please,
and, *right across from me*, fell on his knees;
He *caught the eye* of every person there,
Such warmth and zeal he put into his prayer;
His transports were extreme, his sighs profound;
Each moment he would stoop and kiss the ground;
And when I left, he always went before
To offer me holy water at the door.
I gave him gifts; but in his modest way,
He'd give me back a part and humbly say:
"That is too much, that's twice too much for me;
I am not worthy of your sympathy";
And then when I refused to compromise,
He'd give half to the poor, *before my eyes*.]

The impostor's presence is characterized by perpetual, hyperbolic, and frenzied motion. Because his power rests upon his ability to captivate Orgon's gaze, he must continually reinvent himself to become a constant source of entertainment, an ever changing ambulatory spectacle. Cléante's fervent appeal to distinguish between the mask and the face can have no effect on his brother-in-law, who has become dependent upon the illusion for its own sake. Orgon's stubborn clinging to his devotion to Tartuffe is far less a factor of his stupidity than of a pressing need to escape the banality of everyday life and the rationalistic discourse of the likes of Cléante. Tartuffe offers him just such an escape into a theatrical play world. This is why the legitimacy of the mask of piety remains a nonissue for Orgon, who desires nothing more than to be charmed, enthralled, and bedazzled.

Having lost sight of the boundaries between reality and illusion, between ethics and esthetics, Orgon will seek to expand his authoritative powers into the realm of the illusory. Before announcing his intention to marry his daughter Mariane to Tartuffe, he begins by testing her docility. When asking her what she thinks of the man, Orgon cautions her to mind her words. Mariane instinctively realizes that she must make use of mimetic discourse in order to placate her father's whims:

> Hélas! j'en dirai, moi, tout ce que vous voudrez.
>
> (II,1)

> [Alas! I'll say whatever you want me to.]

This simply means that, like many other ingenues in Molière's theater, she will allow her father to speak for her, informing her discourse with his own wisdom. Such behavior conforms to the father's expectations ("C'est parler sagement" II,1) [That's a good girl], but when he reveals the language that he wants his daughter to adopt, she must rebel on the basis of its inauthenticity. Her rather meek refusal is already an acknowledgment of her own identity: an individuality that refuses to merge with or rather be subsumed by the father's will:

> *Mariane:* Il n'en est rien, mon père, je vous jure.
>   Pourquoi me faire dire une telle imposture?
> *Orgon:* Mais je veux que cela soit une vérité;
>   Et c'est assez pour vous que je l'aie arrêté.
>
> (II,1)

> [Mariane: But that's not so, I swear it. Why
>   Do you want to have me to tell you such a lie?

Orgon: But you forget: I want it to be true.
My mind's made up, and that's enough for you.]

Deluded by Tartuffe's example, the patriarch now not only wishes to assert his authority within the parameters of reality, but to legitimize falsehood itself, magically transforming the imaginary into fact by the sheer force of his will. Such an assertion of patriarchal authority obviously leads one to question the political legitimacy of such a transgression. According to Riggs, "Orgon wants to be a moral ventriloquist. He intends for the voice of his will to speak and act through the members of his household ... His attitude toward his daughter amounts to what neo-Freudian critics would call 'castration.' He silences her and disposes of her person and her subjectivity as he sees fit. His dominance depends on her feminization. Her feminized body is mutilated—metaphorically, her tongue is cut out ... Molière links ostentatious asceticism to suppression of the female."[5]

It is interesting to note how quickly the servant girl Dorine picks up on this issue. Her remarks are subversive precisely because they question the *credibility* of the rumors of Mariane's betrothal to Tartuffe and ultimately of Orgon himself:

> *Dorine:* Vraiment, je ne sais pas si c'est un bruit qui part
> De quelque conjecture, ou d'un coup de hasard;
> Mais de ce mariage on m'a dit la nouvelle,
> Et j'ai traité cela de pure bagatelle.
> *Orgon:* Quoi donc! la chose est-elle incroyable?
> *Dorine:*   A tel point
> Que vous-même, monsieur, je ne vous en crois point.
>
>   (II,2)

> [Dorine: There is a rumor going around here,
> Chance or conjecture, I have no idea;
> But when I heard these two were to be wed,
> I just assumed someone was off his head.
> Orgon: What? Do you doubt it then?
> Dorine: Indeed I do;
> Yes, even though I've heard it now from you.]

Dorine's refusal to believe is simultaneously a refusal to acknowledge Orgon's claim to extend patriarchal authority into the realm of the imaginary. He can force his daughter to wed the impostor, but he cannot control her feelings. Likewise, Orgon can impose silence on Dorine, but he will find it impossible to prevent her from thinking:

Orgon: Et tout résolument, je veux que tu te taises.
Dorine: Soit, mais ne disant mot, je n'en pense pas moins.

(II,2)

[Orgon: And I don't want another word from you.
Dorine: All right, but just the same, my thoughts are there.]

Once again, the patriarch attempts to impose his will through the
stifling of feminine discourse and although, once again, woman
is forced to remain outside of language and the symbolic, her
alienation does not extend to the realm of feelings and thoughts,
the shelter of her own authenticity. The servant girl makes a theatrical display of her case, by continuing to talk to herself onstage.
It is interesting to note that such nonaddressed discourse elicits
Orgon's curiosity more than her direct attacks do.

Having failed, however, to convince Orgon of the limited nature
of patriarchal authority, Dorine finds it necessary to elucidate the
possible consequences of his tyranny:

Et ne devez-vous pas songer aux bienséances,
Et de cette union prévoir les conséquences?
Sachez que d'une fille on risque la vertu,
Lorsque dans son hymen son goût est combattu;
. . . une femme a toujours une vengeance prête.

(II,2)

[And shouldn't you consider what is seemly,
And fear the consequences most extremely?
The danger to a girl's virtue is great
When she is wed to an unwelcome mate;
. . . women have their vengeance close at hand.]

As Charles Mauron has pointed out, the fear of adultery and
cuckoldry is an obsessive and frequently recurring theme in Molière's theater.[6] In terms of Hegelian dialectics, it is the oppressor's
fear of the oppressed. In any relationship of power, the master
paradoxically depends upon his subordinates' continued subservience for the maintenance of his hegemony. The wife, in this case,
is thus negatively empowered to destroy her husband's authority
through public exposure and ridicule. If the concepts of virtue
and free will are symbiotically interdependent, then virtuous
woman cannot exist in an oppressive marital state, for she lacks
the self-determination to be virtuous of her own accord. At the
very heart of the matter lies the danger that such a state of affairs

represents for the male authority figure, be he father or husband, whose honor depends upon the fiction of feminine virtue. Although Dorine's words of warning are prompted by Mariane's impending mismatch, they foreshadow Elmire's own attempts to regain the power that she has lost through Tartuffe's intrusion in the family circle.

It should be noted that Mariane remains utterly silent during the entire scene between Dorine and Orgon. When Dorine reproaches her for her reticence, Mariane retreats behind the pretext of absolute obedience to her father's will. Although the ingenue seems horrified at the prospect of marrying the impostor, her alienation is such that she manifests very little incentive to change the order of things. Her attitude changes radically upon encountering Valère. It is essentially Mariane who initiates the misunderstanding between herself and her lover by coquettishly refusing to mark her dismay at the projected marriage to Tartuffe. Ironically, the timid ingenue now shows herself to be the more assertive and certainly the more stubborn of the two, as she battles it out with Valère. Her refusal to declare herself is true to character, but in this scene she uses the strategy to her advantage, demonstrating thereby the veracity of Dorine's words: even the weak and oppressed have their means to power.

Le Tartuffe is perhaps the most sensual of Molière's comedies, for in it woman's greatest source of empowerment is her physical desirability, which has a disturbing effect on the impostor. His well-known lines to Dorine,

> Couvrez ce sein que je ne saurais voir . . .

> [Cover those breasts that offend my eyes . . .]

lead her to conclude

> Vous êtes donc bien tendre à la tentation;
> Et la chair sur vos sens fait grande impression!

> (III,2)

> [You must be very weak against temptation
> And very prone to fleshly stimulation.]

Having been "unmanned" rather than "unsexed" by his enthrallment for Tartuffe, Orgon is no longer susceptible to Elmire's influence. Instinctively she appeals to the surrogate patriarch, sensing perhaps his vulnerability to her charms. But Elmire's pri-

vate intercession on behalf of her stepdaughter Mariane may not
be as innocent as it would initially appear. Mme Pernelle has already chided her for her coquettishness:

> Vous êtes dépensière, et cet état me blesse,
> Que vous alliez vêtue ainsi qu'une princesse.
> Quiconque à son mari veut plaire seulement,
> Ma bru, n'as pas besoin de tant d'ajustement.
>
> (I,1)

> [You spend too much, and I'm distressed to see
> You dressed the way a princess ought to be.
> If it's your husband that you seek to please,
> My dear, you don't need all these fineries.]

Although one may be aware that Mme Pernelle's sour-natured
disposition causes her to greatly exaggerate her family's faults, it
is nevertheless obvious that some of what she says is true: Orgon's
young wife knows how to enhance her natural advantages and
does indeed enjoy the attention of other men. This is proven by
Tartuffe's efforts to discourage her suitors. In her critique of
Freudian theory, Irigaray challenges Freud's contention that
women have a natural tendency toward physical vanity: "Woman's
physical vanity, which compensates for her original sexual inferiority, is said to be caused by 'penis-envy.' Let us accept the hypothesis. But, here again, *we may question whether woman has a choice
of being or not being vain about her body* if she is to correspond to
the 'femininity' expected of her. Does not her sexual 'usefulness'
depend upon her being concerned about the qualities or 'proper-
ties' of her body? If she is to solicit, support, and even swell the
sexual pleasure of the male consumer?"[7]
Since the astute Dorine has already penetrated the impostor's
secret passion for Elmire, it is not unlikely that the self-possessed
young wife is equally conscious of her effect on Tartuffe. She in
any case makes herself available to him in an intimate setting:

> J'ai voulu vous parler en secret d'une affaire,
> Et suis bien aise, ici, qu'aucun ne nous éclaire.
>
> (III,3)

> [I want to talk to you in secrecy,
> And I am grateful for this privacy.]

This suggestion of intimacy is further heightened by Elmire's proposal that they make themselves comfortable:

Mais prenons une chaise afin d'être un peu mieux.

(III,3)

[But let's sit down, here is a chair.]

Tartuffe is quite naturally led to believe that her desire to be alone with him and her appeal for him to open up his heart to her are direct sexual overtures. One might question whether he misinterprets her innocent words or whether he is being skillfully manipulated into an avowal of his passion by the very object of his desire. The general trend is to view Orgon's wife as a virtuous woman whose naïveté gets her into a compromising situation. A far more interesting hypothesis would be to allow for the possibility of an alluring and sensual coquette who uses her charms in a desperate bid to regain a voice in the sociopolitical arena.[8]

There can be no doubt as to Elmire's sensuality. Upon her husband's return from his voyage she immediately retires to her chambers in order to greet him "in private." When Tartuffe fondles her knee she exclaims:

Ah! de grâce, laissez, je suis fort chatouilleuse.

(III,3)

[Please don't, I'm very ticklish. That's enough.]

Such an indirect acknowledgment of her susceptibility to sexual arousal can only fuel the impostor's desire.

Elmire's initial motivation may simply be to test her power of persuasion over an admirer, but once the full extent of Tartuffe's infatuation becomes known to her, she understands the feasibility of a far more subtle strategy, one through which she envisages the possibility of regaining her lost dominion over Orgon.

As a woman, however, Elmire faces the dilemma of transforming her physical desirability—essentially a passive state—into political action. One might distinguish here, as does Irigaray, between "passivity" and "passive aims": "When it really comes down to it, then, woman will not choose, or desire, an 'object' of love but will arrange matters so that a 'subject' takes her as his 'object'."[9] Elmire's powerless position within her marriage has been established. Her dwindling influence over Orgon is inversely proportional to Tartuffe's rise within the family power structure. Even for the impostor, Elmire's status will be no greater than that of a desirable object. As she cannot expect to exert direct influence over her husband, her course of action can only be indirect and oblique. Elmire can only hope to neutralize the impostor's grip on power through the authority of the patriarch, but she can only attempt to gain access to her husband's attention through Tartuffe. She is in a double-bind situation from which at first there would appear to be no way out. This double bind is due to the exclusive nature of the bonding between Orgon and Tartuffe. Orgon's play world admits of no other object of desire and no other participants. No one is allowed within the confines of his ludic circle.

Elmire's desirability will be the key to the penetration and disruption of Orgon's play world. She will thus offer herself to the coveter's gaze, hoping thereby to captivate and enthrall the enthraller himself. The success of such an undertaking will result in the inflation of the desired object's worth. Elmire's value will become "appreciated" (given a price) within the play world by one of its members and therefore her existence (if only as object) will be acknowledged. This is only possible, of course, because of Tartuffe's illusive participation in the fraternal bond with Orgon. Were he himself as mesmerized by Orgon's presence as the latter is by his, then their play world would be hermetically and impenetrably sealed and masculine desire would result in a homosexual embrace.[10]

Elmire's self-willed transformation into an object of desire will be instrumental in her struggle to regain a voice in family matters, but this is only possible if her sexually compelling presence remains elusive and intangible—behind the dazzling image there is an absence: "[Woman ensures] this *double game* of flaunting her body, her jewels, in order to hide her sex organs all the better. For woman's 'body' has some 'usefulness,' represents some 'value' only on condition that her sex organs are hidden. Since they are something and nothing in consumer terms. Are pictured in fantasy, what is more, as a greedy mouth. How can one trade on something so empty? To sell herself, woman has to veil as best she can how price-less she is in the sexual economy."[11] Only on this condition will she retain her autonomy, offering only a troubling reflection and forcing her desirer into perpetual pursuit. Thus, she will retain control of the situation through passive resistance, transforming powerlessness into action in a remarkable *tour de force*. As Elmire succinctly puts it:

Il suffit pour nous de savoir nous défendre.

(III,5)

[Enough to check familiarities.]

Her elusiveness is reflected in the language of her encounter with the impostor. Whereas Tartuffe perpetually attempts to transform spiritual abstractions into physical realities, Elmire fends off his advances by continuously averting the sexual allusions and reasserting the intangible rewards of religious piety. By doing so, however, she gains control of the dialogue by forcing ever more transparent declarations of intention from her lover until he has stripped himself bare of his hypocritical pretensions, openly revealing his lust for Elmire. This distinctly feminine use of negative empowerment is based primarily on *distraction*, whereas masculine power is generally equated with action. To distract man in order to prevent him from political action—fragmenting his hegemony and transforming him obliquely into an agent of woman's will: this is the basis of Elmire's will to power. Feminine ingenuity makes manifest use of its limitations in order to surpass them and employs passivity to gain indirect access to the political order.

Having gained a strategic advantage over Tartuffe, Elmire attempts to blackmail him into renouncing his marriage to Mariane in return for her silence on this matter to her husband. In other words, she tries to exert power over her suitor by threatening to fragment his exclusive bond with Orgon from within. Elmire's silence can therefore be viewed as a conservative half measure that would still allow the men's play world to remain intact. In the eyes of Orgon's son Damis, however, her reticence is an offense, an insult to her husband's honor. He is quick to pick up on the underlying connection between Elmire's so-called reluctance to disturb her spouse's peace of mind and the threat of outright duplicity and cuckoldry. Dorine has already warned of the possible consequences of a mismatch and Orgon would do well to heed the threat to his honor implicit in Elmire's behavior. It becomes apparent that in a different context, Orgon's wife would have the astuteness and the wherewithal to become a skillful adulteress, easily undermining her husband's authority.[12] Damis's response to Elmire's appeal to keep silent about Tartuffe's lecherous intentions is laced with irony, implying perhaps that she may have underlying motivations:

> Vous avez vos raisons pour en user ainsi,
> Et pour faire autrement, j'ai les miennes aussi, . . .
>
> (III,4)

> [You have your reasons for this compromise,
> But I have mine for doing otherwise.]

Orgon's boundless admiration for the impostor Tartuffe has been discussed at some length. The close friendship, the brotherhood, between Elmire's husband and her suitor leads quite naturally to a perpetual convergence of their desire, unilateral though it may be. Far from being a marginal factor, this becomes an essential element of the fraternal bond. Orgon seeks to imitate his mentor in every way possible, hoping thereby to become one with him, to achieve perfect identification. His subsequent discovery that his honorary brother is his rival leads to his total bewilderment. His lengthy hesitation before intervening on his wife's behalf is partially attributable to the ambivalence of his jealousy. If Tartuffe is indeed the object of Orgon's desire, then Elmire is her own husband's rival and in this capacity gains sudden stature and consideration as an adversary. If, on the other hand, Orgon considers Tartuffe as a brother with whom he identifies and whom he spontaneously imitates to the greatest degree possible, then the latter's desire for his wife would serve to rekindle Orgon's own passion for Elmire, through a process of mimetic desire. McKenna discusses the relationship between illusion and mimetic desire in the following passage:

> Orgon's existence, which Dorine has correctly diagnosed as madness, is imaginary in just such a Lacanian sense: he mistakes the Symbolic for the Real. Whence the structural homology between Lacan's "Mirror Stage" and Girard's dialectics of mimetic desire, where "Le désir selon l'autre" (Girard) takes another for its model of autonomous selfhood: it takes the other, whole in its apparent otherness (as is the reflection of the self in the mirror for Lacan's *infants*) as Wholly Other, or, much the same thing, Holy Other, this delusion being the ground of Orgon's worship of Tartuffe.[13]

Either way, Elmire's presence can no longer be dismissed or discounted. The impostor's appreciation of her has once again given her a space and an identity that will henceforth intrude upon the exclusivity of the fraternal bond.

Orgon's confusion or rather the ambivalence of his jealousy can explain the ease with which Tartuffe regains ascendancy over him through language and gesture ("Quoi! ses discours vous *séduiront* au point. . ." III) [What! His words *seduce* you to this point. . .] He may indeed be more jealous of Elmire's intrusion in his exclusive relationship with Tartuffe than of Tartuffe himself. It is the impostor who skillfully reveals to him the necessary consequence of his indictment. If Orgon accepts Damis' accusation, he must banish his brother from his household and his presence. This would mean the shattering of his play world and its fraternal intimacy. So terrifying is this perspective that instead of expelling the culprit, Orgon seeks to consolidate their intimacy, thereby reaffirming their solidarity and the exclusivity of the bond. To this effect, he banishes his son and alienates his entire family:

> Ce n'est pas tout encor, pour les mieux braver tous,
> Je ne veux point avoir d'autre héritier que vous,
> Et je veux de ce pas en fort bonne manière,
> Vous faire de mon bien donation entière.
> Un bon et franc ami, que pour gendre je prends,
> M'est bien plus cher que fils, que femme et que parents.
>
> (III,7)

> [Nor is that all; to spite them through and through,
> I want to have no other heir than you;
> And legally—I don't intend to wait—
> I'll see that you inherit my estate.
> A good true friend, my son-in-law-to-be,
> Is dearer than my son, wife, kin to me.]

By a similar process, Tartuffe's own desire for Elmire is generated by the mimetic process. However generous his benefactor may be, Orgon's possessions are a constant reminder to the impostor of his de facto inferiority. Tartuffe does not simply want to acquire Orgon's possessions, he wants to assume his identity. Despite his lack of genuine friendship for the master of the house, the zealot cannot refrain from being subject to mimetic desire, not out of admiration but out of envy. This is why it is the sensual wife Elmire and not the younger Mariane who arouses his unbridled passion. The woman is more desirable than the nubile adolescent because she is viewed as an exclusive and nontransferable possession validating and symbolizing Orgon's dominance.

By proffering her physical presence while eluding sexual contact, Elmire is able to gain control of the situation momentarily by driving Tartuffe to distraction. The impostor is forced to temporarily discard the mask and to lay himself at her mercy. When she threatens to reveal the truth to Orgon, Tartuffe can only count upon her generosity and forgiving nature. The following lines prove his vulnerability and defenselessness, yet underline by the same token his self-assurance in assuming selflessness to be an inherent feminine trait:

> Je sais que vous avez trop de bénignité,
> Et que vous ferez grâce à ma témérité

Que vous m'excuserez sur l'humaine faiblesse,
Des violents transports d'un amour qui vous blesse . . .

(III,3)

[I know that you are gracious and benign,
And will forgive this recklessness of mine,
Blame human weakness for the violence
Of this my love, at which you take offense . . .]

Tartuffe's confidence in Elmire's complicity also rides on the notion that she herself is a guilty party in this affair:

Et si vous condamnez l'aveu que je vous fais,
Vous devez vous en prendre à vos charmants attraits.

(III,3)

[And if you think I've put myself to shame,
It's your bewitching charms that are to blame.]

The impostor's transferral of guilt and displacement of responsibility onto the alluring woman, though very much a part of the rhetoric of gallantry, is also a direct reference to the role of woman as temptress and is in constant contradiction with Tartuffe's other characterization of woman as a divine and ethereal being. Although these two faces of woman are rather commonplace, it must be noted that Elmire's sexual appeal is seen as a constant source of blame throughout the play. Her only means of averting defamation is to transform her physical desirability into a source of power.

By the end of the third act, Orgon has managed to strengthen his fraternal bond with Tartuffe by securing it within the boundaries of an exclusive circle and by concomitantly alienating and expelling "fils, femme et parents." This system is founded upon the exclusion of the feminine, articulating a notion of male integrity or wholeness that can be disrupted by the presence of the disunifying other: woman. Without Elmire, the intensity of the identification between Orgon and Tartuffe would threaten to disintegrate into a homoerotic relationship.

The patriarch's desire to subvert the parental role by substituting Tartuffe for his own son Damis would thereby eliminate the generational conflict in which the son not only serves as a constant reminder of the father's own mortality, but in which his inevitable succession to the seat of power represents the impending threat of a hostile takeover—hostile because the patriarch has no intention of relinquishing his right to command. By replacing Damis with Tartuffe, Orgon falsely assumes that he is transferring power to an identical other, thereby reaffirming his tenacious grip on hegemony and symbolically reaffirming his immortality. However, the introduction of Elmire, or rather her intrusion, into the ludic circle, inhibits the centripetal attraction that draws Orgon irresistibly to annihilation in an embrace with sameness. Although the threat of rivalry is temporarily allayed by Orgon's summary dismissal of the charges against Tartuffe, mimetic desire will resurface and establish clearly defined parameters of difference between them in the challenge of one man to another. The paradoxical nature of this system is precisely that the desire for differentiation is contingent upon the convergence of that desire.

When Elmire protests that Damis' accusation of Tartuffe was only too true, Orgon remains unconvinced for the following reason:

> Vous étiez trop tranquille, enfin, pour être crue;
> Et vous auriez paru d'autre manière émue.
>
> (IV,3)

It is apparent that having become accustomed to Tartuffe's mimetic flamboyance, Orgon's imagination can only be captivated by hyperbolic action. Elmire's understated claims remain all too unconvincing. As in *Le Malade imaginaire,* feminine discourse is summarily dismissed as devoid of content or meaning, yet in the previously cited passage, Orgon inadvertently reminds Elmire that she might still have recourse to playacting as a means of access to the play world.

There seems to be a recurring belief subtending Molière's comedies that feminine presence is a more powerful signifier than feminine language. The heroine's final attempt to resort to the mimetic is a reminder of her exclusion from the realm of the symbolic and a reaffirmation of her will to power. It is through her use of gesture and mime that Elmire will eventually disturb and disrupt the male bond.

The fifth scene of the fourth act reminds the spectator, if need be, of the very physical nature of Elmire's presence and of the way in which she makes use of her body to fascinate and subdue her opponent. Even her language becomes physical by insinuating agitation, sexual arousal and intimacy:

> Mon Dieu! que votre amour en vrai tyran agit! . . .
> Et qu'en un trouble étrange il me jette l'esprit!

Quoil de votre poursuite on ne peut se parer.
Et vous ne donnez pas le temps de respirer.

(IV,5)

[My, but your love is the despotic kind,
And puts me in a troubled state of mind!
Must you pursue at such a frantic pace?
And am I not allowed a breathing space?]

Tartuffe shows himself to be acutely aware of the corporeality of Elmire's language in his reply to her advances:

C'est sans doute, madame, une douceur extrême
Que d'entendre ces mots d'une bouche qu'on aime;
Leur miel dans tous mes sens fait couler à longs traits
Une suavité qu'on ne goûta jamais.

(IV,5)

[Of course, Madame, it's very sweet to hear
Such words as these spoken by lips so dear:
Their honeyed flavor floods my every sense.
Such bliss I never did experience.]

Elmire's words have become materialized, transformed into honey to be consumed and savored. The effect of the flow of this substance through Tartuffe's senses is nothing short of orgasmic. The language of this scene is so intensely physical, that I would have to agree with the following comment by Spingler: "That the physical consummation does not actually take place is less significant than the fact that Elmire has consented to it."[14]

In her last desperate bid to convince her husband of Tartuffe's true intentions, Elmire devises a scheme that forces her husband to view her interplay with the impostor from the standpoint of an outsider. Hidden beneath the table, Orgon assumes the ridiculous position of the cuckold who must silently bear witness to his own undoing and to his exclusion from the intimate circle in which his wife now plays a triumphant role by displaying her ascendancy over the man who has come to be Orgon's own master, within a play world of her own creation. Her trump card, however, is her designation of Orgon as master of ceremony. She effectively relinquishes her right to put a halt to her own seduction, thereby placing her fate squarely in the hands of Orgon:

J'aurai lieu de cesser dès que vous vous rendrez,
Et les choses n'iront que jusqu'où vous voudrez.

C'est à vous d'arrêter son ardeur insensée
Quand vous croirez l'affaire assez avant poussée,
D'épargner votre femme, et de ne m'exposer
Qu'à ce qu'il vous faudra pour vous désabuser.
Ce sont vos intérêts, vous en serez le maître. . . .

(IV,4)

[As soon as you're convinced, just let me know,
And that will be as far as things will go.
It's up to you to check his wild desire
When matters are as clear as you require,
To spare your wife, and not expose her to
More than you need to disillusion you.
Your interest is at stake; you are the judge. . . .]

Elmire must now continue to play out her role in a scene over which she has no control. In so doing, however, she forces her spouse to take action by reminding him that her vulnerability is inextricably bound to his own.[15] Once again she shows her aptitude for transforming weakness into a weapon. Orgon is called upon to reaffirm his role as dominant male within the family structure by disassociating himself unequivocally from the man to whom he had relinquished his functions. The violence of the effort involved in breaking the fraternal bond is conveyed by the patriarch's delay in coming forth to denounce the impostor and prevent the otherwise inevitable seduction. Elmire's own gamble should not be underplayed, for she stakes her self-esteem and her integrity on her ability to win back her ascendancy over Orgon, whose inner turmoil is caused by the immediacy of his disintoxication and his return to reality.

The suddenness of Orgon's final disillusionment is contrasted by the prolongation of the illusion in Mme Pernelle's continued obstinacy. The patriarch's words of disbelief are now echoed by those of his mother and he in turn feels the frustration of having his discourse discredited. Mme Pernelle's own voice is then echoed by Dorine's sarcastic counterpoint. Not only does this give the disquieting impression that the repercussions of Orgon's obsession have gone beyond the confines of its initial boundaries, but it also provides him with a feminine echo, displaying the extent of his feminization. It is interesting to note that the temporary upheaval of traditional sexual roles within the domestic sphere is viewed as a true menace to the family's very existence and continuation in history.

Elmire may have gained credibility within the domestic realm, but in a gesture of self-denial characteristic of her general disposition, she returns to silence in the end, satisfied that her spouse will now resume his leadership role within the family structure and that her discourse, momentarily heeded, will no longer prove necessary. Although *Le Tartuffe* exposes the underlying threat of adultery that subtends the husband's vulnerability, Elmire has internalized her own subservience to the patriarchal order and her behavior toward her spouse admits of continual self-censorship.

Beyond the private sphere, Elmire cannot hope to assert authority in any form. Therefore, any attempt to help reestablish her husband's faltering credibility in the public domain would be futile. Orgon's disenfranchisement is directly and doubly attributable to male bonding. Not only has he made Tartuffe the sole heir to his estate, but he has confided in him as well. Tartuffe now holds the key to his benefactor's social disgrace. Orgon has agreed to conceal important documents for his friend Argas, who had incurred the monarch's wrath and who was subsequently sent into exile. Not only does Tartuffe's revelation of this incident reveal the patriarch's proclivity for male bonding, but it shows him to be the victim of a double bond. In addition to everything else, his personal allegiance to Argas represents a threat to royal authority. Although Orgon's gesture of friendship might appear noble within the private sector, its subversive nature comes to light under the public gaze. If Orgon's relationship to Tartuffe has imperiled the very structures of domestic order, his relationship to his exiled friend, generous though it may have been, shows the extent to which the supersedence of the private over the public and the exclusivity of intimacy jeopardize the reigning political order as well. The subject's gaze is turned inward toward its reflection in an identical other rather than outward to the king himself.

As powerful and courageous a character as she may be, Elmire remains an upholder of conservative patriarchal values. She may have managed to save Orgon from his domestic problems by casting light on the true nature of the impostor, but it will take the intervention of the monarch himself to pardon him for his public insubordination. In a fascinating study, Spingler exposes the king's intervention as the logical culmination of preceding plot patterns, linking thereby the seduction scene (IV,5) to the *dénouement:* "Orgon and his family have become trapped in a play suspended between rival endings in which the power of closure has been lost. They become caught in a performance which they themselves may have contrived and initiated but over which they

have lost control. We find in the play a sequence of events consti-
tuting a central pattern in which spectators-in-the-play intervene
in an attempt to extricate other players trapped in performance."[16] By pardoning Orgon and thereby assuring the reestablishment of the latter's patriarchal hegemony, the king
concomitantly solidifies his own power basis, which is both autho-
rial (he rewrites the play's ending) and dictatorial. He guarantees
the resurgence of his "vives clartés" (V,5), for he is the embodiment of supreme reason, order and light, those civilized ideals in
opposition to the murkiness of sexual enthrallment and the disorder of the senses represented by the feminine or feminized
faction.

7

Le Misanthrope: Strategies of Marginality and Centrality

Pourvu que votre coeur veuille donner les mains
Au dessein que je fais de fuir tous les humains
Et que dans mon désert, où j'ai fait voeu de vivre,
Vous soyez, sans tarder, résolue à me suivre.
                                    —*Le Misanthrope* V, 4

The somewhat marginal nature of Molière's play *Le Misanthrope*[1] in relation to his other comedies is suggested by the critical opinion of his contemporary, Boileau:

Dans ce sac ridicule où Scapin s'enveloppe,
Je ne reconnais plus l'auteur du *Misanthrope*.[2]

[In that ridiculous sack in which Scapin hides,
I cannot recognize the *Misanthrope*'s author.]
(Translation by author)

The critic thus establishes a distinction between lower and higher forms of comedy within Molière's opus, designating *Le Misanthrope* simultaneously as the prototype of a nobler, albeit less comical play. The contrast thus established is reflected by the idiosyncratic structure of a play that centers on a humorless individual who rejects the idea of play in any form, yet who finds himself surrounded by characters who unabashedly admit their adherence to the rules of the game.

For reasons that I shall attempt to uncover, Alceste finds a perverse form of masochistic pleasure in his self-willed exclusion from the circle of play and consequently from society at large. He rejects the overtures of his good friend Philinte and seeks from the very outset to extricate himself from the confines of an unauthentic code of social behavior. His apparent masochism in revel-

144

ling in his so-called rejection can be seen to have a twofold cause, the first being perhaps the most obvious. Alceste is obsessed with a desire for transparency, purity, and perfection. Within a corrupt society, he views himself as the One, the Integral: a perfect coincidence of action and intention, of word and meaning. Such a view would obviously promote the notion of authenticity in the absolute. Any deviation between meaning and form is strictly playful and ornamental, can be viewed as a perversion of authenticity, and must be discouraged and rejected. Social play is therefore a form of prostitution, a contagious evil that contributes to the debasement of mankind through a form of reduction to the lowest possible common denominator, precisely because it is predicated upon collusion and convention:

> Non, non, il n'est point d'âme un peu bien située
> Qui veuille d'une estime ainsi prostituée,
> Et la plus glorieuse a des régals peu chers
> Dès qu'on voit qu'on nous mêle avec tout l'univers.
> Sur quelque préférence une estime se fonde,
> Et c'est n'estimer rien qu'estimer tout le monde.
>
> (I,1)

> [No, no, a soul that is well constituted
> Cares nothing for esteem so prostituted;
> Our vanity is satisfied too cheap
> With praise that lumps all men in one heap.
> Esteem, if it be real, means preference,
> and when bestowed on all it makes no sense.]

What is further revealed in this passage is Alceste's passionate desire for recognition, a desire founded upon the will to be distinguished from the common masses. He is in search of a form of recognition that can only be achieved by an act of departure or rupture. Having thus signaled his singularity, he fully expects to be admired for his heroic stature as a misfit in a corrupt society. His efforts are misguided, however, for in the sociable seventeenth century, of which the play is a reflection, the self-pitying lamentations of the solitary misfit can only be subject to ridicule, or as Larry Riggs observes: "Alceste would like to be his own source, and the source of all that surrounds him. He actually attempts to reverse the relationship between individual and group by imposing his condemnation—his misanthropy—as the defining context wherein *others* must exist. He wants to be the audience in whose gaze all performances find their meaning."[3] By isolating himself from the fold, Alceste seeks inversely to become a marginal focal point, thus forcing the displacement of social recognition and admiration outside of its normally accepted boundaries. But society's judgmental criteria, predicated upon the rules of play as identified by Huizinga, insure at the very best the indifference of the participants to the outsider and occasionally their incomprehension and hostility to his behavior. To say this is not an attempt to minimize the courageous nature of the hero's attempt at sincerity. His efforts are, however, trivialized by the very nature of the adversary, who is mediocre at best. Also, Alceste's self-imposed exile from polite society is essentially a preventive strategy, for it is founded upon the not particularly heroic fear of rejection by others.

The hero is haunted by an underlying fear of disguised language and masked behavior. In spurning polite gestures and civilized language as frivolous, he also repudiates their primary effectiveness in deflecting overt aggression. His heroic project consists in substituting the pugnacious assertiveness of "masculine" discourse, for the circuitous hypocrisy of "effeminate" discourse and behavior. Eliante is the only character to recognize and render homage to Alceste's quixotic endeavors:

> Dans ses façons d'agir il est fort singulier,
> Mais j'en fais, je l'avoue, un cas particulier,
> Et la sincérité dont son âme se pique
> A quelque chose en soi de noble et d'héroïque.
>
> (IV,1)

> [His actions are peculiar and extreme,
> But, I admit, I hold him in esteem,
> And the sincerity that is his pride
> Has a heroic and a noble side.]

His good friend Philinte, however, captures the futility of Alceste's quest in his reply: "Le monde par vos soins ne se changera pas" (I,1) [Your efforts will not change the world, you know,]; thereby attempting to dissuade the latter from a pursuit doomed to failure in a play world devoid of heroic ideals as well as signaling his own tendency to champion the stability of the prevailing order. If the social graces can be regarded occasionally as vain embellishments, Alceste's misguided desire for complete honesty is futile as well, for it will generate no imitators. By placing himself squarely outside the circle of play, he will inevitably become the third party in the comic triangle, in other words, the object of ridicule. Rufus

Marsh makes the following observation on this subject: "The fool can affront his society with impunity to the extent that he serves as the willing butt of its laughter. Alceste, on the other hand, insists on being taken seriously."[4]

The traditional concept of laughter as a social corrective, castigating those whose divergence from the norm threatens the foundations of society, subtends the entire play. The hero's presence is subversive in that he reveals the fragility of a world built upon falsehood. By refusing to play the game, Alceste threatens to shatter the illusions upon which seventeenth-century polite society has secured its foundations. Alceste's extremism not only places him outside the ludic realm, but requires that he claim the title of outsider himself. If he seems so intent upon submitting to injustice and violence in order to decry it, it is because he still adheres to the belief that singularity is enviable rather than ridiculous. In other words, Alceste believes that he lives in the world of tragedy, not comedy. Noel Peacock attributes ·the public's misunderstanding of the comic dimensions of *Le Misanthrope* primarily to this factor: "Critics have sometimes taken Alceste's self-assessment literally. The character behaves and talks as if he is in an 'action illustre'. Alceste thinks that his situation is tragic. But, as we shall see, it is the character, and not the author, who has misunderstood the *genre*."[5] Yet, paradoxically, without the parameters of the play world, Alceste's quest for marginality would be invalidated. According to Riggs: "The play clearly ridicules the idea that there can be opposition between an individual and his social environment, except within socially defined limits. Individuation itself is actually a function of collective existence. It is this complex aspect of context—generating and nourishing, as well as limiting, individuation—that Alceste tries to ignore."[6] Alceste thus depends upon the very structures that he would seek to destroy, and his quest to generate imitators is fraudulent at best.

Alceste's desire for spectacular heroic martyrdom is echoed by his masochistic tendencies in love. Célimène's presence is emblematic of the play world in which she thrives. She is a mirror image of the society that Alceste abhors even though it holds him in morbid fascination. The perversity of the relationship is even more acute than one would at first imagine. Alceste "loves" Célimène not in spite, but *because of* her deficiencies. By acknowledging her shortcomings, the misanthrope indirectly unveils his moral superiority over the woman he is courting. Not only does this allow him to wallow in self-pity, but it reinforces his impression of moral self-righteousness and heroic stature: the spectacular contrast between the two is designed to display Alceste to his full advantage. Furthermore, it heightens his desire to shape and inform his female partner, thereby molding her according to his will and creating, godlike, a reflection of himself:

> Sa grâce est la plus forte et sans doute ma flamme
> De ces vices du temps pourra purger son âme.

(I,1).

> [Her grace remains too strong. My love, no doubt,
> Will yet prevail and drive these vices out.]

Jacques Guicharnaud comments on the ambivalence of this antagonism: "Pour le reste du monde, Alceste s'oppose et maintient cette opposition à la fois par ses descriptions hyperboliques et par sa passivité; pour Célimène il vise à l'assimilation complète. Il n'y a pour lui que le mal, qui est autrui dans son altérité même, et le bien, qui est lui-même; son monde est simple, mais ne permet pas la reconnaissance d'autrui comme valeur indépendante."[7] [Alceste opposes the rest of the world and maintains this opposition both through his hyperbolic descriptions and his passivity; as regards Célimène, his aim is total assimilation. For him the only realities are evil, represented by others in their otherness, and good, represented by himself; his world is simple, but does not allow for the recognition of otherness as an independent value.] (Translation by author)

Although Philinte declares that Eliante would be a more suitable companion, Alceste realizes that her admirable qualities would force his begrudging recognition and deflect admiration from his own person, whereas Célimène's stubborn independence of spirit not only provides him with fuel for his self-righteous ire, but allows him to envisage a more challenging project. It is therefore not surprising that he does not resort to the courtship of Eliante, even when all prospects of a relationship with Célimène are dashed.

Oronte's appearance in the next scene allows the spectator to draw more subtle inferences on the nature of the protagonist's obsession. The former's obsequious praise is accompanied by a bid for Alceste's friendship:

> Oui, mon coeur au mérite aime rendre justice,
> Et je brûle qu'un noeud d'amitié nous unisse.

Je crois qu'un ami chaud, et de ma qualité,
N'est pas assurément pour être rejeté.

(I,2)

[Yes, yes, I would see merit have its due;
In friendship's bond I would be joined with you,
An ardent friend, as nobly born as I,
Can surely not be easily passed by.]

Alceste, however, who equates singularity with superiority, rejects Oronte's overtures on that basis. The hero's overriding concern is to establish a safe distance between himself and the players
surrounding him. It is through his presence that the boundaries
of the play world are defined and enforced. Alceste recoils at the
very mention of human contact, which would bring about his
debasement through the contagion of mediocrity. Of course,
Oronte's flattery and his generous offer to speak of Alceste at
court are only symptoms of his foolish vanity and not of genuine
feeling or admiration. Yet the protagonist's reaction to such fool-
ishness is neither one of mockery nor of scorn, but virtually one
of physical repulsion toward a union that would jeopardize the
shelter of his isolation.

Oronte's famous sonnet is interesting in that it situates Alceste's
homophobia within a linguistic framework. Oronte himself rather
fatuously characterizes his attempted authorship as "doux, ten-
dre[s] et langoureux" [sweet, tender and languorous], thereby
providing the cues for Alceste's appraisal. The would-be poet's
efforts are predicated upon desire for recognition or at the very
least the appearance of recognition. Alceste's critical commentary
emphasizes above all else the writer's vulnerability in exposing
himself to ridicule:

Il faut qu'un galant homme ait toujours grand empire
Sur les démangeaisons qui nous prennent d'écrire;
Qu'il doit tenir la bride aux grands empressements
Qu'on a de faire éclat de tels amusements,
Et que, par la chaleur de montrer ses ouvrages,
On s'expose à jouer de mauvais personnages.

(I,2)

[A gentleman must have the will to fight
Our universal human itch to write,
That he must overcome his great temptations
To make a fuss about such recreations,

And that our eagerness for self-display
Can give us many a sorry role to play.]

Paradoxically, Alceste's own fear of persecution and exposure is concomitantly a desire for recognition *through* persecution. By consciously placing himself outside the boundaries of playful activity, he courts attention and curiosity while avoiding the contagion of human contact.

Furthermore, Alceste condemns Oronte's verses for their unnatural, artificial, affected, overly ornate, and effeminate style. He advocates the use of a simpler, more transparent terminology, in which words and meaning coincide and in which the truth is the surest guarantor of excellence—the language of his forefathers: "Nos pères, tout grossiers, l'avaient beaucoup meilleur . . ." (I,2) [Our fathers' taste, though crude, was far more sane. . .] The nature/civilization dichotomy here is essentially subverted. The positive value attributed to nature is accompanied by its association with the masculine order, whereas the excesses of society, viewed with apparent disapproval, are unequivocally associated with the feminine principle. Masculine language can therefore be viewed as frank—robust and straightforward, pure and structured— whereas feminine discourse is devious, frivolous, affected, and essentially meaningless and irrational by comparison: "Alceste's argument is then very simple: if the same words of praise are used for every single individual in society, it can only mean two things: either all men are equal, or words are no longer a proper representation of a man's worth. Alceste will certainly not admit that men are equal; therefore, he concludes that words have lost their meaning."[8]

The association drawn here is, of course, more commonly reversed: woman and nature, man and the rational civilized order. Cixous points this out in the following passage: "So, between two houses, between two beds, [woman] is laid, ever caught in her chain of metaphors, metaphors that organize culture . . . ever her moon to the masculine sun, nature to culture, concavity to masculine convexity, matter to form, immobility/inertia to the march of progress . . ."[9] Alceste nostalgically evokes the archaic order of his patriarchal predecessors, which has been supplanted and perverted through the growing influence of women. This view is partially substantiated by the societal structures represented in the play. Célimène's coterie is composed of a number of male satellites revolving around her dominant feminine presence. They are the reflection of her brilliance, not she of theirs.

The end of the first act is punctuated by Alceste's abrupt departure. Not only does this reinforce the concept of marginality, but his terse utterances—"plus de société," "point de langage" [finis between us, not another word]—demonstrate quite effectively how his attempts at an ideal form of transparent language will inevitably reduce him to silence and exile.

Alceste's first encounter with Célimène is marked by an open hostility that nullifies his professed tenderness for the heroine. Moreover, his desire to "parler net" [speak frankly]—in other words, to divest language of euphemisms and attenuating ornamentation—is linked to undisguised aggression and ruthless candor. Again, one is forced to recognize that the hero's attachment to Célimène is the by-product of his need to display supremacy. The contrast thus established between the lovers is instrumental in highlighting what the hero perceives to be his distinctive integrity.

Although the young widow has never committed herself to an exclusive relationship with any man and has thereby managed to some degree to retain her independence, it is interesting to note that it is her openness, a quality Alceste would otherwise cherish in language ("Parlons à coeur ouvert . . .") [Let's speak openly . . .], that is subject to Alceste's admonishments:

> . . . mais votre humeur, madame,
> Ouvre au premier venu trop d'accès dans votre âme;
> Vous avez trop d'amants qu'on voit vous obséder,
> Et mon coeur de cela ne peut s'accommoder.
>
> (II,1)

> [. . . but what is my dismay,
> Madame, that the first comer makes his way
> Into your heart? By suitors you're beset;
> And I cannot see this without regret.]

or again: "C'est que tout l'univers est bien reçu chez vous" (II,1). It is the heroine's accessibility that fuels his jealousy, but it is concurrently the only stratagem that allows her to retain control of the situation by presenting an image, a fleeting presence that is only an illusory reflection, an absence drawing others into its void. As a woman, her value is dependent on her inaccessibility as an object of desire and possession, and also, paradoxically, on her accessibility to the masculine gaze that valorizes her. As Patricia Cholakian points out: "But she cannot effectively liberate herself from male domination because of her emotional dependence on her suitors, who reassure her that she is desirable as a woman. Without their presence, Célimène would be nothing."[10]

If Célimène's behavior infuriates Alceste, it is because she does not discriminate between her lovers, thereby refusing to permit him to affirm his separate but superior identity. In other words, Célimène's strategy is a democratization process that breaks down stratification and places all of her lovers on equal footing. Although Alceste's desire for Célimène is predicated upon that of her other suitors and is therefore mimetic in nature, it is also a sign of the hero's eccentricity.

Alceste's world is one of tragedy, in which ethical values govern behavior and choice, whereas Célimène's playful conduct places primary importance on aesthetics and appearances, as Alceste sarcastically points out:

> Mais au moins, dites-moi, madame, par quel sort
> Votre Clitandre a l'heur de vous plaire si fort.
> Sur quel fonds de mérite et de vertu sublime
> Appuyez-vous en lui l'honneur de votre estime?
> Est-ce par l'ongle long qu'il porte au petit doigt
> Qu'il s'est acquis chez vous l'estime où l'on le voit?
> Vous êtes-vous rendue, avec tout le beau monde,
> Au mérite éclatant de sa perruque blonde?
>
> (II,1)

> [But by what spell, Madame, if I may know,
> Does your Clitandre contrive to please you so?
> In worth and virtue is he so supreme
> That you should honor him with your esteem?
> His little finger nail is very long:
> Is that way your regard for him is strong?
> Has his blond wig, which has such great effect
> Upon society, won your respect?]

The primary obstacle to true communication between the lovers is their respective adherence to entirely divergent and even contradictory rules of conduct. Their use of language reflects this incompatibility on a linguistic level. While Alceste values unadorned discourse as a direct and true reflection of one's innermost feelings, Célimène views language playfully. Speech is not binding, but can be altered at will and according to the situation at hand: "De tout ce que j'ai dit je me dédis ici" (II,1). [All I have said, I here and now deny.] From Alceste's point of view, such an utterance can only be viewed as heretical and unorthodox, for his

mistress breaks the very rules upon which continuity and consistency of meaning must be predicated. For the hero, language is
essentially monolithic: a reflection of the Integral and Indivisible
Self. When called upon to retract his critical objections to Oronte's
sonnet, Alceste emphatically refuses to do so in the following
terms, thus echoing his mistress' use of the word "dédire":

> Je ne me dédis point de ce que j'en ai dit . . .
> Je n'en démordrai point . . .
> J'irai, mais rien n'aura pouvoir
> De me faire dédire.
>
> (III,6).

> [I won't take back a single thing I said, . . .
> I won't back down; . . .
> I'll go; but I shall not unsay
> One thing I've said.]

Furthermore, Alceste's desire for isolation and his need to set
himself apart is paralleled by Célimène's need to be surrounded
by others. These opposite modes of social behavior and interaction are the direct result of their similar determination to assert
their superiority. Alceste's position is peripheral to the circle of
play, whereas that of Célimène is central, but both seek to subjugate the social gaze. Célimène's success and her lover's failure at
such an endeavor are emblematic of the dialectics of exclusion
and inclusion in the comic realm. In order to gain consideration
within the play world it is necessary to maintain the fraternal bond
that unites the joke-maker and the laugher against the object of
ridicule, who is excluded, or who in this case excludes himself,
from participation in the ludic events. Only those privy to the
shelter of the comic circle can witness and mock those who cannot
enjoy the same exclusive membership.

This interplay between marginality and centrality is echoed by
an altercation in scene 3 of act 2. Throughout the play, Alceste's
physical presence on stage is a constant visual reminder of the
tension between inclusion and exclusion, for he is continuously
on the brink of departure. When he threatens to leave due to
Clitandre's arrival, Célimène orders him to stay:

> *Célimène:* Où courez-vous?
> *Alceste:* Je sors.
> *Célimène:* Demeurez.
> *Alceste:* Pour quoi faire?

Célimène: Demeurez.
Alceste: Je ne puis.
Célimène: Je le veux, je le veux.
Alceste: Non, il m'est impossible.

(II,3)

[Célimène: Where are you going?
Alceste: Leaving.
Célimène: Stay.
Alceste: What for?
Célimène: Stay here.
Alceste: I can't.
Célimène: I want you to.
Alceste: No more.]

The terseness of the dialogue represents the dialectical antagonism between the protagonists: Alceste's immobility is the direct result of the bipolarity of his concomitant longings for centrality and marginality. Caught between contradictory impulses to remain and depart, he finds it impossible to do either. Célimène mocks his inertia with her sarcasm: "Vous n'êtes pas sorti?" (II,4) [You haven't left?] The heroine's own insistent commands are the result of her need for dominant centrality, but she is dependent for this on the very presence of her satellites, whose gaze substantiates and validates her desirability, and whom she attempts to control through her personal magnetism. Alceste is caught between his desire to disengage himself from Célimène's mesmerizing presence (a presence that reduces him to a mere reflection of her brilliance) and his will to dominate the controlling presence, thereby asserting his superiority in the absolute. In his study of the gestural structure of three of Molière's comedies, G. Donald Jackson makes the following discovery:

Les déplacements du *Misanthrope* se groupent autour du thème de la recherche ou du refus de la compagnie d'autrui, de la fuite ou de l'accueil. [Les] mouvements typiques [d'Alceste] continueront à exprimer le refus de la présence d'autrui . . . La recherche de la compagnie d'autrui est associée à des déplacements de la plupart des autres personnages . . . Il est remarquable que Célimène ne figure pas dans cette catégorie. On aurait cru que ce serait elle qui, par excellence, rechercherait la compagnie des autres. Elle le fait sûrement, mais par le discours. C'est le moins "mouvementé" des personnages de la pièce. Mais, en revanche, c'est elle qui plus que tout autre personnage, et de loin, commente, valorise et dévalorise les entrées, les sorties et les déplacements des autres.[11]

[The stage movements of *The Misanthrope* revolve around the theme of the quest for, or the refusal of the company of others, of flight or reception. Alceste's typical movements will continue to express the refusal of the presence of others. The search for the companionship of others is associated with the displacements of most of the other characters. . . . It is remarkable that Célimène is not represented in this category. One would have thought that she would be the one in particular to seek the company of others. She certainly does so, but through discourse. She is the least mobile of the characters in the play. But it is she who, more than any other character, and by far, comments upon, validates and devalues the entrances, the exits and the movements of others.] (Translation by author)

Having failed in his attempt to depart, or rather having succumbed to his mistress' orders to remain, Alceste issues a hasty series of imperatives in order to regain a semblance of authority: "Aujourd'hui vous vous expliquerez."—"Vous vous déclarerez."—"Vous prendrez parti."—"Non, mais vous choisirez" (II,4). [You shall explain yourself today.—You shall say your say.—You'll make up your mind.—No, you *shall* choose.] However, given Célimène's disregard for the value of committed discourse, Alceste's attempts at forcing her to pronounce herself are ludicrous at best.

This is not to say that Célimène disregards the power of linguistic discourse. In fact, her refusal to pronounce, declare, or choose is equivalent to a rejection of the limitations of the language of commitment and the ensuing loss of personal freedom. Furthermore, her awareness of the central importance of language is reflected in her malicious commentary on various members of her entourage. Damon, the reasoner, is a bombastic orator whose esoteric utterances mask the insignificance of his message. Timante's main flaw is to turn the most commonplace phrases into mysterious secrets, whereas Géralde's discourse is characterized by continual name-dropping. Bélise's stupidity renders her conversation sterile and unbearably boring and Adraste is a chronic complainer, while Damis' laborious efforts at uttering witticisms mar his verbal expression. Célimène's critique of her contemporaries contains an implicit stylistic analysis of the various modes of unauthentic discourse and echoes her lover's own analytical commentary of Oronte's sonnet. Her perceptiveness can be viewed as an ironic reflection of Alceste's own aversion to insincerity. However, Célimène's capricious behavior remains inadmissible and unauthentic in Alceste's view, because she hastily retracts her opinions when the object of criticism is present. It is this playful ability to retract language, to take it back and alter it to suit the occasion, that Alceste abhors, rather than the criticism itself. In other words, the hero refuses to believe in the relativity or subjectivity of language, preferring to confer upon it immutable significance. He wants to place language outside of time and space, in the realm of absolute and transcendent value.

By withholding approval of others, Célimène retains her dominant position as the universal source of all judgment. This strategy to retain her superior status is strangely analogous to that of Alceste himself. Yet there is one main difference: Célimène requires the acquiescence and the complicity of those surrounding her. Alceste voices his objection to her tactics and attributes most of the blame for her behavior to her accomplices:

> . . . vos ris complaisants
> Tirent de son esprit tous ces traits médisants;
> Son humeur satirique est sans cesse nourrie
> Par le coupable encens de votre flatterie,
> Et son coeur à railler trouverait moins d'appas
> S'il avait observé qu'on ne l'applaudît pas.
>
> (II,4)

> [. . .your fawning laughter
> Affords her wit just the applause she's after.
> Her bent for character assassination
> Feeds constantly upon your adulation;
> For satire she would have less appetite
> Were it not always greeted with delight.]

It becomes increasingly apparent that Alceste, who has little compassion or understanding for the foibles of humankind, is not so much infuriated by what is said, but by the bond of complicity formed between the joke-maker and the witness. It is precisely such a bond that marks off the play world from that of serious values and helps to define Alceste as an outsider looking in. Nina Ekstein suggests that "For Célimène, portrait-telling is both a social activity and a means of reigning over her salon. Her portraits are not confidences, but a form of entertainment for her guests: she becomes the center of attention through her talents as a portraitist . . . The scene has a ritual quality: the victims are seemingly sacrificed by the high priestess with the active collusion of the spectators."[12] Célimène's centrality to the play world becomes imperiled then only when her duplicity is revealed, for the roles of joke-maker and cheat are fundamentally incompatible. If the joke-maker is invested with the power to forge the rules of the game, s/he must subscribe to at least one limitation in not being allowed to break them.

If complicity is the key word to Célimène's code of conduct, contradiction is the cornerstone of Alceste's behavior. Although he fancies himself the herald of authenticity and sincerity, Alceste's maniacal desire to assert his superiority by distancing himself from vulgarity results in opposition for opposition's sake. As Célimène puts it:

> L'honneur de contredire a pour lui tant de charmes
> Qu'il prend contre lui-même assez souvent les armes,
> Et ses vrais sentiments sont combattus par lui
> Aussitôt qu'il les voit dans la bouche d'autrui.
>
> (II,4)

> [For him contrariness offers such charms,
> Against himself he often turns his arms;
> And should another man his views defend,
> He will combat them to the bitter end.]

The supreme irony of such a strategy is that the hero's search for authenticity becomes subordinate to his desire for differentiation. The truth he professes to speak is as mutable as that of Célimène: it changes in accordance with the targeted audience. In spite of himself, Alceste adopts a playful and relativistic form of discourse that forces him to be contrary to his own principles and ultimately to his innermost self.

As has been indicated, Alceste's concomitant desires for marginality and centrality in the play world of his peers leads to an emotional and behavioral impasse. Despite a pressing desire to shun human companionship, the hero feels a compelling need to remain within the social sphere. When Clitandre and Acaste refuse to part company with Célimène, Alceste stubbornly vows to outlast even the most assiduous suitor by being the last to leave. As Riggs points out: "Because of his desire to possess Célimène and to be individuated, Alceste is bound to others in a relationship that is inescapable, and even mimetic, as well as contradictory."[13] The hero's insecurity is in direct relationship to his need to control the situation through his vigilant presence, although he has an opposite longing to dominate through his peripheral presence as object of desire. It is ironically at this precise moment that Alceste is called away to settle his dispute with Oronte. His reluctance to abandon the stage to his rivals is quite apparent, while his departure triggers a sense of relief among Célimène and her consorts.

Alceste views his ambivalent quest for the truth, which he continuously redefines so as to remain opposed to each new interlocutor, as an uncompromising adherence to immutable objective standards. However, this behavior is merely a rather transparent pretext for an unremitting territorial desire to mark off his separate space.

For Alceste, the language of love is one of harsh and straightforward criticism, for he believes that the true lover's judgment remains untainted by subjectivity. It is Eliante who attempts to mitigate his opinion by revealing the inherently relativistic nature of sentiment:

> L'amour, pour l'ordinaire, est peu fait à ces lois,
> Et l'on voit les amants vanter toujours leur choix;
> Jamais leur passion n'y voit rien de blâmable,
> Et dans l'objet aimé tout leur devient aimable;
> Ils comptent les défauts pour des perfections,
> Et savent y donner de favorables noms.

(II,4)

> [Love tends to find such laws somewhat austere,
> And lovers always brag about their dear;
> Their passion never sees a thing to blame,
> And everything is lovely in their flame:
> They find perfection in her every flaw,
> And speak of her with euphemistic awe.]

In so doing she inevitably infers that Alceste's love for Célimène is perhaps merely a devious form of self-indulgence. It becomes increasingly apparent that Alceste's brand of truth is incompatible with the rules of social conduct and that to become a player in the ludic sphere one has to learn how to lie, or at least to distort the truth. What is most interesting, however, is that the protagonist's uncompromising adherence to the truth is highly unauthentic and that, within this comedy, the playful adaptations of veracity are much closer to genuine authenticity. This may allow one to draw certain inferences regarding the varying definitions of truth within the ludic and the tragic spheres respectively.

By virtue of her centrality, it becomes Célimène's prerogative to define the truth, and we have seen that she does so in a playful manner, ever redefining it to suit her purposes and the circumstances at hand. Yet in order to retain her hegemony, her continued stage presence is a vital necessity. Her brief absence at the beginning of act 3 is a major tactical error. Assured of her ascendancy over her lovers ("L'amour retient ici nos pas . . ." III,2) [Love will not let us go . . .], she leaves them alone for only a moment in order to escort Alceste to the door. But it is precisely during this scene that a secret bond is formed between the rivals. Acaste and Clitandre concur that to give without a return on one's investment is of little interest to them:

> Mais les gens de mon air, marquis, ne sont pas faits
> Pour aimer à crédit et faire tous les frais.
> Quelque rare que soit le mérite des belles,
> Je pense, Dieu merci, qu'on vaut son prix comme elles,
> Que, pour se faire honneur d'un coeur comme le mien,
> Ce n'est pas la raison qu'il ne leur coûte rien . . .
>
> (III,1)

> [But men of my class are not made to yearn
> For anyone, Marquis, without return.
> However fair the girls, however nice,
> I think, thank God, we too are worth our price;
> If they would claim the heart of one like me,
> They should in reason pay the proper fee . . .]

Acaste thus echoes the words of Dom Juan and substantiates Cixous' definition of a masculine economic order of give-and-retrieve.[14] The heroine's lovers form a merger in order to minimize their losses, thereby undermining her hegemony. Quite in contrast to Alceste, Acaste is described as a carefree individual ("Toute chose t'égaye, et rien ne t'inquiète" III,1) [You're free from worriment and full of glee] whose rivalry with Clitandre takes on the characteristics of a playful competition, subject to the gamelike rules of winner-take-all. The ludic quality of their quest for Célimène is predicated on an underlying awareness of the temporary or evanescent nature of the play world's boundaries:

> Oui, mais trouvant ailleurs des conquêtes faciles,
> Pourquoi pousser ici des soupirs inutiles?
>
> (III,1)

> [When elsewhere easy conquests meet your eyes,
> Why linger here to utter useless sighs?]

It is interesting to note that this display of masculine solidarity among rivals is paralleled by a rift between Célimène and her female rival Arsinoé. Cholakian observes that "All the men in the play are thus bound by codes which honor fair play and respect the territorial rights of other men. No such codes exist between the women in the play . . . Each recognizes in the other a member of an inferior caste—the female sex. Célimène flatters and manipulates her male friends because in her eyes they are of value. The female, who possesses no value in her eyes, is not worth flattering."[15] The common economic interests that forge the bond between the male antagonists are contrasted to the opposing interests of the women. Célimène describes Arsinoé's behavior in the following manner:

> Elle veut que ce soit un vol que je lui fais,
> Et son jaloux dépit qu'avec peine elle cache,
> En tous endroits sous main contre moi se détache.
>
> (III,3)

> [And she pronounces this a kind of theft.
> In jealous spite, which she can hardly bear,
> She covertly attacks me everywhere.]

The male rivals' efforts to band together in order to protect their interests by conceding victory to the dominant male do not constitute a feminine strategy, for the female characters of *Le Misanthrope* seem incapable of such solidarity. It is therefore fitting that Arsinoé condemns Célimène's empowerment as a theft. She also attempts to minimize Célimène's physical and personal appeal by referring to the ineluctable laws governing the masculine economy of give-and-take:

> Et de là nous pouvons tirer des conséquences,
> Qu'on n'acquiert point leurs coeurs sans de grandes avances,
> Qu'aucun pour nos beaux yeux n'est notre soupirant,
> Et qu'il faut acheter tous les soins qu'on nous rend.
>
> (III,4)

> [From this I think we safely may conclude
> That such devotion springs from gratitude,
> That no one courts us for our lovely eyes,
> And that we pay a price for all their sighs.]

Arsinoé's envy can be related in a sense to a more general and pervasive contempt for the female gender. According to Irigaray, "Given that woman has been unable to work out her envy in the way justice demands, she would indeed be unfamiliar with 'the condition subject to which one can put envy aside.' Woman's 'envies' would not find an economy, a right, a system or law, to regulate the ways in which those envies could or could not be expressed. Indeed, the needs and desires of the little girl have remained 'latent': curbed, inhibited, repressed, converted into hatred (of the mother), contempt (for the female sex), etc."[16]

It must not be forgotten, however, that it is not sensual gratification that Célimène seeks, but domination. To ensure this, she must remain ever present yet ever elusive behind the beautiful image she projects. It is precisely because Arsinoé can project no such image that she cannot comprehend the effectiveness of her rival's strategy.

Often likened to a feminine Alceste, Arsinoé is the very antithesis of Célimène. Having lost her desirability as a means to empowerment and self-assertion, she wields moral judgment as a means to exert dominion over others. Although Arsinoé's thinly veiled attack and Célimène's hostile reply are symmetrically inverted reflections of one another, it is most important to note the way in which they seem to constitute a direct application of Alceste's plea for direct and authentic dialogue. This only serves to emphasize the aggressively hostile nature of the hero's project:

> *Arsinoé:* Madame, et je vois bien, par ce qu'elle a d'aigreur,
> Que mon sincère avis vous a blessé au coeur.
> *Célimène:* Au contraire, madame, et si l'on était sage,
> Ces avis mutuels seraient mis en usage:
> On détruirait par là, traitant de bonne foi,
> Ce grand aveuglement où chacun est pour soi.
>
> (III,4)

> [Arsinoé: And since, Madame, it is so very tart,
> I see my frank advice has stung your heart.
> Célimène: Why, not at all, Madame; if we were wise,
> Such chance for mutual counsel we would prize;
> And honesty would banish from our mind
> The blindness toward oneself that plagues mankind.]

Célimène's professed admiration for Alceste's unmasked language is followed immediately by a scene in which the hero's own tolerance for the harshness of unmitigated truth is put to the test. When Arsinoé offers to give him proof of Célimène's infidelities, Alceste admonishes her for the very same lack of sensitivity that he himself frequently advocates in his quest for authenticity:

Cela se peut, madame: on ne voit pas les coeurs;
Mais votre charité se serait bien passée
De jeter dans le mien une telle pensée.

(III,5)

[Perhaps, Madame, the heart we cannot know;
But could you not in charity decline
To plant such a disloyal thought in mine?]

The true ironic counterpoint to all this, however, occurs in act 4, scene 3, during a violent confrontation between Alceste and Célimène. The former accuses his mistress of betrayal and seems to have lost all sense of measure in his excessive rage. His jealousy has been spawned, of course, by an anonymous letter in Célimène's handwriting and given to him by Arsinoé as proof of his vulnerability.

Alceste's desire for consistency and integrity is short-circuited by the emotional intensity of this confrontation. His sudden decision to have Eliante become the surrogate object of his desire is an insulting and vindictive gesture aimed at Célimène's preoccupation with centrality. Eliante fully understands that she is being used as a pawn in this lovers' quarrel and points out the impossibility of controlling emotion through reason. In his anger, Alceste becomes increasingly dramatic and hyperbolic:

Que toutes les horreurs dont une âme est capable
A vos déloyautés n'ont rien de comparable;
Que le sort, les démons et le Ciel en courroux
N'ont jamais rien produit de si méchant que vous.

(IV,3)

[Nothing can match, no, not the ugliest crimes,
The faithlessness you've shown these many times;
The worst the Fate, Hell, wrathful Heaven could do
Never made anything as bad as you.]

By contrast, Célimène's ability to retain her self-control is reflected once again in her use of playful language, to which Alceste heatedly responds: "Ah! ne plaisantez point, il n'est pas temps de rire . . ." (IV,3). [No, no, this is no time for pleasantries . . .] Whereas Célimène's mockery displays her command of the game, the hero's mimicry of tragic discourse is, by his own admission, indicative of his loss of control: "Je n'ai point, sur ma langue, un assez grand empire" (V,1). [My tongue will not obey me as it should] In other words, only the comic idiom allows the player to retain control in the ludic sphere. Alceste's grave admonitions and accusations of infidelity are countered by the heroine's playful reply: "Et si c'était une femme à qui va ce billet?" (IV,3) [But if it's written to a lady friend?]

Once again the language employed is purposefully evasive, sowing seeds of doubt where certainty is desired. According to one critic, "The salient quality of language for Célimène is ambiguity. It does not serve the function of communication since its intent is not to purvey meaning, but to mystify."[17] The one trait characteristic of comic discourse seems to be its mutability and its total disregard for consistency of meaning. It is language engaged in continuous metamorphosis, forcing the listener into a never ending pursuit of elusive meaning.

In other words, Célimène's discourse is a perfect reflection of herself, for it refuses definition in order to retain its freedom. Her discourse is at the same time a perfect example of feminine language as defined by Irigaray: "'She' is indefinitely other in herself. This is doubtless why she is said to be whimsical, incomprehensible, agitated, capricious . . . not to mention her language, in which 'she' sets off in all directions leaving 'him' unable to discern the coherence of any meaning . . . It is useless, then, to trap women in the exact definition of what they mean, to make them repeat (themselves) so that it will be clear; they are already elsewhere in that discursive machinery where you expected to surprise them."[18] Such a flight from definition allows Célimène to retain perfect control over her pursuers.

As a result, Alceste is forced to beg his mistress to put his mind to rest, even if that should require a bold-faced lie:

> De grâce, montrez-moi, je serai satisfait,
> Qu'on peut pour une femme expliquer ce billet.
>
> (IV,3)

> [Please show me how this letter could be meant
> For any woman, and I'll be content.]

The hero willingly gives up his claim to authenticity and integrity in favor of his desire for consistency of meaning, be it ever so false. Célimène's ultimate refusal to provide Alceste with a plausible explanation of the letter is a manifestation of her power within the ludic sphere.

The heroine's centrality is furthermore evidenced by her ability to define the judgmental standards within the comic realm. Her derision separates the laughers from the objects of ridicule. It is perhaps small wonder that Alceste bitterly regrets his impotence and sees his only means of empowerment as a debt of recognition. The problem, as he sees it, is that Célimène is self-sufficient and economically independent: nothing he might give her could reestablish the balance of power:

> [Je voudrais que] j'eusse la joie et la gloire, en ce jour,
> De vous voir tenir tout des mains de mon amour.
>
> (IV,3)

> [Twould be my pride and joy, all else above,
> To have you owe everything to my love.]

By his own admission, Alceste's love is inherently destructive, not only of Célimène's autonomy, but of her entire identity. He would like her to owe him everything, and by inference, to become a faithful reflection of her creator. As Célimène points out: "C'est me vouloir du bien d'une étrange manière!" (IV,3) [You surely wish me well in your own way!]

Alceste's forced exit at the end of the fourth act is further evidence of the bipolar attraction of marginality and centrality. Though he professes to seek self-willed isolation, he finds it difficult in the extreme to disengage himself from the centripetal force of Célimène's presence. The stalemate resulting from his own ambivalence will be resolved in the final act, when the power structures of the ludic sphere implode, causing a shift from comedy to melodrama.

In the first scene of the final act, Alceste bursts upon the scene venting his rage against the inequities of mankind. What is revealed, however, in his discourse, is the self-willed nature of his exclusion. Whatever price he has had to pay, it has bought him the right to vociferate against humanity.

> Mais pour vingt mille francs j'aurai droit de pester
> Contre l'iniquité de la nature humaine.
>
> (V,1)

> [But for those twenty thousand francs I'll buy
> the right to rail against man's wicked state]

Subtending the hero's claim to marginality is, as might have been expected, the desire for immortality. By removing himself from the play world, Alceste seeks to divert attention away from Célimène and onto himself, becoming a living exemplum, a model victim of society's injustice.

> Quelque sensible tort qu'un tel arrêt me fasse,
> Je me garderai bien de vouloir qu'on le casse:
> On y voit trop à plein le bon droit maltraité,
> Et je veux qu'il demeure à la postérité
> Comme une marque insigne, un fameux témoignage
> De la méchanceté des hommes de notre âge.
>
> (V,1)

> [The wrong it does me is so manifest,
> I won't appeal it; no, I'll let it rest.
> It shows the right downtrodden and maligned,
> And I want it exposed to all mankind
> As a clear testimony and display
> Of all the evil of the present day.]

Alceste desires to put himself on display outside of the boundaries of the comic circle, thereby disrupting the game by focusing on a strictly moralistic perspective. His miscalculation stems from his lack of personal magnetism.

Alceste's failure to rivet the attention of the participants leads him to adopt an alternate strategy. He will attempt to co-opt the central object of desire, that is Célimène, into accompanying him into exile, thereby appropriating the mesmerizing presence of the one toward whom all eyes are turned. In doing so, he once again overestimates his own desirability. For Célimène, whose identity and empowerment rest upon centrality, the hero's attempt to dislodge her from the seat of power can only be viewed as a form of living death:

> Moi, renoncer au monde avant que de vieillir,
> Et dans votre désert aller m'ensevelir!
>
> (V,4)

> [What! *I* renounce the world before I'm old,
> And molder in some solitary hold?]

Alceste's failure to persuade Célimène to follow him on his lonely quest is perhaps none too surprising, but within the male contingent the need to dislodge female ascendancy from within the parameters of the play world becomes increasingly acute. The heroine has effectively maintained her grip on power by preserving the delicate balance of mimetic desire: "Conserver tout le monde est votre grande étude!" (V,2) [You don't need everyone under your sway.] The fragile nature of this equilibrium can be attributed to the fact that individual desire is predicated upon collective desire. Her ascendancy collapses the moment her suitor Oronte disengages himself from her circle of influence by freely "giving" her back to Alceste. Thus, the disillusionment of one individual will have a domino effect. In order to achieve this result, however, Célimène's male satellites, who had previously bonded together out of common interest, besiege, surround, and effectively immobilize her central presence, forcing her into pronouncement. Although she still doggedly refuses to engage in committed discourse, her silence itself will be interpreted by her suitors, who thereby rob her of her ability to command evasive discourse. Cornered on all sides, Célimène is stripped of her freedom of choice, her elusiveness, and consequently her desirability. It is precisely at this point in the narrative, that her final consent to marry Alceste is emblematic of her fall from power.

The hero's rejection of this long-awaited prize is an important key to the play's interpretation. It allows one to question yet again the authenticity of his love for the heroine, for he only consents to such an arrangement on his own terms. Célimène's extradition from the comic realm becomes a precondition for the reaffirmation of Alceste's empowerment:

> Pourvu que votre coeur veuille donner les mains
> Au dessein que je fais de fuir tous les humains
> Et que dans mon désert, où j'ai fait voeu de vivre,
> Vous soyez, sans tarder, résolue à me suivre.
>
> (V,4)

> [Provided only that your heart agree
> To flee human society with me,
> And that you'll follow me without delay
> To the seclusion where I've vowed to stay.]

Alceste understands that as long as she remains within the parameters of an essentially playful society, the coquette (who is essentially a female embodiment of the cheat) will always retain the potentially dangerous power to reassert her dominion.

Although within the comic sphere marriage is traditionally symbolic of reunification and harmonious integration of diverging principles, it does not entirely protect men from their wives' indiscretions. Furthermore, Alceste's unwavering desire is to attain the status of hero *outside* the confines of the ludic circle. If marriage ultimately represents the consecration of a new and playful societal order, then *Le Misanthrope* ends on a discordant note. Alceste's refusal to acknowledge the fundamental rules of the game qualifies him as a spoil-sport whose presence is disruptive and undesirable. His alienation will eventually lead to self-willed exclusion and exile. As for Célimène, whose exit also marks the end of the play, we know that she will resurface in one form or another, for she owes her resilience to her mutability.

Once again, the play world is more tolerant of the cheat than the spoil-sport, because the former breaks the rules while acknowledging their importance on the surface, whereas the latter disregards them altogether, thereby shattering the carefully constructed illusion. The stalemate between Célimène's strategy of centrality and Alceste's marginality, however, has left the prevailing societal structures intact.

The reaffirmation of the stability of the established order is represented by the marriage of Philinte and Eliante: the two characters whose conciliatory presence is emblematic of an attitude of tolerance, acceptance, and somewhat dreary compromise. Eliante resigns herself to a loveless marriage rather than continue life as a single woman devoid of societal status. Gone is the threat of the female cheat's disruptive presence. Just as the contradictory Alceste has been replaced by his conciliatory counterpart Philinte, the constant advocate of propriety, so too has Célimène been replaced by Eliante, the very image of complacency and subservience within the domestic patriarchal order.

8

Le Malade imaginaire:
The Symbolic and the Mimetic

L'on n'a qu'à parler avec une robe et un bonnet, tout galimatias
devient savant, et toute sottise devient raison.
—*Le Malade imaginaire* III, 14

Many critics indulgently dismiss Molière's apparent lack of attention to structural unity as unimportant in view of his comic genius,
which liberates him from the constraints facing ordinary play-
wrights. Without arguing against the poetic license of genius, I
should like to point out that this view of Molière's plays as a series
of sketches favoring the display of comic character does very little
justice to his talent for plot construction. I hope to have justified
this point of view already in my analysis of *Le Bourgeois gentilhomme,* which, along with *Le Malade imaginaire,* has been cited as
one of Molière's most dismembered plots. Naturally, the negative
perception has a great deal to do with the fact that both plays
are *comédies-ballets.* The incorporation of music and dance into a
broadly farcical main plot may appear somewhat arbitrary, and
Molière's attempts at careful integration of the interludes seem,
at least initially, very casual. Paradoxically, this flagrant lack of
integration is, as I shall try to prove, a very important feature of
the structural unity of *Le Malade imaginaire.* The key to the play's
fundamental symmetry lies in uncovering the dialectics of opposition between two radically different ludic spheres that are largely
determined by gender.

The first scene of act 1 is of critical importance to our understanding of Argan, for the spectator is made aware of the semiconscious nature of his game. The fact that the protagonist is
engrossed in monologue indicates his self-absorption within an
illusory circle of his own creation. On the other hand, his need

168

to be surrounded by others manifests his desire for an audience: "Il n'y a personne. J'ai beau dire, on me laisse toujours seul; il n'y a pas moyen de les arrêter ici"[1] (I,1). [There's nobody here. No matter what I say, they always leave me alone; there's no way to keep them here.] He is therefore presented as a comedian, but as one who is only semiconscious of his playacting. His infantilism and helplessness are merely attention-getting artifices that allow him to manipulate his audience. This child-subject cannot be satisfied with self-appraisal. He needs the gaze of others to substantiate his being. Argan therefore simultaneously depends upon and controls this gaze. Carol Mossman points out the paradoxical nature of Argan's manoeuvre: "If, on the one hand, Argan has wished himself into a position of total dependence on his family, the family is in turn forced to focus its attention on this counterfeit child."[2]

Argan is an invalid who measures the state of his health by the number of medications he has ingested. "Si bien donc que, de ce mois, j'ai pris une, deux, trois, quatre, cinq, six, sept et huit médecines et un, deux, trois, quatre, cinq, six, sept, huit, neuf, dix, onze et douze lavements; et l'autre mois, il y avait douze médecines et vingt lavements. Je ne m'étonne pas si je ne me porte pas si bien ce mois-ci que l'autre" (I,1). [So this month I've taken one, two, three, four, five, six, seven, eight doses of medicine and one, two, three, four, five, six, seven, eight, nine, ten, eleven, twelve enemas; and last month there were twelve doses of medicine and twenty enemas. I don't wonder that I'm not as well as this month as last.] This comical use of inverted logic points to the equivalence of pleasure and pain. This masochistic propensity of Argan, for whom illness is a veritable source of pleasure, is a means whereby to become the center of attention in a circle of ludic activity of his own creation. According to Philip Berk, "He has the pleasure of knowing . . . that his helplessness is willed and therefore a function of his strength."[3] One should never underestimate Argan's puerile behavior and seeming dependency, which serve as a pernicious smoke screen for authoritarianism. His patriarchal powers remain intact, perhaps all the more so because of the false security his childish disposition inspires in his entourage.

Although Argan's play world may seem utterly foolish to those who do not share in his obsessions, absorption is intense for those who take any game and its rules seriously. Ralph Albanese describes the carefully constructed demarcation line between reality and play in the following terms: "L'univers chimérique dans lequel il s'enferme doit être perçu, on le verra, comme une stratégie de défense contre les impératifs de l'univers réel."[4] [The chimerical universe in which he encloses himself must be perceived, we shall see, as a defensive strategy against the demands of the real world.] (Translation by author) It is participation or nonparticipation in Argan's play world that marks the delineation between the two groups of opponents within the play. The attributes and activities of the two circles of adversaries, though diametrically opposed, will eventually overlap and fuse. It is in this respect that Molière reveals his true talent for plot construction.

A primarily male society has formed around the patriarch Argan, consisting of members of the medical profession: Diafoirus Père and Fils, M. Fleurant, and Docteur Purgon. Béline's rather marginal presence within this society will be examined at some length later on. One thing that these male characters share is their serious regard for their profession. Indeed, even the skeptical Béralde must concede that Purgon's intentions are sincere, in spite of their disastrous consequences. "Votre Monsieur Purgon, par exemple, n'y sait point de finesse; c'est un homme tout médecin de la tête jusqu'aux pieds; un homme qui croit à ses règles plus qu'à toutes les démonstrations des mathématiques, et qui croirait du crime à les vouloir examiner . . . Il ne faut point vouloir mal de tout ce qu'il pourra vous faire; c'est de la meilleure foi du monde qu'il vous expédiera, et il ne fera, en vous tuant, que ce qu'il fait à sa femme et à ses enfants, et ce qu'en un besoin il ferait à lui-même" (III,3). [Your Monsieur Purgon, for example, doesn't try to fool anybody: he's a man who's all doctor, from head to foot, a man who believes in his rules more than in all the demonstrations of mathematics, and who would think it a crime to want to examine them; . . . You mustn't bear him ill will for anything he may do to you; it's in the best faith in the world that he'll expedite you; and in killing you he will do only what he's done to his wife and children, and what, if the need arose, he would do to himself.]

This impression of Purgon is confirmed in scene 5 of act 3, when Béralde, Argan's more sensible brother, attempts to dismiss the overeager M. Fleurant, who has prepared yet another of Purgon's prescribed enemas. Purgon's outrage is vented in a litany of imprecations and threats of impending doom. By association, Argan is characterized as rebellious, insubordinate, even sacrilegious. His subsequent excommunication from the sacred realm of medicine leaves him feeling the anguish of an outcast from that very group of which he was initially the center. The equivalence between the science of medicine and religious doctrine established by the text, demonstrates once again the utter seriousness of the endeavor and the ethical overtones that the participants confer upon their activity, but most importantly it indicates the exclusive nature of enclosure within the ludic circle.

Diafoirus Père is portrayed as obsequious, conservative, and unjustifiably proud of his foolish son Thomas. Unwittingly, he reveals the faults of the very person he desires to praise: "Il n'a jamais eu l'imagination bien vive, ni ce feu d'esprit qu'on remarque dans quelques-uns; mais c'est par là que j'ai toujours bien auguré de sa judiciaire, qualité requise pour l'exercice de notre art. Lorsqu'il était petit, il n'a jamais été ce qu'on appelle mièvre et éveillé. On le voyait toujours doux, paisible et taciturne, ne disant jamais mot, et ne jouant jamais à tous ces petits jeux que l'on nomme enfantins" (II,5). [He has never had a very lively imagination, nor that sparkling wit that you notice in some; but it's by this that I have always augured well of his judgment, a quality required for the exercise of our art. When he was small, he was never what you'd call mischievous or lively. He was always mild, peaceful and taciturn, never saying a word, and never playing all those little games that we call childish.] Thomas' predicament is that he is intrinsically colorless, having no imagination, no gift for spontaneity, and no desire to play. His inability to reason for himself is demonstrated by his rote memorization of medical theory and his constant need for parental guidance. One of the main attributes of all those within Argan's sphere is a humorless disposition. Because the boundaries of ludic activity are largely undiscernible to them, their playacting is executed in dead earnest. This confusion between reality and play, medicine and comedy, is further illustrated by Thomas' proposal to take Angélique to a dissection for an evening's entertainment. Toinette rebukes him in the following manner: "Le divertissement sera agréable. Il y en a qui donnent la comédie à leurs maîtresses; mais donner une dissection est quelque chose de plus galant" (II,5). [That will be a delightful entertainment. There are some who put on a play for their sweethearts, but to put on a dissection is a much more gallant thing.]

With the exception of Béline, Argan's cohorts all abide by the laws of medicine in utter devotion. As his name indicates, Purgon's practice is almost exclusively based on purgative remedies. When he threatens Argan, it is with severe digestive disorders. Based on medical theories of the time, one can assume that Argan suffers primarily from melancholia, attributed to a malfunction of the spleen, which produces inordinate amounts of black bile and black vapors. Hellebore, a medicinal laxative plant, was the habitual cure for this ailment, although it is interesting to note that the other commonly prescribed cure was laughter. Thus, melancholy patients were often enjoined to attend comic plays. The evacuation of anguish could hence be a physical or a psychic phenomenon. Purgon's heavy reliance on enemas can be attributed to his insensitivity to the comic spirit.

The constant cleansing of Argan's digestive track has a theatrical effect. It allows the protagonist to interrupt the action at frequent intervals, riveting the audience's attention on his physical presence. According to Albanese, "L'hypocondrie permet à Argan de faire de son corps un pur objet d'exhibition, de l'ériger en spectacle . . . La passivité de son corps est telle que l'on assiste à un processus permanent de prise et d'évacuation de médicaments sous forme de substances malignes."[5] [Hypochondria allows Argan to turn his body into an object of pure exhibition, to erect it as a showpiece . . . The passiveness of his body is such that one witnesses a permanent process of ingestion and evacuation of medications in the form of malignant substances.] (Translation by author) Small wonder that Béline heaves a sigh of relief at the simulated death of her loathsome husband: "Un homme incommode à tout le monde, malpropre, dégoûtant, sans cesse un lavement ou une médecine dans le ventre, mouchant, toussant, crachant toujours, sans esprit, ennuyeux, de mauvaise humeur, fatiguant sans cesse les gens, et grondant jour et nuit servantes et valets" (III, 12). [A man who was a nuisance to everyone, dirty, disgusting, always with an enema or a dose of medicine in his stomach; always blowing his nose, coughing, and spitting; devoid of wit, boring, bad-humored, constantly wearying people, and scolding all the servants day and night.] The audience is left with an impression of uncleanliness, humorlessness and irritability. The constant process of ingestion and excretion is in essence destructive, draining Argan physically, emotionally, and financially, and proving the ineffectiveness of the cure.

Béline forms a striking contrast to the other members of Argan's clan. Argan's wife accurately perceives the delineation between reality and play, and her astuteness is a measure of her effectiveness as a player. Unlike the other characters surrounding Argan, Béline's game is consciously hypocritical and motivated by self-interest. Angélique's youthful stepmother is a cheat, a female incarnation of the trickster. The false player pretends to be playing the game and, on the face of it, still acknowledges the rules of the game. This is why Argan is so much more lenient toward

Béline than toward the other members of his family who refuse to condone his fantasies and who reveal the relative fragility of the play world in which he has shut himself up with others. In contrast to Mme Jourdain, Béline is an example of a wife whose speech is listened to and whose opinion is respected, but this is only because she has made herself the receptacle of her husband's projections and an echo of her husband's voice. Béline says what Argan wants to hear and it is only at this cost, the cost of losing her identity in speech, that she retains his interest. However, Béline's loss is a short-term sacrifice for a long-term gain. Like Tartuffe, her ultimate goal is to gain control of the family fortune by disinheriting the rightful heirs. Her strategy is to help Argan reinforce and define the boundaries of his play world by casting out the dissenting others. By reflecting her husband's gaze, allowing it thereby to turn back on itself, and by offering herself as the mirror in which the narcissistic gaze can consume itself, Béline becomes an object of fascination for Argan.[6]

Béline's role as wife-mother to Argan, in spite of her youth, casts a murky shadow over the nature of their matrimony. Béline refers to her husband as "mon pauvre mari" [my poor little hubby] and "mon petit fils" [my sweet boy (son)] in almost the same breath, whereas her husband refers to her as "mamie" [my dear], which is homonymous with "mamy" [granny]. The ambiguity of Argan's own assertion that he would require the assistance of Purgon in order to conceive a child with Béline has been interpreted by some as an abdication of paternal power and a desire to return to the irresponsibility of childhood: "Tout le regret que j'aurai, si je meurs, mamie, c'est de n'avoir point un enfant de vous. Monsieur Purgon m'avait dit qu'il m'en ferait faire un" (I,7). [The only regret I'll have if I die, my darling, is not to have a child by you. Monsieur Purgon told me he'd have me have one.] However, this allusion to Argan's sexual impotence allows one to draw the conclusion that the protagonist's enthrallment with his wife is purely narcissistic and that this willed impotence represents not an abdication, but a reaffirmation of paternal authority through the vehicle of the false child, namely Argan, who is controlled by and controls his mother; who desires his mother, but only as an extension of himself.

There is an interesting correlation between Béline's specular role and Argan's desire to sire her child: "The point being that man is *the* procreator, that sexual *production-reproduction* is referable to his 'activity' alone, to his pro-ject alone. Woman is nothing but the receptacle that passively *receives* his *product* . . ."[7] The reabsorption of femininity into maternity is a stultifying reduction process allowing man to assimilate the otherness of woman into Mother, the complement of man's primary narcissism.

The opposing cast of characters includes Cléante, Angélique, Louison, and Toinette: all those whose actions are directed against Argan's egocentric fantasies. Although Béralde takes the side of the younger generation, he will be only marginally involved in their plotting. Béralde's function is primarily dramatic. Though he may sympathize with the young, he belongs to Argan's generation and he will attempt to exploit the advantages of age by acting as go-between for the two groups of opponents. His moralizing tone indicates his adherence to the serious values of an older generation, yet his long-windedness has very little real effect on his brother. Unlike the comic spirit, didactic reason has not the ability to divert (entertain), and it is precisely a diversion from his obsession that Argan so vitally needs. The thematic value of Béralde's position as intermediary is thus established by the seriousness of his logical argumentation, while he remains nonetheless a proponent of the healing power of comedy.

It is therefore significant that it is Béralde who initially suggests the equivalence of comedy and medicine. In his view, medical practice is a superfluous art, for the body has the inherent power of healing itself. The primary function of doctors is not to heal, but to name, to enumerate, and to classify diseases: "Ils savent la plupart de fort belles humanités, savent parler en beau latin, savent nommer en grec toutes les maladies, les définir et les diviser; mais, pour ce qui est de les guérir, c'est ce qu'ils ne savent point du tout . . . Toute l'excellence de leur art consiste en un pompeux galimatias, en un spécieux babil, qui vous donne des mots pour des raisons et des promesses pour des effets" (III,3). [Most of them know a lot in the humanities, know how to talk in fine Latin, know how to name all the diseases in Greek, define them, and classify them; but as for curing them, that's what they don't know how to do at all. . . . and the whole excellence of their art consists of a pompous mumbo-jumbo, a specious chatter, which gives you words for reasons and promises for results.] Medicine is thus closely connected to the nominative function of linguistic discourse, as well as to the art of deception and disguise. It is in this respect that medical practice is truly an art similar to that of comedy, based on illusion rather than substantive acts. Doctors can be seen as comedians whose sense of self-importance leaves them prey to self-deception. As Albanese points out, the doctors "font de leur art l'objet d'une érudition puérile and sclérosée, une expérience essentiellement discursive et formaliste."[8] [turn their art into the object of sterile and ossified erudition, into an essentially discursive and formalistic experience.] (Translation by author)

In his endeavor to free his brother from the tenacious ascendancy of medical practitioners, Béralde addresses him with the following exhortation: "Songez que les principes de votre vie sont en vous-même, et que le courroux de Monsieur Purgon est aussi peu capable de vous faire mourir que ses remèdes de vous faire vivre" (III,6). [Remember that the principles of your life are in yourself, and that the wrath of Monsieur Purgon is as little capable of making you die as are his remedies of making you live.] Béralde's alternative to physical purgation is, of course, the intake of comedy, the true means for the elimination of psychic anguish. The medicinal value of pleasure and laughter operates by means of diversion, allowing for a psychic discharge of anxiety. Not content to prove his point in the abstract, Béralde has brought with him a band of Egyptians for Argan's entertainment: "Ce sont des Egyptiens, vêtus en Mores, qui font des danses mêlées de chansons où je suis sûr que vous prendrez du plaisir; et cela vaudra bien une ordonnance de Monsieur Purgon" (II,9). [They are Gypsies dressed as Moors, who put on dances mingled with songs. I'm sure you'll enjoy them, and they'll do you as much good as one of Monsieur Purgon's prescriptions.] Béralde also highly recommends that his brother attend a comedy by none other than Molière. This metaliterary allusion allows the spectator to consider for a moment the benefits of his own activity. The correlation between mental and physical well-being is further emphasized by Argan's distraction after viewing the spectacle: he momentarily forgets that he is unable to walk without his cane.

At this point in the play the theme of medicine as comedy and comedy as medicine has been firmly established by Béralde, who thus provides an important link between the two circles of ludic activity present within the play. It is this link that accounts for the very central importance of this character and his somewhat lengthy discourse. It will now be up to the others to put his suggestions to work.

If the art of medicine is the bond between the members of Argan's group, the art of comedy is certainly the common link between their adversaries. Indeed, Angélique and Cléante's first encounter takes place at the theater. As Toinette reminds Cléante, "l'on vous a dit l'étroite garde où elle est retenue, qu'on ne la laisse ni sortir, ni parler à personne, et que ce ne fut que la curiosité d'une vieille tante qui nous fit accorder la liberté d'aller à cette comédie qui donna lieu à la naissance de votre passion" (II,1). [you've been told of the tight guard she's kept under, how they don't let her go out, and that it was only the curiosity of an elderly aunt of hers that got us permission to go to that play that was the scene of the birth of your passion . . .] According to Berk: "the gesture of liberation transports Angélique to the comédie, quintessentially a place of art and illusion, but where too nature can run its course, a locus of freedom and love not unlike the pastoral *locus amoenus* of medieval and Renaissance romance. It is then at the theater that are born the forces that will oppose Argan's hypochondria."[9] Comedy is thus associated with liberation from the constraints of Argan's hegemony.

With the exception of the suitor Cléante, the circle of comedians is primarily composed of women: Angélique, Louison, and Toinette, who plays the leading role. Nor should we forget Béline's role as comedienne and tactician within the opposing group. The exclusion of women from the medical circle is partially attributable to what is perceived as their inability to grasp the symbolic. Hélène Cixous contends that "woman is said to be 'outside the Symbolic': outside the Symbolic, that is outside language, the place of the Law, excluded from any possible relationship with culture and cultural order."[10] Though outside the symbolic, women are not outside the mimetic. Deprived of language, they employ their bodies as signs. Jane Gallop comments upon the relation between the Kristevan semiotic and the Lacanian imaginary in the following terms: "Both are defined in contradistinction to 'the symbolic'; the semiotic is revolutionary, breaks closure, and disrupts the symbolic . . . It is noteworthy that the male theorist sees the paternal as disruptive, the maternal as stagnant, whereas the female theorist reverses the positions."[11] Although Molière's female characters seem to share a common aversion to participating in a man's game that has lost sight of its playful origins, they are not at all adverse to forming a play world of their own. From Argan's point of view, these characters are spoil-sports, refusing as they do to participate in his circle of fantasy. By withdrawing from his game, they reveal the falsehood of his hypochondria and shatter the illusion of his play world. This is all the more distressing to Argan, as he has lost sight of the temporal and spacial limitations of his game.

The women, however, do gradually form a locus of play of their own. It is not surprising that Cléante, the lone male participant in this circle, is initially met with distrust. It is interesting to note that his presence in the female locus is structurally analogous to

Béline's presence within the masculine circle of medical practitioners. It is the more worldly Toinette who cautions Angélique
against the perils of love and the deceit of men: "Hé! hé! ces
choses-là, parfois, sont un peu sujettes à caution. Les grimaces
d'amour ressemblent fort à la vérité, et j'ai vu de grands comédiens là-dessus" (I,4). The doubt thus cast upon the authenticity
of Cléante's intentions is further heightened by his first appearance on stage under the assumed identity of Angélique's music
instructor. Cléante is in fact a consummate actor, the "grand co-
médien" of Toinette's warning. However, any initial ambivalence
toward Cléante is immediately tempered by admiration for his
skill, especially in view of the contrast established between himself
and Thomas Diafoirus. Unlike his rival, Cléante is creative, playful, spontaneous, boldly imaginative, and he is, besides, a skillful
improvisor. Whatever the initial distrust, one cannot help but be
drawn to such a beguiling entertainer.

Despite Cléante's charismatic presence, it is the servant girl
Toinette who is the most protean character of all: changing roles
to suit the moment. Toinette's inferior social status affords her
freedom from behavioral norms in spite of her economic dependency. Béline's reluctance to fire her spirited maid in spite of Argan's insistence demonstrates the soubrette's indispensable
position in the household. Furthermore, Toinette's freedom is attributable to her status as unattached female. She is the only
woman in the play unfettered by a male consort or a father and
thus the only woman who is able to speak for herself. This allows
her to assume the leadership of the group opposing Argan's
wishes. The brief appearance of her suitor Polichinelle in the first
interlude only serves to emphasize her complete detachment. She
has no interest in her aging admirer and merely summons him
to use him as an emissary. Furthermore, no actual encounter will
take place at any time between Toinette and Polichinelle. Such
freedom will allow her to assume a number of different identities
in the course of the play.

When she first appears on stage, summoned by her master, she
pretends to have knocked her head against a shutter. This tactic
allows her to continuously interrupt Argan's discourse with her
cries of pain, frustrating thereby his desire to quarrel with her:
"Tais-toi donc, coquine, que je te querelle" (I,2). [Will you shut up,
you hussy, and let me scold you?] Like Jourdain's servant Nicole,
Toinette makes a mockery of her master's attempts to impose
his authoritative voice while stifling hers. However, unlike Nicole's
involuntary convulsions, Toinette's behavior is willfully disruptive.

By her own admission, she can turn the tears on and off: "Si vous querellez, je pleurerai" (I,2). [If you scold me, I'll cry.] She opposes her own form of body language to paternal authority, forcing the father into silence by blocking the reception of the message and forcing him to shout to the point of hoarseness. The effectiveness of a command is shown to be inversely proportional to the loudness of its transmission.

Toinette's second role as Angélique's confidante is equally one at which she excels. Understanding the ingenue's need to talk about her love, to recreate emotions through speech, and to gain self-confidence through approval, Toinette keeps her replies to a monosyllabic minimum, laced with gentle irony. Her only statement of any length cautions Angélique to distinguish the mask from the person, reality from illusion. The accomplished actor must never confuse the two. It is therefore appropriate that it be Toinette who issues such a statement.

In the next scene, Toinette will step in for Angélique, whose reticence leaves her prey to her father's commands. The servant will speak for her mistress, giving voice to the latter's objections to a marriage with Thomas Diafoirus. She will play her role for her while Angélique remains silently present. Finding, however, that paternal authority prevails and that Argan discredits her ability to reason, Toinette will usurp the voice of the father, taking over the prerogative to issue commands, the masculine voice:

> *Argan:* Je lui commande absolument de se préparer à prendre le mari que je dis.
> *Toinette:* Et moi, je lui défends absolument d'en faire rien . . . Quand un maître ne songe pas à ce qu'il fait, une servante bien sensée est en droit de le redresser.
>
> (I,5)

> [Argan: I absolutely command her to prepare to take the husband I say.
> Toinette: And *I* absolutely forbid her to do anything of the sort. . . . When a master doesn't think what he's doing, a sensible servant has the right to correct him.]

Argan immediately detects the subversiveness of this intrusive move into absolutist political discourse and counters with: "Viens, viens, que je t'apprenne à parler!" (I,5) [Come here, come here, I'll teach you how to talk.] What Argan really wants is to teach Toinette to speak like a woman who allows a man to in-form her speech. The servant has overstepped the boundaries of propriety by using the traditionally masculine imperative voice.

Although Toinette uses very little circumspection to reply to her master, her behavior changes radically in the presence of Béline. Both women are playacting, but Toinette is the more skillful of the two, as she is able to deceive the deceitful wife. Toinette has vowed to employ her talents in the service of young love. Her machinations will lead to the gradual integration of spectacle within the structural framework of the play. This integration parallels the disintegration of Argan's illusory circle of play and the gradual shifting of his loyalties from the medical clan to that of the comedians, the final substitution being that of comedy for medicine.

The intention of the prologue, for example, is obvious. Molière makes no attempt to disguise the obsequious flattery directed at his benefactor, the king, for whose entertainment this comedy has been devised. In a pastoral setting, shepherds and shepherdesses sing of the ailment and fatal suffering of love, as well as of its pleasures, laughter, and games. Despite the fact that for most spectators the transition between the artificial convention of the bucolic scene and Argan's first appearance on stage seems tenuous, the juxtaposition of pleasure and pain, vaguely sketched out in the prologue, will form one of the major thematic building blocks of the play.

Another point of interest that is frequently overlooked is that it is presumably the shepherds and shepherdesses of the prologue who perform *Le Malade imaginaire,* which can therefore be perceived from its inception as a play within a play, a royal *divertissement.* The main plot is thus on a plane of illusion once removed from that of the eclogue, and yet, strangely enough, the vivid realism of Argan's first monologue makes the audience perceive the preceding ballet as the less "real" of the two. Nonetheless, a framework is established from the outset, whereby *Le Malade imaginaire* is presented first and foremost as a theatrical diversion. It is interesting to note that this framework will remain open, for the play will never return to the initial pastoral illusion and thus one loses sight of the pretext for the play.

The pretext for the first interlude can be located within the first act. Toinette needs to advise Cléante of the impending marriage between Angélique and his rival. To this effect, she summons her admirer Polichinelle. Although the first interlude appears somewhat better integrated than the prologue, its introduction of music, mime, and rhythmic movement gives it a more stylized atmosphere than that of the rest of the play. Once again, the martyrdom of love is evoked; however, this time Polichinelle's laments are interrupted by a beating in the vein of farce. More importantly, Toinette's message to Cléante will never be transmitted and Argan will remain unaware of the events. Cléante will have to appear of his own volition in the next scene to hear of his misfortunes. Thus, the pretext for the first interlude seems to be rather transparent: the simple desire to add a gratuitous comic spectacle to the play, the justification being solely the pleasure it affords.

Aside from Toinette, with her frequent role playing, Cléante is the first character to offer a formal comic presentation. His impromptu opera is the first true spectacle to occur within an act of the play and to be carefully integrated, as it contributes directly to plot development. Argan insists upon witnessing his daughter's music lesson, adding a comment on his appreciation of the fine arts. This claim will soon reveal itself false, as the protagonist has little patience for the impertinent love duet. The previously silent Angélique now comes alive under the tutelage of her lover, as he coaxes her to break her silence and teaches her what to say/sing. Cléante's thinly disguised commentary on paternal tyranny irritates Argan who puts a halt to the spectacle. Once again, comedy is a vehicle for the freedom to communicate and the liberation from external constraints. Even more pertinent is the fact that the operatic subject matter is that of the play itself. Cléante thus affords us a glimpse at a miniature version of his own reality-as-comedy.

Argan's growing irritation at his daughter Angélique's insubordination is further compounded by his discovery that the music master has visited her within the confines of her private chambers. His attempt to force his younger daughter Louison into a sisterly betrayal is countered by her pretending to be dead. For one so young, she is an accomplished actress in her own right and shows an awareness of female solidarity. This time, Argan is taken in by a deception that has aroused his greatest fear, that of death. He is so jarred by his daughter's comedy that he momentarily forgets his own ailment: "Ah! que d'affaires! je n'ai pas seulement le loisir de songer à ma maladie" (II,8). [Oh, what a lot of troubles! I don't even have time to think about my illness.]

Argan's state of confusion is so great by this time, that he barely has the energy to counter the next offensive by Béralde, who has brought a band of gypsies to distract and amuse his brother. The song and dance constitute the second interlude, which again removes Argan for a moment from his troubled illusions. Integration is more complete than for the first interlude. Not only does the spectator understand the motives for the introduction of the diversion, but s/he also witnesses its effects on Argan.

The healing effect of comic diversion may have been proven to the audience, but Argan's conversion will be obtained with greater difficulty. The first step in extricating him from the doctors' grip will be taken by Béralde. By dismissing M. Fleurant, Argan's brother causes the ire of Docteur Purgon, who will subsequently expel Argan from his circle of support. As Gérard Defaux points out, "Ce n'est pas lui qui quitte la médecine mais, avec un Purgon offensé, la médecine qui le quitte."[12] [It isn't he who abandons medicine but, with an offended Purgon, it is medicine that abandons him.] (Translation by author) At this crucial moment, Toinette's intervention becomes imperative, for fear that the patient find some way to regain his medical sanctuary by placating the offended physician. Toinette understands that the only means of shattering Argan's play world is from within, by invading his ludic space and gaining his confidence within his own frame of reference. She is also perceptive enough to understand that the only way to gain stature and credibility in Argan's mind is to assume a masculine identity. By donning the disguise of a physician—that is, through the mimetic—Toinette gains access to the symbolic and consequently to authoritative discourse. Understandably, this is a concession on her part, as her ability to reason was established from the start. In his study of *Le Malade imaginaire,* Marc Fumaroli corroborates this assertion by stating that Béralde and Toinette change their tactics in the following manner: "Dès lors les deux complices, 'le génie du foyer' Toinette et le 'bon enchanteur' Béralde, doivent se rabattre sur une autre voie. De la *démonstration* au sens logique et rationnel, ils vont passer à la *démonstration* au sens esthétique."[13] [From this point on, the two accomplices, the "household genie" Toinette and the "kindly enchanter" Béralde, must resort to other means. From the logical and rational *demonstration,* they must pass on to an aesthetic *demonstration.*] (Translation by author)

Toinette's strategy is simple. Initially she discredits Purgon and his consorts by proposing remedies contrary to those that have been prescribed. Having accomplished this, she proceeds to discredit her own remedies by prescribing such a drastic cure that even Argan must flinch at its execution: "Voilà un bras que je me ferais couper tout à l'heure si j'étais de vous" (III,10). [That's an arm that I'd have cut off right away, if I were you.] It should not escape notice that Toinette's proposed remedy is a thinly disguised form of castration. The maid servant thereby calls upon the father to do in actuality what he has already done symbolically: relinquish the phallus and the accompanying paternal power by assuming the role of the unsexed child. Argan is thus forced to finally distinguish between reality and his fantasy world, when all of his concerted efforts have so far been focused on erasing the boundaries between the two. Mossman concludes: "I suggest that by erasing the barriers between reality and illusion, between adult and child, begetter and begotten, Argan is attempting to deny the fact of his mortality."[14] Argan is also jarred into recognizing that his infantilism was never in fact an abdication of power, but a pernicious means of consolidating it. Toinette's suggested castration is a means to feminine empowerment since the phallus is said to constitute the *a priori* condition of all symbolic functioning. Naturally, Argan will refuse this final solution. Although by now the disintegration of Argan's play world is nearly complete, one further step will prove necessary.

Béline's importance within the circle of Argan's illusions has been discussed at some length. As long as her presence reflects the image of himself that he wants to see, Argan can retreat to her mirror gaze as he projects himself into the space she provides for him. This mother figure is the last remaining shelter from the harshness of reality. In order to pry Argan loose from his narcissistic contemplation, it becomes necessary to afford him a view of Béline as Other. This can only be done by enlisting his participation in a subterfuge. Argan must become Other himself—a comedian—but in order to do so he must first subdue his overriding fear of death: "N'y a-t-il point quelque danger à contrefaire le mort?" (III,11) [Isn't there some danger in pretending to be dead?] The effort involved in acting out his own death is cathartic and relieves some of his morbid anguish. It allows him to merge with the image of death rather than be riveted by it. Argan's abandonment by the doctors and his subsequent disengagement from Béline leaves him nowhere to turn for refuge but to the opposing clan.

The final shift in loyalties is momentarily delayed by the protagonist's obstinacy, as he consents to his daughter's betrothal to Cléante but only on condition that Cléante become a doctor himself: "Qu'il se fasse médecin, je consens au mariage. Oui, faites-vous médecin, je vous donne ma fille" (III,14). [Let him become a doctor and I'll consent to the marriage. Yes, become a doctor and I'll give you my daughter.] Thus, Argan's permutation takes place within the structural permanence of illusion. Although his obsession with medicine does not seem to have diminished and in this respect no change is apparent, he does seem to have grasped the playful nature of the transformation and the inherent kinship between comedy and medicine. If the authority of medicine rests upon the art of deception, disguise and language, then it is essentially a theatrical art: "En recevant la robe et le bonnet de médecin, vous apprendrez tout cela . . . L'on n'a qu'à parler, avec une robe et un bonnet, tout galimatias devient savant, et toute sottise devient raison" (III, 14). [As you receive the doctor's cap and gown, you'll learn all that . . . One has only to talk with a cap and gown on. Any gibberish becomes learned, and any nonsense becomes reason.] To which Toinette slyly adds: "Tenez, monsieur, quand il n'y aurait que votre barbe, c'est déjà beaucoup; et la barbe fait plus de la moitié d'un médecin" (III, 14) [Look here, sir, if all you had was your beard, that's already a lot and a beard makes more than half a doctor], thereby obliquely acknowledging the inherent kinship between the masculine identity and the realm of the symbolic. However, if comedy proves more effective than medicine, it is ultimately because it makes use of magical, poetic, and evocative language rather than nominative discourse; of creation and mimesis rather than symbolic representation. When considered from such a vantage point, it is obviously Cléante the inveterate actor, not the unimaginative Thomas, who will afford the better cure.

It is not enough, however, for Argan to surround himself with comedians: he needs to exchange one fantasy for another, becoming a comedian himself. His stubborn clinging to his former illusion, his insistence on surrounding himself with doctors, forces a bilateral compromise. Though he may have to make do with make-believe doctors, the comedians must comply with his obsessions. Béralde exhorts his brother to become a doctor himself, thus reiterating his previous plea that he cure himself from within. As a doctor-comedian, Argan will internalize and assimilate comedy, the ultimate remedy. Thus, the ingestion and incorporation of comedy-as-medicine is symbolically represented onstage by the donning of a doctor's gown, and the fusion of the initially separate play worlds of the symbolic and the mimetic is complete. Although the solution is fantastic, it is eminently logical within the context of the play. Healing will take place in an atmosphere of complete comic liberation and rebirth authorized by carnival. Beralde explains that "Ce n'est pas tant le jouer que s'accommoder à ses fantaisies. Tout ceci n'est qu'entre nous. Nous y pouvons aussi prendre chacun un personnage, et nous donner ainsi la comédie les uns aux autres. Le carnaval autorise cela" (III, 14). [But niece, it's not so much our making fun of him, than accommodating ourselves to his fancies. All this is just between us. We can also each of us take a part, and thus put on a comedy for one another. Carnival time authorizes that.] The term "entre nous" stresses the exclusivity of the play world's membership and the awareness of its temporal and spatial limitations.

In spite of the liberating experience of comedy, the structural paradigm of patriarchy remains intact. For the women in particular, the experience of freedom has definite temporal limitations. Having managed to extricate Argan from the shelter of his hypochondria, Toinette will now, at Béralde's behest, relinquish her leadership position within this group, deferring to the Father. The power switch is marked by the third interlude, which can be seen as an initiation ritual confirming Argan's adherence to this new group in which a fusion of comedy and medicine has taken place. It is interesting to note that it is Béralde, Argan's male sibling and member of the older generation, who seeks to firmly establish the patriarch's centrality to this new group: "Les comédiens ont fait un petit intermède de la réception d'un médecin, avec des danses et de la musique; je veux que nous en prenions ensemble le divertissement, et que mon frère y fasse le premier personnage" (III,14). [I have some actors who have composed a little act about accepting a man as a doctor, with music and dances. I want us to enjoy the entertainment together, and I want my brother to play the leading part.] It must be remembered that Argan has never entirely lost his grip on power and that his shift to Toinette's group was contingent upon his retention of the male hegemony. Hence his stubborn insistence on retaining the right to give his daughter away. In fact, his switch becomes an imperative move in his struggle to retain paternal power. Although the author seems to recognize woman's ability to perform and improvise in the realm of the mimetic, the inaccessibility of the symbolic leaves her outside of authoritative discourse, outside of any possible relationship to the cultural order. This engenders a void that will ultimately be filled by Argan's appropriation of comedy.

Paralleling this development—that is, the progressive fusion of the initially separate worlds of comedy and medicine—the spectacular elements and most notably the play's interludes, which are initially almost separate entities, become increasingly incorporated into the fabric of the plot, as the play ends on a note of delirium. Thus, Le Malade imaginaire, the last opus of a brilliant comic playwright, with its complete integration of metadramatic reflections on the nature and value of comedy, can been regarded as one of the most autoreferential of Molière's works: comedy ingesting itself. In the words of Defaux; "Molière, en rejoignant dans sa dernière comédie la grande et ancienne tradition du rire médical, nous apprend, après Hippocrate, L. Joubert et Rabelais, que le rire est non seulement le propre de l'homme, mais encore son salut, sa plus belle sagesse et sa dignité."[15] [By joining in his last comedy the great and ancient tradition of medical laughter, Molière teaches us, after Hippocrates, L. Joubert and Rabelais, that laughter is not only characteristic of mankind, but his salvation, his greatest wisdom and his dignity as well.] (Translation by author) I will simply add that the word "homme" in this citation could be viewed as gender specific.

9

Conclusion: *Les Femmes savantes* and the Problem of Carnal Knowledge

Nous saurons toutes deux imiter notre mère:
Vous, du côté de l'âme et des nobles désirs,
Moi, du côté des sens et des grossiers plaisirs;
Vous, aux productions de l'esprit et de lumière,
Moi, dans celles, ma soeur, qui sont de la matière.
—*Les Femmes savantes* I, 1

This study has focused on the role of female characters in relation to the parameters of the male-dominated play world. We have seen that within the gender-delineated power struggle, female attempts to invade the ludic circle have been by and large successfully countered, though at times not until the very last moment, and occasionally thanks to feminine complicity with the masculine order or reluctance to assume a permanent dominant role. Another constant seems to be the use of sexuality as an effective means to feminine empowerment, although there are innumerable strategic variants on this theme. What has been stressed is woman's difficulty in gaining direct access to the channels of knowledge and power, and a definite masculine tendency to inform the feminine according to his own selective ideology. Therefore, Molière's female characters frequently have recourse to a secondary and indirect form of persuasion by permitting themselves to be transformed into objects of desire, thereby gaining control of the masculine gaze.

In *Les Femmes savantes*, Molière explores yet another alternative form of feminine empowerment. The female contingent attempts to establish dominion by entering and ostensibly "intruding" upon the male bastion of erudition, thereby confronting men within their own space and on their own terms. As James Gaines has pointed out in a recent article:

Les Femmes savantes adds an important dimension to the social dynamics of Molière's theater, for it is his only comedy to feature a struggle between two equally developed social units . . . The balanced forces of the household and the coterie confront each other in a series of carefully orchestrated and rigorously sustained skirmishes. On one level, the measured discourse of *Les Femmes savantes* reminds the audience of that of a courtroom, for each party is given equal time to present its case and to argue for the survival of the way of life it represents.[1]

William Howarth not only corroborates this point of view, but also sees the play's dialectical debates as the primary cause for its weakened comic effect:

> Whereas in the *Précieuses,* the heroines had proclaimed their folly with every word they uttered, this is by no means the case in *Les Femmes savantes.* Bélise is a case apart, but the feminist aspirations of both Philaminte and Armande have to be taken seriously. Hence the prominence given the dialectical exchanges between Henriette and Armande, Philaminte and Clitandre, Clitandre and Trissotin, and the importance of the whole role of Ariste . . . The impression we receive of a diffuseness of comic effect, of a lack of that comic focus we are used to note not only in the major verse plays, but also in *L'Avare, Le Bourgeois gentilhomme,* or *Le Malade imaginaire,* can be confirmed, in however crude a way, by a statistical analysis of the various roles.[2]

It is primarily for this reason and because of the ambivalent nature of the outcome, that I have reserved the exegesis of *Les Femmes savantes* for my concluding chapter. More than any other of Molière's plays, this comedy offers a view of a world in which a balance of power is carefully established between feminine and masculine circles of play.

In the opening lines of *Les Femmes savantes,* marriage is equated almost exclusively with the sexual act by the *précieuse* Armande. She admonishes her sister Henriette that the very word "marriage" is offensive, as it conjures up images of physical contact:

> Ne concevez-vous point ce que, dès qu'on l'entend,
> Un tel mot à l'esprit offre de dégoûtant,
> De quelle étrange image on est par lui blessée,
> Sur quelle sale vue il traîne la pensée.
> N'en frissonnez-vous point?
>
> (I,1)[3]

[Can you not conceive how disgusting to one's feelings is the very mention of the word? Think what shocking thoughts it brings to mind! Into what dirty paths it drags one's ideas! Do you not shudder at it?]

The sign is confused with the signified: a concrete, physical reality that is both visual and audible, and tactile as well. The desire within *précieux* circles to separate the physical from the spiritual is predicated upon a Manichaean perception of reality in which immanence is evil and transcendence good. Concrete reality can therefore be invoked only indirectly, through abstractions and allusions, metaphors and paraphrases. According to Riggs, however, Armande's speech "is full of figurative expressions whose meaning depends on their basis in material, especially sexual, experiences. The scene dissolves the screen between the rhetoric and motive, since her language inadvertently but obsessively refers to what it is trying to hide."[4]

Ironically, the perception of a culture/nature dichotomy in which feminine materiality opposes masculine spirituality leads one to conclude that preciosity, generally perceived as a preponderantly feminine movement, seeks to suppress its own feminine "nature" in favor of the masculine cultural ideology.

At the very core of the problematics engendered by *Les Femmes savantes* is the institution of marriage itself. It is naturally founded upon physical contact between two members of opposite sex, or "carnal knowledge." From the *précieux* point of view, however, carnal knowledge posits a dichotomous coupling of opposites in which *scientia*, or knowledge, is not grasped intellectually, but is acquired through the senses. The female becomes quite literally the receptacle of the male and the knowledge thus transmitted is purely sensorial in nature. In this model the direction of the flow is always from man to woman and never the reverse. Thus, the repulsion experienced by Armande at the very mention of the word "marriage" can be ascribed in part to the contamination engendered by the coupling of the animal and the spiritual, the monstrous nature of the unholy union between the elevated spheres of intellectual pursuit and debased carnal appetites:

> Laissez aux gens grossiers, aux personnes vulgaires,
> Les bas amusements de ces sortes d'affaires.
> A de plus hauts objets élevez vos désirs,
> Songez à prendre un goût des plus nobles plaisirs,
> Et, traitant de mépris les sens et la matière,
> A l'esprit, comme nous, donnez-vous toute entière.

(I,1)

[Leave such contemptible amusements to common people and vulgar persons. Raise your hopes to loftier ambitions, try to cultivate a taste for the noblest accomplishments, and, looking with scorn upon things of the senses and of matter, give yourself up entirely, as we do, to intellectual pursuits.]

What Armande is in fact advocating is a woman's right to gain direct access to the realm of knowledge without the intermediary of a masculine tutor. Her fear of physical contact can be at least partially equated to a fear of spiritual and intellectual domination as well. Her strategy for retaining ascendancy over men is through inaccessibility. She prefers the "adorateur" [admirer] to the "époux" [spouse]:

> Cet empire que tient la raison sur les sens
> Ne fait pas renoncer aux douceurs des encens;
> Et l'on peut pour époux refuser un mérite
> Que pour adorateur on veut bien à sa suite.
>
> (I,1)

[The rule that reason sways over the senses does not necessitate the renouncement of the pleasures of adulation; one may refuse a man of merit for a husband, whom one would willingly have in one's train as an admirer.]

The male suitor must substitute sublimated erotic language for impossible physical contact. Riggs clearly defines the true nature of such a relationship: "'Préciosité' thus ritualizes a relationship of domination and submission. Submission to the object of the erotic aspirant's idealized ardor, or his submission to being dominated by another person, is somewhat disguised by the relationship's ostensible function, which is to practice and ceremonialize, in language, mastery over 'nature'."[5] Ostensibly, the platonic relationship seems to be the only means of avoiding the physical contamination that would lead to feminine subservience, yet here for once Armande's tactics seem to backfire. Her suitor Clitandre simply opts for the path of least resistance by transferring his love to the more receptive Henriette.

It is interesting to note that Henriette's definition of marriage stresses in a rather subtle manner the possibility of indirect feminine empowerment through marital ties:

> Et qu'est-ce qu'à mon âge on a de mieux à faire
> Que d'attacher à soi, par le titre d'époux,
> Un homme qui vous aime, et soit aimé de vous . . .
>
> (I,1)

[What can I do better, at my age, than bind myself in the ties of
wedlock to a man whom I love and who loves one in return?]

Henriette's vision of conjugal bliss is strictly egalitarian as it
stresses not only mutual affection but the active role of the wife
in "attaching" the man. In other words, both women seem to be
concerned to some extent with avoiding complete subservience to
a male counterpart.

During their discussion, Henriette also pinpoints the fallacy
subtending Armande's line of argumentation. By denying the materiality of one's existence one denies the very basis or the physical
nature of that existence. Abstract thought that has no basis in
concrete reality is sterile and unsubstantial. The language used to
express it becomes solipsistic. Devalorization of matter as vulgar,
animalistic, and instinctual is tantamount to devalorization of the
Mother as a life-giving source:

> Mais vous ne seriez pas ce dont vous vous vantez,
> Si ma mère n'eut eu que de ces beaux côtés;
> Et bien vous prend, ma soeur, que son noble génie
> N'ait pas vaqué toujours à la philosophie.
> De grâce, souffrez-moi, par un peu de bonté,
> Des bassesses à qui vous devez la clarté;
> Et ne supprimez point, voulant qu'on vous seconde,
> Quelque *petit savant* qui veut venir au monde.
>
> (I,1)

[But you would never have become all you boast of being, if my mother
had only possessed spiritual qualities; and well it is for you, sister, that
her noble genius was not always taken up with philosophy. I beg of
you to exercise some indulgence towards me and allow in me those
earthly qualities to which you owe birth. Do not, by trying to make
me copy you, hinder the advent of some tiny savant who may wish to
come into existence.]

In this particular instance the maternal principle is the channel
through which the male intellect is generated.

Henriette's insistence on the precedence of matter over thought
is an attempt to reestablish the preeminence of the feminine principle. Paradoxically, however, in order to do so she must promote
the values of the masculine hierarchy of which she is the unknow-
ing victim. Armande's quest for knowledge, on the other hand, is
an attempt to eradicate sexual difference by emulating men:

A sa place [de la reproduction], [Armande] prône la production: elle revendique pour la femme un rôle presque masculin et, ce faisant, elle se masculinise et devient une caricature. Se refusant d'être le support de l'ordre, peut-elle être autre chose qu'une exclue, une opprimée? Oppression à laquelle d'ailleurs elle participe elle-même puisque, comme les autres, elle est convaincue—c'est à dire la force des idées régnantes—qu'une femme n'est rien par elle-même: il lui faut s'attacher soit à un homme soit à la philosophie et trouver dans cet attachement son identité.[6]

[In its stead [of reproduction], [Armande] advocates production: she insists on an almost masculine role for woman, and, in so doing, she becomes man-like herself and, by the same token, a caricature. In refusing to become the support of the prevailing order, can she be anything other than marginal and oppressed? Oppression in which she participates herself, since, like the others, she is convinced—to show the tenacity of the reigning ideology—that a woman is nothing by herself: she must either tie herself to a man or to philosophy and find her identity in this bond.] (Translation by author)

Both options are inherently problematic. The girls' mother, Philaminte, is referred to as a woman who has learned to reconcile nature and culture within her life, whereas the two sisters represent a split in which each one embodies only one side of the animus/anima opposition:

> Ainsi, dans nos desseins, l'une à l'autre contraire,
> Nous saurons toutes deux imiter notre mère:
> Vous, du côté de l'âme et des nobles désirs,
> Moi, du côté des sens et des grossiers plaisirs;
> Vous, aux productions d'esprit et de lumière,
> Moi, dans celles, ma soeur, qui sont de la matière.
>
> (I,1)

[Thus shall we both, in our contrary ways, imitate our mother: you on the side of the spirit and of noble desires, I, through the coarser pleasures of the senses; you, by the productions of light and reading, I, sister, in more material ways.]

For Armande, "the idyllic space of women together is supposed to exclude the phallus. The assumption that the 'phallus' is male expects that the exclusion of males be sufficient to make a nonphallic space. The threat represented by the mother to this feminine idyll might be understood through the notion that Mother, though female, is none the less phallic. So, as an afterthought, not only men, but Mother must be expelled from the innocent, non-phallic paradise."[7] Therefore, the daughter denies Philaminte's reproductive maternal function. Armande is, of course, not the only sister to accept a fragmented vision of woman. Henriette's amazing lack of intellectual curiosity is symptomatic of her alienation, of her lack of awareness of what Kristeva determines to be her need of language, "of the paternal symbolic order, to protect herself from the lack of distinction from the mother."[8] Without it, she runs the risk of reabsorption into the Mother and loss of self.

Although the one-sidedness of the two sisters might be attributed to immaturity, while the mother could potentially be viewed as a well-balanced individual in whom nature and culture are in a state of equilibrium, it is interesting to note that the play's rhetorical stance favors Henriette, the apologist for feminine materiality. Not only Armande but her mother as well are "guilty" of having transgressed feminine propriety by invading masculine territory. Strangely enough, it is not the acquisition of knowledge by women that is condemned by Clitandre, but the overt display of erudition. In other words, women may acquire knowledge, but they must not make ostensible use of it:

> Je consens qu'une femme ait des clartés de tout:
> Mais je ne lui veux point la passion choquante
> De se rendre savante afin d'être savante;
> Et j'aime que souvent, aux questions qu'on fait,
> Elle sache ignorer les choses qu'elle sait:
> De son étude enfin je veux qu'elle se cache,
> Et qu'elle ait du savoir sans vouloir qu'on le sache.
>
>   (I,3)

[I like a lady to have some knowledge of all questions; but I have no patience with the detestable passion of wishing to be learned for the sake of being thought so; I would rather she at times feigned to be ignorant, when questioned, of things she knows; in short, I would rather she concealed her knowledge, and possessed it without wishing people to know that she did . . .]

David Shaw reminds us, however, that Clitandre's point of view echoes the words of Madeleine de Scudéry herself: "If these famous lines sound a little patronizing today, this would not have been the case in 1672: for Molière, through Clitandre, is actually echoing the sentiments of one of the most gifted and respected feminists of his age."[9]

Under the guise of a concession to liberalism, Clitandre effectively seeks to neutralize feminine knowledge. What good, after all, is uncommunicable knowledge severed from the free interchange and transmission of ideas? Paradoxically such erudition becomes knowledge for its own sake: the very type that Clitandre overtly condemns. His condemnation of ostentation is based upon the sure awareness that knowledge is power and that concealment not only allows men to maintain an illusion of power, but effectively safeguards the reality of an exclusively masculine hegemony.

It is obvious, therefore, that from Clitandre's perspective the relationship between Philaminte and Chrysale is inherently perverse, for it represents a complete subversion of "the natural order." The play offers a fascinating example of a household governed exclusively by women and in which the patriarch's goodness is equated with an abdication that could potentially lead to a state of complete anarchy within the family circle. Henriette explains that:

> Mon père est d'humeur de consentir à tout;
> Mais il met peu de poids aux choses qu'il résout;
> Il a reçu du ciel certaine bonté d'âme
> Qui le soumet d'abord à ce que veut sa femme.
> C'est elle qui gouverne; et, d'un ton absolu,
> Elle dicte pour loi ce qu'elle a résolu.
>
> (I,3)

[. . . my father is of a very yielding disposition, but little reliance can be felt that he will carry out what he consents to do. Heaven has endowed him with a gentle nature that submits itself first to the wishes of his wife; she is the ruler and she lays down the law with no uncertain voice when she has made up her mind.]

Although Chrysale's affability makes him appear more sympathetic than his shrewish wife, the implicit judgment that a man can be too good, whereas there are no inherent boundaries to the complacency of women, subtends the play's rhetorical stance.

Philaminte's reign of terror is supported by her sister Bélise's presence, a situation that merely confirms the predominance of women and echoes in its structural symmetry the sisterly relationship between Armande and Henriette. If Philaminte has been able to reconcile at least minimally the material and the intellectual facets of her life, Bélise appears to have lost all touch with reality, thereby foreshadowing what might some day become of Armande. Thus, the old maid's physical sterility becomes emblematic of the intellectual sterility of the salon as well. Divorced from the life-engendering reality principle, the coterie advocates playful knowledge that serves a purely decorative and self-referential purpose. The trivialization of feminine knowledge is an effective means of neutralizing it as a vehicle to empowerment. Nonetheless, subtending Clitandre's earlier remarks is the acknowledgment and the concomitant fear of women's ability to inform themselves.

The fact that Bélise has lost touch with reality is exemplified in scene 4 of act 1, when she misconstrues Clitandre's declaration of love for Henriette as a veiled avowal of passion addressed to herself. The play's portrayal of Philaminte as a phallic mother who has emasculated the father figure is in distinct contrast to the "charmante douceur" [charming sweetness] of Bélise's madness. In order to maintain her unorthodox authority within the conjugal union, Philaminte is required to live in a continual conflictual state. However, the status of old maid is seen as unnatural as well. Bélise's suppression and sublimation of sexual desire have led to a form of psychosis that presupposes that a woman without a man is somehow incomplete, uninformed, and needy. Once again, this view corroborates the definition of woman as lack, void, or receptacle.

The inner emptiness thus generated creates a mental imbalance that causes Bélise to consider herself the object of all masculine desire. Such overcompensation is a direct result of prolonged virginity where the old maid attempts to assume personal responsibility for her state, thus gaining illusory empowerment rather than accepting the devalorization that accompanies a woman's undesirability, for in the society in which Bélise lives, masculine appreciation is the only thing that gives a woman value. This means, however, that Bélise must conceal her own desire from others, as well as from herself, in order to retain her illusion of control, for such an avowal would put her in the position of supplicant. She can only hope to achieve an indirect and illusory form of empowerment through the democratization, or the leveling, of all male roles. As Gaines explains: "Deprived of husband and suitors by unspecified circumstances, she has collapsed all male roles into one category—that of secret admirers."[10]

Bélise's misinterpretation of Clitandre's discourse as a series of detours and indirect allusions is due in large part to the fluidity of her own hysterical speech, her formless language, which denies the possibility of a systematic ontology. Ironically for someone who abhors the thought of physical contact, Bélise has learned to read or interpret her so-called lovers' *body* language:

> Contentez-vous des yeux pour vos seuls truchements,
> Et ne m'expliquez point, par un autre langage,
> Des désirs qui, chez moi, passent pour un outrage.
>
> (I,4)

[. . . let it be enough that your eyes alone interpret your passion and do not explain to me in any other language aspirations which I look upon as insulting.]

Bélise favors the semiotic as a more immediate expression of Clitandre's internal drives over the symbolic representation of the paternal order, which short-circuits fluid desire by affixing it to an object.

Keeping in mind this analysis of the principal players in the feminine faction, the inherently conflictual nature of the conjugal relationship, insofar as it reflects the aforementioned nature/culture dichotomy, also bears closer investigation. Although he cowers before his wife's overbearing willfulness, Chrysale attempts to save face by maintaining an illusion of patriarchal authority in the company of his friend Ariste. The former's affection for the suitor Clitandre stems from a bond of friendship with the suitor's father. Chrysale alludes nostalgically to their youth:

> Nous donnions chez les dames romaines,
> Et tout le monde là parlait de nos fredaines.
> Nous faisions des jaloux.
>
> (II,2)

[We were much smitten with the Roman ladies, and our pranks were the talk of the whole place: we caused many jealous hearts.]

Not only was this a time of freedom from the tyranny of marriage, but a time of intimate male bonding:

> Et puis, son père et moi n'étions qu'un en deux corps.
>
> (II,4)

[. . . his father and I were one in spirit, though two in body.]

The feminine conquest not only serves as visible proof of masculine dominance, but also as a distraction from the temptation of enclosure within an exclusively fraternal order. Chrysale's nostalgia for a self-contained masculine circle of play is a temporary diversion from his present subservience and is accompanied by a defiant attitude toward his wife's authority. When Ariste reminds him that it might be advisable to consult Philaminte in selecting his future son-in-law, Chrysale dismisses his advice with uncharacteristic bravado:

Je réponds de ma femme, et prends sur moi l'affaire.

(II,4)

[I will answer for my wife, and take the business upon myself.]

He demonstrates the desire to uphold the right to speak for his wife, thus substituting his discourse for hers.

With Philaminte's first onstage appearance the difference between her language and her sister's becomes immediately apparent. In contrast to Bélise's use of circuitous language, Philaminte's discourse is peremptory and authoritative. Her imperious presence, alluded to in the first act, is confirmed by the accumulation of imperatives in her first two replies, followed by the statement:

Je ne veux point d'obstacle aux désirs que je montre.

(I,6)

[I will not brook any opposition to my wishes.]

Chrysale had not anticipated such an immediate clash of wills concerning the dismissal of the maid Martine whose grammatical mistakes have offended his wife. This takes him off guard, and despite assurances that he will protect his servant, he is totally ineffectual in his efforts to do so. His long-winded but futile rebuttal of Philaminte's desires leaves him drained of the energy needed to defend the interests of Clitandre. Thus, the more important issue is rapidly dismissed.

Aside from its import from the point of view of the logic of dramatic tension, the row over the maid's dismissal is equally important from a syntagmatic perspective. The argument focuses primarily on the function of discourse. In Martine's opinion, for instance, language has one function only: the literal communication of practical information. Ornamentation and embellishments are incidental and ancillary:

Quand on se fait entendre, on parle toujours bien;
Et tous vos biaux dictons ne servent pas de rien.

(II,6)

[To make oneself understood is good enough for me; all your fine
sayings don't do me no good.]

Her own understanding of language is purely literal, as she mistakes grammatical abstractions for concrete realities. It is Chrysale
who defends the materiality of language in support of Martine,
whereas Philaminte and Bélise argue in favor of its spirituality.
Once again, the precedence of matter over spirit is championed,
but this time by the male protagonist:

Je vis de bonne soupe, et non de beau langage.

(II,7)

[I live by good soup, and not on fine language.]

Material existence is indeed and irrefutably the precondition
for thought, and food is more vital than spiritual nourishment.
Still, Chrysale's fondness for a good meal makes him appear
somewhat pedestrian and sophomoric, as his adversaries are
quick to point out:

Que ce discours grossier terriblement assomme!
Et quelle indignité pour ce qui s'appelle *homme*,
D'être baissé sans cesse aux soins matériels,
Au lieu de se hausser vers les spirituels!
Le corps, cette guenille, est-il d'une importance,
D'un prix à mériter seulement qu'on y pense?

(II,7)

[How terribly shocking this coarse conversation is! What a degrada-
tion it is to see one who calls himself a man always stooping to material
cares, instead of lifting himself up towards immaterial things! Is this
rubbishy body of ours of sufficient importance, of sufficient value, to
deserve even a passing thought?]

It is obvious that what is most shocking to Bélise and Philaminte
stems from their association of masculinity and spirituality. From
this perspective, Chrysale falls short of the standards of masculinity, though he may call himself a man: they equate the family's
failure to form a cohesive unit to the patriarch's unwillingness to
assume his own essential spirituality. Chrysale, on the other hand,

attributes the subversion of traditional roles to the women's transgression of the preestablished boundaries of proper feminine behavior, which does not include the acquisition of knowledge. Both parties argue in favor of one principle to the exclusion of the other. While the women uphold the preeminence of mind over matter:

> L'esprit doit sur le corps prendre le pas devant . . .
>
> (II,7)

[. . . the mind ought to take precedence over the body.]

Chrysale stubbornly insists:

> Oui, mon corps est moi-même et j'en veux prendre soin.
>
> (II,7)

[Yes, my body is myself, and I mean to take care of it.]

The cultivation of reason in women is considered by Chrysale and his contingent an anomaly akin to folly or madness. The acquisition of knowledge is a right reserved to men (the "docteurs de la ville"), whereas in women it is viewed as a transgression and a contradiction in terms:

> Raisonner est l'emploi de toute ma maison,
> Et le raisonnement en bannit la raison.
>
> (II,7)

[. . . to reason is the chief occupation of everyone in my household, and reasoning has banished reasonableness.]

Chrysale's belief arises primarily from the fact that the main function of the female of the species is considered to be reproduction through carnal knowledge, accompanied by the physical nourishment and care of others, rather than production itself. In this light, self-nourishment and self-fulfillment imperil the family structure that depends essentially on the mother's abnegation, self-denial, and generosity. Her traditional confines are those of household concerns, whereas philosophy and authorship do afford her a boundless freedom from spatial constraints:

> Nulle science n'est pour elles trop profonde,
> Et céans beaucoup plus qu'en aucun lieu du monde;
> Les secrets les plus hauts s'y laissent concevoir.
>
> (II,7)

[No science is too deep for them. It is far worse in this house of mine than anywhere else in the world: the loftiest secrets are understood. . . .]

Thus, the women's spirituality is a vehicle for liberation and the antithesis to the limitations of materiality. However, it is also, according to Chrysale, an escape from the boundaries of rationality and a flight into sheer lunacy. Philaminte claims:

> Et j'ai vu clairement des hommes dans la lune.
>
> (III,2)

[I have plainly seen men in the moon.]

According to their male critics, these women seem to lack the ability to confine their imagination within a rational structure: this is both their strength and their downfall. Freedom, therefore, becomes co-terminus with madness in the feminine realm.

Because the women suffer from their marginality and their enclosure within the domain of strict domesticity, they seek vindication by establishing their own circle of play governed by rigid laws and restricted exclusively to an intimate grouping of friends:

> Nous serons, par nos lois, les juges des ouvrages;
> Par nos lois, prose et vers, tout nous sera soumis:
> Nul n'aura de l'esprit, hors nous et nos amis.
> Nous chercherons partout à trouver à redire,
> Et ne verrons que nous qui sache bien écrire.
>
> (III,2)

[Our laws will make us judges of each work produced; whether prose or verse, it will be subjected to the test of our laws; no one save us and our friends will have any wit; we shall try to find fault all round, so that no one will be capable of writing well but ourselves.]

It becomes apparent that literary achievement is a mere pretext for the establishment of an inner circle in which women trade their marginality for centrality, in accordance with masculine traditions of exclusivity. The women's quest for knowledge is the direct result of their intellectual confinement and of their desire to open the doors to the secret realm of erudition. Albanese refers to their enclosure in the following terms: "Leur non-adhérence aux rôles sexuels stéréotypés les voue au ridicule frappant celles qui refusent d'habiter un espace féminin soigneusement circonscrit; elles sont en outre perçues comme des femmes se livrant à une stratégie de sur-compensation justifiant leur manque de qualités féminines 'naturelles'."[11]

By establishing their own inner circle, however, they not only recreate the iniquities of the masculine hegemony, but inadvertently enclose and limit themselves of their own volition: "En somme, si l'enthousiasme pour le savoir et la confiance engendrée par sa possession s'associent à une certaine générosité verbale, au désir de partager son savoir, la volonté du pouvoir savant mène à une sorte d'avarice intellectuelle où l'idée d'accumulation est primordiale et l'idée de partage est nécessairement exclue."[12] [To sum up, if enthusiasm for knowledge and the confidence engendered by its possession can be associated with a certain verbal generosity, with the desire to share one's knowledge, the scholarly will to power leads to a type of intellectual avarice where the notion of accumulation is primordial and from which the ideal of sharing is necessarily absent.] (Translation by author) Thus, generosity, so often associated with feminine behavior, is absent from this feminine circle of play. One might even contend that to refuse and deny the phallic position, as in the case of the *précieuses,* may mean to merely conceal it and be all the more phallic, whereas blatantly to assume it, as in the case of Chrysale, may mean to dephallicize.

Language becomes the key to admission into the learned society and the primary basis for power, control, and exclusion: "Personal impulse and desire are 'controlled' by linguistic formulae. Because this language is synthetic, it must be taught. Thus, it becomes the basis for a hierarchization of human faculties, for the designation of the great majority of people as 'lacking', and for a power structure."[13] Moreover, the primary flaw of the feminine play world and the ultimate cause of its collapse is internal. It is not necessarily because they have included male members in their circles, but it is most certainly attributable to the fact that they have made these men the focal point of their admiration. Thus, their liberation is illusory at best, and may in fact be an alternate form of servitude, all the more pernicious because it passes itself off as its opposite.

As an example of the ambivalence that can arise, Vadius and Trissotin have become objects of sublimated sexual desire and although they share equal consideration from the lady admirers, such a well-balanced distribution of favors among two rivals is too unnatural to be enduring. Almost by definition, a plurality of men in a feminine context degenerates very rapidly into a rivals' battle for domination, which takes place in the form of attacks on Trissotin's literary "offspring." Thus, from the outset sedition is at the very core of the alternate feminine play world created by Philaminte and Bélise. However, it would also seem that the women view the inclusion of the literary rivals as a requirement to give value and weight to their intellectual endeavors. In other words, their erudite society's inner core is sensed as a void needing to be in-formed by men and is a reflection of the dynamics of carnal knowledge: women gaining knowledge though the in-corporation of men. Riggs makes the following pertinent observation:

The learned ladies believe they are using the power of words, but they are being used by it. Having seduced its objects/subjects and convinced them of their autonomy, the ideology of reason—through its "priest", Trissotin—ministers to the subjects it has called into being. The metaphorical suggestions of consumption and penetration through the ears destroy the textual disguise behind which the celebrants try to hide, and permit Molière to show us the internalizing of an ideology. The scene serves a deconstructive or anti-hegemonic purpose by referring ineluctably to actual motive and showing the savantes' relationship with Trissotin as one based on power, submission and pleasure. Trissotin's words pass through the ladies, in through their ears and, as they repeat them, out through their mouths. We are thus shown an enactment of persons being "created" as subjects by a discourse which "ventriloquizes" them. They are "fertilized" by Trissotin and they reproduce the poem—the newborn child.[14]

As a further overt manifestation of empowerment, Philaminte has usurped the patriarchal prerogative to impose a husband on her daughter. If the father's authority in this domain is a means to retain control over his daughter's future by means of a sexual surrogate, the matriarch's choice of Trissotin can be seen as a vicarious means of creating an intimate bond with the poet through a daughter who is, after all, a reflection of herself, without the necessity of direct sexual contact. The excitement she experiences in Trissotin's company is nothing short of orgasmic:

De mille doux frissons vous vous sentez saisir.

(III,2)

[It makes a thousand gentle shiverings thrill through one.]

Furthermore, Philaminte unwittingly espouses the notion of carnal knowledge by insinuating that her daughter Henriette, who is singularly lacking in intellectual curiosity, might experience a spiritual awakening through physical contact with a husband such as Trissotin:

> J'ai donc cherché longtemps un biais de vous donner
> La beauté que les ans ne peuvent moissonner,
> De *faire entrer chez vous* le désir des sciences,
> De vous *insinuer les belles connaissances;*
> Et la pensée enfin où mes voeux ont souscrit,
> C'est d'attacher à vous un homme plein d'esprit . . .

(III,4)

[I have, therefore, been searching for a long time for a method whereby you might become possessed of that beauty which the years cannot destroy, a means of *inspiring* you with a desire for learning, of *equipping you with a knowledge of great things,* in short, I have made up my mind to unite you with a man of great intellect . . .]

Ariste cites Chrysale's abdication of power and his impotence as the direct cause of the subversion of traditional family roles. Philaminte has taken over the patriarchal function by default and wishes to impose the pedantic poet Trissotin as a husband on her daughter Henriette. She views the ensuing power struggle as a battle between form and matter, body and spirit:

> Je lui montrerai bien aux lois de qui des deux
> Les droits de la raison soumettent tous ses voeux,
> Et qui doit gouverner, ou sa mère ou son père,
> Ou l'esprit ou le corps, la forme ou la matière.

(IV,1)

[I will soon show her to which of the two the laws of reason make her submit, and whether she shall be ruled by her father or her mother, mind or body, form or matter.]

What is interesting from this point of view in the mother's interchange with the pedant is the allusion to his giving birth to a poem:

> *Trissotin:* Hélas! c'est un enfant tout nouveau-né, madame:
> Son sort assurément a lieu de vous toucher,
> Et c'est dans votre cour que j'en viens d'accoucher.
> *Philaminte:* Pour me le rendre cher, il suffit de son père.
> *Trissotin:* Votre approbation lui peut servir de mère.

(III,1)

[Trissotin: Alas! It is but a new-born babe, Madam. Its fate should, assuredly, touch you, since it was in your courtyard that I was delivered of it.
Philaminte: That you are its father is sufficient to endear it to me.
Trissotin: Your approbation supplies it with a mother.]

The author is thus equated to a life giver whose offspring, though an abstraction, is considered in very material terms. This reversal of the theme of carnal knowledge, due to the subversion of sexual roles—in which the spiritual coupling between Philaminte ("la mère") and Trissotin ("le père") results in the father giving birth to a newborn child—leads to our perception of an effeminized Trissotin. The father, of course, can only generate an abstraction and the mother is required to give it material form. The confusion engendered by this vision of a birthing father assisted in his labor-delivery by a phallic mother conceals the fact that the production-reproduction myth referred to earlier is left intact. Philaminte's ear is the receptacle that passively receives Trissotin's product.

Not only does Trissotin evoke regeneration as a symbolic function, but he assumes the role of nourisher of the spirit as well, in a symbiosis of matter and culture:

> Pour cette grande faim qu'à mes yeux on expose,
> Un seul plat de huit vers me semble peu de chose;
> Et je pense qu'ici je ne ferai pas mal
> De joindre à l'épigramme, ou bien au madrigal,
> Le ragoût d'un sonnet qui, chez une princesse,
> A passé pour avoir quelque délicatesse.
> Il est de sel attique assaisonné partout,
> Et vous le trouverez, je crois, d'assez bon goût.
>
> (III,2)

[A dish of only eight lines seems scanty fare to appease the great hunger I see before me. I think that I shall do well to add to the epigram, or, rather, to the madrigal, the seasoning of a sonnet, which a certain princess thought somewhat delicate. It is seasoned throughout with Attic salt, and you will, I believe, find it passably good.]

It is interesting to note how frequently those wishing to purify language of material references employ those very same allusions to concrete reality in order to create a surprise effect.

In order to challenge his wife's usurpation of patriarchal power and to reassert his dominance, Chrysale assumes the role of teacher in the final act:

Je veux, je veux apprendre à vivre à votre mère.

(V,2)

[I have made up my mind to teach your mother how to behave herself.]

However, when the notary arrives, Chrysale is unable to verbalize his argument, and Martine becomes his spokeswoman. Inarticulate though she may be, the servant girl's recourse to direct verbal confrontation is in and of itself a form of subversion. She literally takes the words out of Chrysale's mouth ("elle lui prend la parole"), thereby assuming, at least temporarily, authoritative discourse. Thus, ironically and paradoxically, patriarchal prerogative is temporarily preserved—and thus devalorized—by an illiterate woman. Although she insists on the preeminence of the patriarchal hegemony, Martine concurrently proves that the powers-that-be cannot be effectively maintained without the woman's consent to divest herself of her rights. Furthermore, the ideal husband, in her opinion, must use his wife as a source of knowledge, or rather as his only book:

Et je veux, si jamais on engage ma foi,
Un mari qui n'ait d'autre livre que moi.

(V,3)

[. . . and if ever I plight my troth I shall choose a husband who wants no other book than myself.]

Thus, although the husband retains the right to impose his authority, he must base his law on a sure knowledge of the woman he has married. The masculine prerogative to inform woman— to give form to matter, to impose knowledge upon substance— is therefore posited upon his ability to read and interpret her innermost being. Failing this, his authority will be peremptory but illusory at best. In other words, carnal knowledge ultimately rests upon an understanding of matter, which takes precedence over form. Form can never be entirely arbitrary, but has to accommodate the matter it wishes to restrain, and it is thus to some degree determined by it.

Chrysale's inability to govern or restrain his wife stems inevitably from a deep-seated marital alienation. His intellectual limitations prevent him from understanding the core of her being. Philaminte simply counters his (or rather Martine's) arguments with the language of absolutism. The ensuing stalemate is re-

solved artificially by the false tidings of the couple's bankruptcy.
Philaminte's intrepidity contrasts markedly with her husband's
emotional outcry, proving once again that she is the primary
source of strength in the relationship. Furthermore, her attitude
thoroughly substantiates the authenticity of her claim to disdain
the material in favor of the spiritual. Trissotin beats a hasty retreat
in light of the family's financial misfortunes, thereby allowing the
play to end with the *pro forma* restoration of paternal authority.
However, it should escape no one's notice that it is Philaminte who
ultimately retains the authoritative voice by being the one to give
away her daughter to the more deserving suitor Clitandre:

> Vous me charmez, monsieur, par ce trait généreux,
> Et je veux couronner vos désirs amoureux.
> Oui, j'accorde Henriette à l'ardeur empressée . . .
>
> (V,4)

[I am delighted, Monsieur, with this generous deed, and I desire to
crown your love. Yes; I give Henriette to the greater affection . . .]

To which the ineffectual and passive Chrysale can only add:

> Je le savais bien, moi, que vous l'épouseriez.
>
> (V,4)

[I knew well enough that you would marry her.]

Gaines observes that at this point:

Taken in by Ariste's ruse and thinking that she can offer her generous
suitor only a life of want and suffering, Henriette puts the time-
honored values of her milieu before the gratification of her personal
needs, and she only agrees to the wedding once the illusion has been
revealed. Such self-control on the part of the bride demonstrates most
conclusively that Molière's theatre reflects an ideology in which the
decision to marry is a commitment to collective goals rather than an
act of self-gratification.[15]

Gaines views the prevailing social structure, however, in a positive
light, for it is "resilient in crises and admirably suited to survival,"
whereas he unequivocally condemns the salon as an upstart social
unit. The conservatism of this approach skirts one of the major
issues elucidated by Elisabeth Lapeyre: "L'ordre accepté a priori
par tous et représenté par la famille de Chrysale est l'ordre patri-

archal, par définition essentiellement répressif."[16] [The order accepted a priori by all and represented by Chrysale's family is the patriarchal order, by nature repressive.] (Translation by author)

Although Philaminte's artificially delineated circle of play has effectively been disrupted by her disillusionment with Trissotin and Vadius, she is one of the very few feminine protagonists to firmly establish her dominance in the bourgeois family circle. I must therefore disagree with critics such as Lapeyre who view the *dénouement* in the following manner: "Philaminte a retrouvé la place qu'on veut bien qu'elle ait: elle est récupérée par la société à travers sa conscience maternelle et retrouve le rôle de la mère compréhensive qui laisse même Chrysale avoir le dernier mot. Elle redevient muette et laisse l'H/histoire se faire sans elle."[17] [Philaminte returns to the place that others allow her to occupy: she is rehabilitated by society through her maternal conscience and resumes the role of understanding mother who even lets Chrysale have the last word. She is silenced and lets HIS/tory continue without her.] (Translation by author) Though the play's rhetoric seems to condemn her grip on the reins of power and to favor perhaps the more moderate and conventional wisdom of Henriette and Clitandre, her retention of power stands, nevertheless, as a monument to feminine potential.

It is true, of course, that the conflict between the two contingents has been temporarily abated. It is true, as well, that the feminine circle has lost its focus and cohesive principle. Yet the mere fact that the familial power structures remain intact—with no evidence supporting the reinstatement of a patriarchal hegemony consecrated by a communal reaffirmation of paternal power and wisdom—leads one to conclude that even after she has been divested of the illusory security and the false empowerment of a play world that merely mimicked the patriarchal hegemony, Philaminte, the primary representative of the coterie, can now stand alone without necessarily relinquishing the reins of power or her intellectual quest. As Gallop reminds us:

It is no answer, no sure-fire solution to have women rather than men assume the position of power. Women are *not* so essentially and immutably 'body' that they are eternally and dependably unrepresentable. In a certain dialectical moment, a certain here and now, the assumption of power by women may crack the impassive, neuter mask of power. But were women to assume power, the representation of power would inevitably alter so as to reassimilate the contradiction, to suture the chink. Perhaps the conflict is always between body—as the inadequate name of some uncommanded diversity of drives and contradictions—and Power, between body and Law, between body and Phallus, even between body and Body."[18]

* * *

Thus, Molière's theatrical exploration of the dynamics of opposition and collusion between the sexes provides us with a multiplicity of models of feminine empowerment within the comic sphere. Having studied in detail various heroines of Molière's creation, let us review in conclusion certain character types that have emerged from this analysis.

The ingenue's presence in relation to the play world remains at best peripheral. Because *L'Avare* evolves within the parameters of economic bartering, it provides an excellent analytical context for a study of the ingenue. Her profound alienation is due primarily to her status as object, whose possession is solicited as prize or reward. Not having attained individual awareness, the ingenue's personality remains largely undifferentiated from her state or status. Her rebellious behavior often takes the form of mutinous silence or retreat, although an outspoken servant girl or an assiduous lover may occasionally prod her into a mild form of assertiveness.

Unlike the ingenue, the servant girl frequently participates as a shrewd countertactician in the ludic sphere. Toinette in *Le Malade Imaginaire* provides an enlightening example of this type of heroine. Her forthright belly laugh would be considered unseemly behavior for heroines of higher rank, who are effectively barred from comic appreciation due to societal norms of impropriety. Toinette's hilarity is, however, not so much a sign of participation in the play world as a direct attack upon it. She is, in fact, not laughing *with*, but *at* the male protagonist. Though her strategies are effective in the short term, they are generally ineffectual in disrupting the male hegemony. From the latter's point of view, such laughter is simply further evidence of woman's otherness.

Women are seen as non-laughers primarily because they are regarded as proponents of the serious moral norms and/or of the common sense of the "real world" outside the realm of play. They refuse to recognize or condone the existence of a separate male society of play. The wife is the most common incarnation of the spoil-sport. She is characterized by her refusal to laugh with the trickster and by her inability to enjoy and participate in the game. So strong is our tendency to be captivated by the machinations of the trickster that we tend to spurn the earnestness of the spoil-sport. Perhaps the ultimate reason is that the latter champions a prosaic reality that ever threatens to destroy the circle of playful illusion. Although the role of spoil-sport is generally a negative one, it becomes a very important positive foil to the dangers of a play world that threatens to exceed its boundaries and that borders dangerously close on tragedy. Done Elvire (*Dom Juan*), Elmire (*Le Tartuffe*), and Mme Jourdain (*Le Bourgeois gentilhomme*) share certain characteristics in this regard, despite enormous outward differences.

A much more threatening presence is that of the comic heroine who tries to fill traditionally male roles. A general observation that holds true for most of Molière's comedies is that the degree to which a female character is perceived as laughable is proportional to the forcefulness of her attempts to invade male territory, be it in her desire for knowledge or social status. Any attempt to be "like" men must be suppressed because it endangers the very existence of the play world, which depends on the dialectics of difference and sameness to retain its exclusivity. Nonetheless, the final scene of *Les Femmes savantes* does seem to suggest the potential for a more permanent form of feminine empowerment to be acquired through knowledge.

Most frightening of all, however, is the shadow of infidelity. It is woman's intrinsic means of retaliation. The female cheat who creates a separate space, a play world analogous to, yet apart from, that of the male characters, is generally the adulteress or the coquette. Her game is played at man's expense, and his public ridicule is symbolized by horns. If Arnolphe (*L'Ecole des femmes*) and Alceste (*Le Misanthrope*) appear somewhat obsessed and daunted by the female cheat, it is because her presence can lead to the disintegration of the male play world by breaking all the rules. In other words, the female cheat is the ultimate and certainly the most effective incarnation of the spoil-sport. Wherever she plays her subversive role, the male protagonist's abrupt departure marks his transition from his carefully constructed play world to the world of bitter reality, and it also marks his refusal to participate in the newly established feminine play world. Thus, it would appear that the ultimate threat to the play world established by the male characters is the creation of a parallel hegemony in which the female trickster wields power through deception. When faced with such a complete reversal of roles, the men refuse to participate and are compelled in turn to become outcasts and proponents of moral norms that are in strong opposition to playful activity.

Notes

CHAPTER 1. INTRODUCTION

1. Sigmund Freud, *Jokes and Their Relation to the Unconscious*, trans. James Strachey (1905; reprint, New York: Norton, 1968): 140–158.

2. Henri-Louis Bergson, *Le Rire* (1900; reprint, Paris: Presses Universitaires de France, 1978): 1–17.

3. Elder Olson, *The Theory of Comedy* (Bloomington: Indiana University Press, 1975): 25–65.

4. Freud, *Jokes*, 137.

5. Ibid., 152.

6. Ernst Kris, "Ego Development and the Comic," in *Psychoanalytic Explorations in Art* (1935; reprint, New York: International Universities Press, 1952): 204.

7. Ibid., 205.

8. Ibid., 205.

9. Charles Mauron, *Psychocritique du genre comique* (Paris: José Corti, 1964).

10. Ibid., 18.

11. Ibid., 32.

12. George Meredith, "An Essay on Comedy," in *Comedy*, ed. Wylie Sypher (1877; reprint, Garden City, NY: Doubleday, 1956): 17.

13. Bergson, *Rire*, 13. Translation from Wylie Sypher, *Comedy*. (Garden City, NY: Doubleday, 1956): 71.

14. John Dryden, "Preface to *An Evening's Love*," in *Four Comedies*, ed. L. A. Beaurline and Fredson Bowers (1671; reprint, Chicago: University of Chicago Press, 1967).

15. Charles Lamb, "On the Artificial Comedy of the Last Century," in *Lamb as Critic*, ed. Roy Park (1822; 1823; reprint, Lincoln, Nebr.: University of Nebraska Press, 1980): 62–68.

16. Lamb, "Notes on Thomas Middleton's *A Fair Quarrel*," in vol. 1 of *The Works of Charles and Mary Lamb*, ed. E. V. Lucas (1818; reprint, London: Methuen, 1912): 45–46.

17. Lamb, "Artificial Comedy," 63.

18. Jean Paul Richter, "Über die Humoristishe Dichtkunst," in vol. 5 of *Werke* (1804; reprint. München: Carl Hanser Verlag, 1963): 124–44.

19. August Wilhelm von Schlegel, *A Course of Lectures on Dramatic Art and Literature*, trans. John Black (1808; reprint, London: H. G. Bohn, 1846): 187.

20. G. W. F. Hegel, *The Philosophy of Fine Art*, vol. 4, trans. F. B. P. Osmaston (1820; reprint, London: G. Bell, 1920): 293–305; 312–30.

21. Johan Huizinga, *Homo ludens* (1950; reprint, Boston: Beacon Press, 1955): 13.

22. Aristotle, *Poetics*, trans. Leon Golden (Englewood Cliffs, N.J.: Prentice-

Hall, 1968): 9. To cite the complete definition: "As we have said, comedy is an imitation of baser men. These are characterized not by every kind of vice but specifically by 'the ridiculous', which is a subdivision of the category of 'deformity'. What we mean by 'the ridiculous' is some error or ugliness that is painless and has no harmful effects. The example that comes immediately to mind is the comic mask, which is ugly and distorted but causes no pain."

23. Northrop Frye, "The Mythos of Spring: Comedy," in *Anatomy of Criticism* (Princeton: Princeton University Press, 1971): 177.

24. Ibid., 163. Frye reduces comic plot to the following archetypal pattern:

What normally happens is that a young man wants a young woman, that his desire is resisted by some opposition, usually paternal, and that near the end of the play some twist in the plot enables the hero to have his will. In this simple pattern there are several complex elements. In the first place, the movement of comedy is usually a movement from one kind of society to another. At the beginning of the play the obstructing characters are in charge of the play's society, and the audience recognizes that they are usurpers. At the end of the play the device in the plot that brings hero and heroine together causes a new society to crystallize around the hero, and the moment when this crystallization occurs is the point of resolution in the action, the comic discovery, *anagnorisis* or *cognitio.*

Though it is evident that Frye has uncovered here one of the most common plot patterns for comedy, one might ask what it is about this rather banal story line that is inherently comical.

25. Huizinga, *Homo*, 11.

26. Ibid., 11.

27. Simone de Beauvoir, *Le Deuxième sexe*, vol. 1 (Paris: Gallimard, 1949): 16–17. Translation from Simone de Beauvoir, *The Second Sex*, vol. I, trans. H. M. Parshley (New York: Alfred M. Knopf, 1957): xvi–xvii.

28. Jeffrey Mehlman, "How to Read Freud on Jokes: The Critic as Schadchen," in *New Literary History* 6, no. 2 (1975): 439–61.

29. Jane Gallop, *Thinking Through the Body* (New York: Columbia University Press, 1988): 37.

30. Joan Kelly, *Women, History and Theory* (Chicago: Chicago University Press, 1984): 8.

31. Luce Irigaray, *Speculum of the Other Woman*, trans. Gillian Gill (Ithaca: Cornell University Press, 1985): 11–132. In this radical "deconstructionist" text, the critic takes on the academic establishment by exposing the flaws and inconsistencies of Freudian phallocentric discourse through a process of dialogic questioning and mimicry.

32. Gail Schwab, "Irigarayan Dialogism: Play and Powerplay," in *Feminism, Bakhtin and the Dialogic*, eds. Dale Bauer and Susan Jaret McKinsky (Albany: State University of New York Press, 1991): 68.

CHAPTER 2. *L'AVARE*

1. Ralph Albanese Jr. argues that "On ne saurait trop insister sur l'âpreté du ton qui caractérise *L'Avare*, pièce noire qui renchérit sur l'atmosphère d'amertume qui empreint *George Dandin*" [One cannot overemphasize the bitter tone characterizing *The Miser*, a black comedy whose atmosphere is more venomous than that of *George Dandin*.] (Translation by author) ("Argent et réification dans

L'Avare," *L'Esprit Créateur* 21, no. 3 [fall 1981]: 35). In a more recent article entitled "Molière and the Sociology of Exchange," Jean–Marie Apostolides claims that "In no other play by Molière does death have a stronger presence than in *The Miser*" (trans. Alice Musick McLean, *Critical Inquiry* 14, no. 3 [1988]: 482).

2. Jean-Baptiste Poquelin de Molière, *Oeuvres complètes,* ed. Pierre-Aimé Touchard (Paris: Seuil, 1962). All further references to the plays of Molière will appear in the text. The source of translation of *L'Avare* is Molière, *Comedies,* trans. Donald M. Frame (Oxford: Oxford University Press, 1968, 1985).

3. Mitchell Greenberg, "Suréna's Melancholy and the End of the Ancien Régime," in *Actes de Baton Rouge,* ed. Selma Zébouni (Paris: Biblio 17, 1986): 127.

4. According to Luce Irigaray, "Woman, in this sexual imaginary, is only a more or less obliging prop for the enactment of man's fantasies. That she may even find pleasure there in that role, by proxy, is possible, even certain. But such pleasure is above all a masochistic prostitution of her body to a desire that is not her own, and it leaves her in a familiar state of dependency upon man. Not knowing what she wants, ready for anything, even asking for more, so long as he will 'take' her as his 'object' when he seeks his own pleasure. Thus she will not say what she herself wants; moreover, she does not know, or no longer knows, what she wants" (*This Sex Which is Not One,* trans. Catherine Porter [Ithaca: Cornell University Press, 1985]: 25).

5. Apostolides, "Sociology of Exchange," 483.

6. Hélène Cixous, "Castration or Decapitation?" trans. Annette Kuhn, *Signs: Journal of Women in Culture and Society* 7, no. 1 (Autumn 1981): 45.

7. Greenberg, *Corneille, Classicism and the Ruses of Symmetry* (Cambridge: Cambridge University Press, 1986): 138.

8. Cixous, "Castration," 48.

9. Simone de Beauvoir, *Le Deuxième Sexe,* vol. 1 (Paris: Gallimard, 1949): 23. English translation from Simone de Beauvoir, *The Second Sex,* trans. H. M. Parshley (New York: Alfred H. Knopf, 1957): xxi.

10. Cixous, "Castration," 43.

11. In an article entitled "Harpagon ou la terre aride", J. Pineau credits Elise with a wilfulness of which there is, however, little evidence in the text. Furthermore, I find his assertion that she surpasses Moliere's other ingenues in strength of character to be unfounded: "Quant à Elise, elle est la seule fille du théâtre de Molière qui s'oppose directement aux vouloirs paternels" [As for Elise, she is the only daughter in Molière's theater to directly oppose her father's wishes.] "Harpagon ou la terre aride," *Revue d'Histoire du Théâtre* 38, no. 4 (1986): 413.

12. Jacques Derrida, "All Ears: Nietzsche's Otobiography," in *The Pedagogical Imperative, Teaching as Literary Genre* (New Haven: Yale University Press, 1982).

13. Cixous, "Castration," 47.

14. Albanese contends that "donner de l'argent c'est nécessairement une diminution de l'être, voire une mutilation, l'avarice étant liée chez lui, selon G. Goldschmidt, à 'la matérialité corporelle de l'identité.'" [To give money is necessarily a diminution of one's being, a mutilation, since avarice is linked, according to G. Goldschmidt, to "the corporal materiality of identity.] (Translation by author) ("Argent," 39).

15. Ibid., 36.

16. According to Albanese, "Harpagon, lui, vit en fonction des impératifs d'une économie monétaire régie par le 'fétichisme de la marchandise,' c'est-à-dire, qu'il se laisse gouverner exclusivement par des valeurs d'échange qui relèguent les êtres humains au stade d'objet inerte" [Harpagon lives by the demands

of a monetary economy dictated by the "fetishism of merchandise," meaning that he allows himself to be governed exclusively by those laws of exchange relegating humans to the status of inanimate objects.] (Translation by author) (ibid., 43).

17. Apostolides, "Sociology of Exchange," 481.

18. "Le prêt à intérêt constitue, enfin, une pratique éminemment 'rentable' en ce sens que l'argent, se reproduisant de lui-même, prend une existence autonome—d'où son objectification comique—et exerce, par là, une fonction déshumanisante." [The interest-bearing loan constitutes an eminently profitable practice, in that sense that money, reproducing itself, takes on an autonomous existence—whence its comic reification—and exerts, by the same token, a dehumanizing function.] (Translation by author) Albanese, "Argent," 42.

19. Gérard Montbertrand, "Territoire et société dans L'Avare et Tartuffe de Molière," French Literature Series 15 (1988): 11.

20. William J. Kennedy, "Comic Audiences and Rhetorical Strategies in Machiavelli, Shakespeare and Molière," Comparative Literature Studies 21, no. 4 (1984): 376.

21. Pineau, "Terre aride," 415.

22. Albanese, "Argent," 41.

23. Apostolides, "Sociology of Exchange," 482.

24. "Dans une vie où la sexualité est totalement absente, il est tentant de voir un rapport amoureux ambigu entre l'avare et sa cassette." [In a life totally devoid of sexuality, it is tempting to see an ambiguous love relationship between the miser and his money-box.] (Translation by author) Albanese, "Argent," 40.

25. In her study of garden imagery in L'Avare, Dorothy Jones contrasts images of fertility and sterility in the ending scene: "No one enters the garden after the cassette has been removed. With their own treasure unearthed, the lovers are free to move elsewhere. They carry within themselves the promise of fruitfulness and new life. Led by their true father, Anselme, they leave Harpagon's barren ground behind to be united with an unseen and loving mother" ("The Treasure in the Garden: Biblical Imagery in L'Avare," Papers on French Seventeenth Century Literature 15, no. 29 [1988]: 526).

CHAPTER 3. DOM JUAN

1. Shoshana Felman, The Literary Speech Act, trans. Catherine Porter (Ithaca: Cornell University Press, 1980): 45–46.

2. Larry Riggs, "The Issues of Nobility and Identity in Dom Juan and Le Bourgeois gentilhomme," The French Review 59, no. 3 (February 1986): 401.

3. David Shaw, "Egoism and Society: A Secular Interpretation of Molière's Dom Juan," Modern Languages 59, no. 3 (September 1978): 121.

4. Felman, Speech Act, 27.

5. Source of translations for Dom Juan: Albert Bermel, trans. The Actor's Molière: Scapin and Don Juan, vol. 3 (New York: Applause, 1987).

6. Riggs, "Ethics, Debts and Identity in Dom Juan," Romance Quarterly 34, no. 2 (May 1987): 141.

7. Hélène Cixous, "Castration," 47.

8. Felman, "Don Juan ou la promesse d'amour," Tel Quel 87 (1981): 22.

9. Marcel Gutwirth, "Dom Juan et le tabou d'inceste," Romanic Review 77, no. 1 (1986): 27.

10. Max Vernet, "Economie, histoire, littérature," *Oeuvres et critiques* 16, no. 1 (1990): 69.

11. Many critics have commented on the bipartite structure of *Dom Juan.* According to Charlotte Shapira, "la pièce se divise en deux parties de grandeur égale: la première moitié dramatise la Séduction triomphante alors que la deuxième moitié est consacrée à la réaction divine, qui conduit à la damnation du héros" ("La Séduction face au ciel dans *Don Juan* de Molière," *Neohelicon* 11, no. 1 [1984]: 347). J.-M. Pelous insists that "de l'ouverture du rideau à la catastrophe finale la représentation s'étend sur deux journées consécutives . . . Cette deuxième journée (qui se confond avec le cinquième acte) n'est donc pas un simple supplément de vie accordé à Don-Juan pour satisfaire aux exigences d'un emploi du temps trop chargé et persévérer dans ses habitudes insouciantes; c'est un second moment du spectacle très différent du premier en ce qu'il restitue au temps la valeur que l'inconséquence du héros lui refusait jusque-là" (Les Problèmes du temps dans le *Dom Juan* de Molière," *Revue des Sciences humaines* 38, no. 152 [octobre-décembre 1973]: 556, 562).

12. Felman, *Speech Act,* 40.

13. Julia Kristeva, "Women's Time," trans. Alice Jardine and Harry Blake, *Signs: Journal of Women in Culture and Society* 7, no. 1 (autumn 1981): 16.

14. John Dunmore, "The Impotence of Dom Juan," *New Zealand Journal of French Studies* 4, no. 2 (November 1983): 5–16. Moreover, Dunmore points out the seducer's failure to accomplish a single seduction.

15. According to Jean-Marie Apostolides, "Dom Juan's power to change his fellow human beings recalls the power of gold when it comes into contact with objects: he transforms people into merchandise, he attributes a quantifiable value to them, and he makes them circulate. This process of market transformation manifests itself in his relationships as seducer with women" ("Sociology of Exchange," 488).

16. According to Irigaray,

Woman takes pleasure more from touching than from looking, and her entry into a dominant scopic economy signifies, again, her consignment to passivity: she is to be the beautiful object of contemplation . . . For woman is traditionally a use-value for man, an exchange value among men; in other words, a commodity. As such, she remains the guardian of material substance, whose price will be established, in terms of the standard of their work and of their need/desire, by "subjects": workers, merchants, consumers. Women are marked phallically by their fathers, husbands, procurers. And this branding determines their value in sexual commerce. Woman is never anything but the locus of a more or less competitive exchange between two men, including the competition for the possession of mother earth. (*This Sex,* 26, 29–30).

17. Felman, "Promesse," 28.

18. Jean-Pierre Dens, "Dom Juan: héroïsme et désir," *French Review* 50, no. 6 (May 1977): 836.

19. Felman, "Promesse," 25.

20. Apostolides, "Sociology of Exchange," 489.

21. Nathan Gross, "The Dialectic of Obligation in Molière's *Dom Juan,*" *Romanic Review* 65 (1974): 188–89.

22. Felman, *Speech Act,* 48.

23. Vernet, "Economie," 66–7.

24. Felman, *Speech Act,* 38.

25. Ibid., 56.

26. As quoted in Felman, "Promesse," 23.

CHAPTER 4. *L'ECOLE DES FEMMES*

1. Translation of *L'Ecole des femmes* from Molière, *Comedies*, trans. Donald M. Frame (Oxford: Oxford University Press, 1968; 1985).

2. Johan Huizinga, *Homo ludens*, 11.

3. Serge Doubrovsky, "Arnolphe ou la chute du héros," *Mercure de France* 343 (1961): 112.

4. James F. Gaines validates this argument in the following terms: "Since Arnolphe defines his own honor in terms of the dishonor, lowliness, and misfortune of those who surround him, one incidence of cuckoldry will be enough to destroy his chimerical ambitions" ("*L'Ecole des femmes:* Usurpation, Dominance and Social Closure," *Papers on French Seventeenth Century Literature* 9, no. 17 [1982]: 616).

5. Patrick Dandrey, "Structures et espaces de communication dans *L'Ecole des femmes*," *Littérature* 63 (1986): 68.

6. Irigaray, *This Sex*, 30.

7. In a study entitled "L'Ingénuité d'Agnès. Etude d'un champ lexical dans *L'Ecole des femmes*" (*L'Information grammaticale* 24 [1985]: 20–27), Françoise Berlan discusses the various meanings of the term "ingénuité" in the seventeenth century and applies these to a careful examination of the use of this word and its derivatives in *L'Ecole des femmes*.

8. Dandrey, "Structures," 77.

9. Marcel Gutwirth contends that "There can be no doubt about it: the shadow thrown by that ignorant waif is the shadow of the infinite power, the inexhaustible resourcefulness, the quicksilver elusiveness of the towering myth with which masculine imagination so readily identifies woman: Nature. Poised against the protean threat, armed with the incorruptible net of his own watchful devising stands man, whose ever inadequate response is Art" ("Molière and the Woman Question: *Les Précieuses ridicules, L'Ecole des femmes, Les Femmes savantes*," *Theatre Journal* 34, no. 3 [October 1982]: 354).

10. Will G. Moore, *Molière, A New Criticism* (Oxford: Clarendon Press, 1949): 38, 107.

11. According to Myrna K. Zwillenberg ("Arnolphe, Fate's Fool," *Modern Language Review* 68 [1973]: 304, 293), "The major thrust of each *péripétie* has been to replace Arnolphe's illusion with a retroactive reality which negates his pretension to power over the present . . . The emphasis on the role of fate in the dénouement deserves immediate consideration. The main characters need not have bothered to exert themselves because none of them bears any responsibility for the *a priori* decision taken by Enrique and Oronte. The final revelation of the two fathers cancels out all the systems; only fate has the last word."

12. Doubrovsky exposes the fallacy subtending Arnolphe's heroic project in the following terms:

> Dans une perspective aristocratique saine, la domination absolue de soi est la condition préalable de toute domination sur autrui. C'est par ce biais qu'une éthique de la violence peut aboutir à une pratique de la magnanimité. Mais Arnolphe, lui, a compris à l'envers: il croit que c'est en étant maître de l'univers qu'on devient maître de soi. C'est la possession d'autrui qui doit permettre de se récupérer soi-même comme maître et comme chef. Dès lors, la dialectique du Maître et de l'Esclave, source vraie de la morale aristocratique, est pervertie en son essence et se trouve remplacée par l'insoluble dialectique de la victime et du bourreau. Au lieu de vaincre, à la manière cornélienne, une liberté

en termes de liberté, Arnolphe va essayer de contraindre un être libre, *de l'extérieur.* ("Arnolphe," 115–16).

[From a healthy aristocratic perspective, the absolute domination of the self is the premise for the domination of others. It is through this channel that the ethics of violence can result in the practice of magnanimity. But Arnolphe has misunderstood: he believes that it is by being master of the universe that one achieves mastery of oneself. The possession of the other allows one to reestablish oneself as master and leader. It follows that the Master/Slave dialectic, true source of the aristocratic value system, is perverted in its essence and is replaced by the unsolvable dialectic of the victim and the tormentor. Instead of achieving a Cornelian victory, a freedom on freedom's terms, Arnolphe will attempt to constrain a free human being from the exterior.] (Translation by author)

13. Bernard Magné contends that in *L'Ecole des femmes* Agnès learns to speak while Arnolphe learns to be silent ("*L'Ecole des femmes* ou la conquête de la parole," *Revue des Sciences humaines* 145 [janvier/mars 1972]: 125–40).

14. Critics who have drawn attention to the illogicality of the play's *dénouement* include well-known authorities such as Jacques Scherer (*Structures de Tartuffe* [Paris, Société d'édition d'enseignement supérieur, 1974]: 207), and René Bray (*Molière, homme de théâtre* [Paris: Mercure de France, 1954]: 218). It is, however, this very illogicality that is eminently logical within a comedy such as *L'Ecole des femmes*, which incorporates the chance factor within its structure.

CHAPTER 5. *LE BOURGEOIS GENTILHOMME*

1. Jesse Dickson, "Non-sens et sens dans *Le Bourgeois gentilhomme*," *French Review* 51 (1978): 342.

2. Gérard Defaux, *Molière ou les métamorphoses du comique: de la comédie morale au triomphe de la folie* (Lexington, Ky.: French Forum Publishers, 1980): 267.

3. Ronald W. Tobin, "Fusion and Diffusion in *Le Bourgeois gentilhomme*," *French Review* 59, no. 2 (December 1985): 241.

4. Hallam Walker reminds us that "The audience of courtiers at Chambord was used to seeing ballets with pastoral or mythical figures, so that the appearance of tailor's apprentices in a dance took them a bit by surprise" (*Molière* [New York: Twayne Publishers, 1971]: 154).

5. Translations of *Le Bourgeois Gentilhomme* from *Molière, Comedies*, trans. Donald H. Frame (Oxford: Oxford University Press, 1968, 1985).

6. Larry Riggs sees *Le Bourgeois gentilhomme* as a response to the blurring and the eroding of the boundaries between the nobility and the bourgeoisie: "The alacrity with which commoners bought 'nobility' reflected its desirability, but also accelerated its decline . . . *Qualité*, or nobility, was, increasingly, a matter of style, and the life of the old nobility at court was increasingly ceremonial. The very theatricality—the vagueness and changeability—of social class in the 1660's made comic theater the ideal medium for exploring the question of class, identity and ethics" (See "Issues of Nobility," 400). In other words, the attributes of the aristocracy become increasingly a matter of aesthetics, illusion, deceit and disguise.

7. Anthony A. Ciccone, "Metalanguage and Knowledge in Molière's *Le Bourgeois gentilhomme*," *Degré Second* 6 (July 1982): 44.

8. Jules Brody, "Esthétiques et société chez Molière," in *Dramaturgie et société: Rapports entre l'oeuvre théâtrale, son interprétation et son public aux XVIe et XVIIe*

siècles, eds. Jean Jacquot, Elie Konigson and Marcel Oddon (Paris: CRNS, 1968): 318.

9. Kenneth S. White, "Hypnotic Language and its Apotheosis: Molière and Ionesco," in *Molière and the Commonwealth of Letters: Patrimony and Posterity,* eds. Roger Johnson, Jr., Editha S. Newmann and Guy T. Trail (Jackson, Miss.: University of Mississippi Press, 1975): 103.

10. Dickson, "Non-sens," 348.

11. Hélène Cixous, "Castration," 42–43.

12. Ciccone, "Metalanguage," 53.

13. Defaux, *Métamorphoses,* 273.

14. René Bray, *Homme de théâtre,* 28, 31.

15. Nathan Gross, "Values in *Le Bourgeois gentilhomme,*" *L'Esprit Créateur* 15 (spring-summer 1975): 108.

16. Harold K. Knutson, *Molière. An Archetypal Approach* (Toronto and Buffalo: University of Toronto Press, 1976): 112.

17. Ronald Tobin insists on the etymology of her name: Dorimène—the "giver". ("Fusion," 240).

18. Defaux, *Métamorphoses,* 272.

19. Though critics tend to agree that the ending represents an evaporation into the world of illusion, they view this process with varying degrees of scepticism or optimism. Riggs argues that "Like Dom Juan, [M. Jourdain] can only 'evaporate' from the world of significances. Madame Jourdain and Cléonte understand that M. Jourdain's attempt to transform his identity is absurd in the profoundest sense: he is abandoning meaning and value" ("Issues of Nobility," 407). E. Kern points out that "Reality is ridiculous, indistinguishable from illusion. Life can be borne only by those who, like the philosophical Philinte or the farcical Sganarelle of *Le Médecin malgré lui,* like 'mamamouchi' Jourdain or 'Doctor' Argan, ally illusion with reality, creating a new reality, genuine and viable, because it functions with the least harm and the most joy" ("Molière and the Tradition of the Grotesque," in Roger Johnson, *Molière Commonwealth,* 520).

20. Michèle Vialet, "*Le Bourgeois gentilhomme* en contexte," *Papers on French Seventeenth Century Literature* 17, no. 32 (1990): 57.

CHAPTER 6. *LE TARTUFFE*

1. Larry Riggs, "Molière's 'Poststructuralism': Demolition of Transcendentalist Discourse in *Le Tartuffe,*" *Symposium* 44, no. 1 (spring 1990): 42–43.

2. Translations of *Tartuffe* from Moliere, *Comedies,* trans. Donald M. Frame (Oxford: Oxford University Press, 1968, 1985).

3. Riggs, "Intimations of Post-Structuralism: Subversion of the Classicist Subject in *Les Femmes savantes* and *Le Tartuffe,*" *Literature Interpretation Theory* 2, no. 1 (July 1990): 69.

4. Andrew McKenna, "*Tartuffe,* Representation and Difference," *Papers on French Seventeenth Century Literature* 16, no. 30 (1989): 79.

5. Riggs, "Demolition," 48–49.

6. Charles Mauron, *Psychocritique du genre comique* (Paris: José Corti, 1964): 130–39.

7. Luce Irigaray, *Speculum,* 113–14.

8. In his review of Brian Bedford's 1981 staging of *Le Tartuffe,* Raymond LePage not only defends the plausibility of the director's heavy emphasis on the

play's eroticism, but he also praises Bedford's innovative approach as being faithful to the tradition of the original production. Most importantly, he emphasizes Elmire's overt sensuality and seductiveness in the British production: "A traditional view would explain [Elmire's] ambivalence as a shrewd tactic: necessary to gain the confidence of a seducer and re-seduce him through his rhetorical paces. Still, one could not help but detect in Bedford's Elmire a sublimated pleasure, the kind of pleasure that a person senses in discovering the truth, of enticing it out into the open, of having it confided in secret" ("Brian Bedford's *Tartuffe:* The Erotic Violence of Hypocrisy," *Theatre Journal* 34, no. 3 [October 1982]: 395).

9. Irigaray, *Speculum,* 113.

10. The possibility of homosexual involvement between Orgon and Tartuffe has always subtended the play's textual surface. The case for such a relationship has been made by many, including Gifford Orwen in *"Tartuffe* Reconsidered" *(French Review* 16, no. 5 [April 1968]: 611–15). Planchon's 1977 production and Bedford's 1981 staging also emphasized this relationship.

11. Irigaray, *Speculum,* 115.

12. Ralph Albanese confirms this impression in the following passage:

> Si la femme d'Orgon en vient à mettre en question la validité du comportement de Damis, ses propres démarches, de leur côté, ne manquent pas de présenter une certaine ambiguïté. A l'arrivée d'Orgon (I,3), ainsi qu'après la dénonciation de Damis (III,6), elle fait des sorties que l'on peut qualifier d'injustifiées. De plus, son silence à ce moment critique est équivoque, car elle ne contredit ni ne confirme cette dénonciation. Au contraire elle se tait au moment où son mari est mis au courant de la perfidie de son conseiller. Enfin, ne pourrait-on pas poser certaines questions sur son besoin de se réunir avec Tartuffe en tête-à-tête aussi bien que sur son insistance à empêcher que la déclaration galante que lui fait l'imposteur ne s'ébruite?

(Le Dynamisme de la peur chez Molière: une analyse socio-culturelle de Dom Juan, Tartuffe et L'Ecole des femmes [University, Miss.: Romance Monographs, 1976]: 125).

13. McKenna, "Representation," 86.

14. Michael Spingler, "The King's Play: Censorship and the Politics of Performance in Molière's *Tartuffe,*" *Comparative Drama* 19, no. 3 (fall 1985): 248.

15. Spingler considers Elmire's strategy to be a grave miscalculation rather than a *tour de force:* "One of Elmire's mistakes has been to place the responsibility of interrupting her scene in the hands of a man whose vulnerability to theater and whose capacity for being enthralled by performance have already been clearly established by his own account to Cléante in Act I of his first meeting with Tartuffe" (ibid., 249). However, Riggs reminds us that "When Orgon is under the table, he cannot be mesmerized by Tartuffe as a mirror sending back a flattering image. He is obliged to *listen* to Tartuffe's discourse as a tissue of speech-acts, designed to undermine his, Orgon's, mastery" ("Intimations," 73).

16. Spingler, "King's Play," 241.

CHAPTER 7. *LE MISANTHROPE*

1. All translations of *Le Misanthrope* taken from: Molière, *Comedies,* trans. Donald M. Frame (Oxford: Oxford University Press, 1968; 1985).

2. Nicolas Boileau, *L'Art poétique,* (1674; reprint Paris: Larousse, 1972): 80.

3. Larry W. Riggs, "Context and Convergence in the Comedy of *Le Misanthrope,*" *Romance Notes* 25, No. 1 (fall 1984): 66.

4. Rufus K. Marsh, "Alceste, *Honnête Homme* or *Faux Honnête Homme?*" *Stanford French Review* 5, no. 1 (spring 1981): 26.

5. Noel Peacock, "Lessons Unheeded: The Denouement of *Le Misanthrope*," *Nottingham French Studies* 20, no. 1 (1990): 12.

6. Riggs, "Context," 66.

7. Jacques Guicharnaud, *Molière, une aventure théâtrale: Tartuffe, Dom Juan, Le Misanthrope* (Paris: Gallimard, 1963): 358.

8. Pierre Force, "What Is a Man Worth? Ethics and Economics in Molière and Rousseau," *The Romanic Review* 80, no. 1 (1989): 19.

9. Hélène Cixous, "Castration," 44.

10. Patricia Francis Cholakian, "The 'Woman Question' in Molière's *Misanthrope*," *The French Review* 58, no. 4 (March 1985): 525.

11. G. Donald Jackson, "Gestes, déplacements et texte dans trois pièces de Molière," *Papers on French Seventeenth Century Literature* 11, no. 20 (1984): 39, 40, 41, 42.

12. Nina Ekstein, "*Le Misanthrope* and *Tartuffe:* Two Critiques of Verbal Portraiture," *Rivista di letteratura moderne e comparate* 42, no. 2 (April-June 1989): 141–42.

13. Riggs, "Context," 69.

14. Cixous, "Castration," 47 (see endnote 13 in Chapter 2 on *L'Avare.*). To reiterate the quotation: "Take Don Juan and you have the whole masculine economy, getting together to 'give women just what it takes to keep them in bed', then swiftly taking back the investment, then reinvesting, etc., so that nothing ever gets given, everything gets taken back, while in the process the greatest possible dividend of pleasure is taken. Consumption without payment, of course."

15. Cholakian, "Woman Question," 527–28.

16. Irigaray, *Speculum,* 117.

17. Ibid., 530.

18. Irigaray, *This Sex,* 28–29.

Chapter 8. *Le Malade Imaginaire*

1. Translation of *Le Malade imaginaire* from: Molière, *Comedies,* trans. Donald M. Frame (Oxford: Oxford University Press, 1985, 1986).

2. Carol A. Mossman, "The Restitution of Paternity in Molière's *Le Malade imaginaire,*" *The South Central Review* 3, no. 1 (spring 1986): 51.

3. Philip R. Berk, "The Therapy of Art in *Le Malade imaginaire,*" *The French Review* 45, Special Issue, no. 4, (spring 1972): 41.

4. Ralph Albanese Jr., "*Le Malade imaginaire,* ou le jeu de la mort et du hasard," *Dix-septième siècle* 154 (1987): 4.

5. Ibid., 6–7.

6. Irigaray suggests that "the desire for the same, for the self-identical, the self (as) same, and again of the similar, the alter ego and, to put it in a nutshell, the desire for the auto . . . the homo . . . the male, dominates the representational economy. 'Sexual difference' is a derivation of the problematics of sameness, it is, now and forever, determined within the project, the projection, the sphere of representation, of the same" (*Speculum,* 26–27).

7. Ibid., 18.

8. Albanese, "Jeu de la mort," 9.

9. Berk, "Therapy of Art," 39.

10. Hélène Cixous, "Castration," 46.

11. Jane Gallop, *The Daughter's Seduction. Feminism and Psychoanalysis* (Ithaca: Cornell University Press, 1982): 124.

12. Gérard Defaux, *Métamorphoses*, 298.

13. Marc Fumaroli, "Aveuglement et déabusement dans *Le Malade imaginaire*," in *Vérité et illusion dans le théâtre au temps de la Renaissance* (Paris: Touzot, 1983): 110.

14. Mossman, "Restitution of Paternity," 54.

15. Defaux, *Métamorphoses*, 301.

CHAPTER 9. CONCLUSION

1. James F. Gaines, "Ménage versus Salon in *Les Femmes savantes*," *L'Esprit Créateur* 21, no. 3 (fall 1981): 51–52.

2. William D. Howarth, "Une Pièce Comique Tout à Fait Achevée: Aesthetic Coherence in *Les Femmes savantes* and *Le Tartuffe*," ed. William D. Howarth *Form and Meaning: Aesthetic Coherence in Seventeenth-Century French Drama* (Amersham, England, Avebury: 1982): 146, 150.

3. Translations of *Les Femmes savantes* from: A. R. Wallen, trans., *The Plays of Molière*, vol. 7 (Edinburgh: John R. Grant, 1907).

4. Larry W. Riggs, "Intimations," 64.

5. Ibid., 64.

6. Elisabeth Lapeyre, "*Les Femmes savantes:* une lecture aliénée," *French Forum* 6, no. 2 (May, 1981): 135.

7. Gallop, *Daughter's Seduction*, 118.

8. As quoted by Gallop, ibid., 115.

9. David Shaw, "*Les Femmes savantes* and Feminism," *Journal of European Studies* 14, No. 1 (1984): 30.

10. Gaines, "Ménage," 57.

11. Ralph Albanese, Jr. "Images de la femme dans le discours scolaire républicain (1880–1914)," *The French Review* 62, no. 5 (April 1989): 745.

12. K. Willis Wolfe, "Pouvoir de pédant, volonté de femme: le renouvellement molièresque d'une tradition comique," ed. Claude Abraham, *Actes de Davis* (Paris, Biblio 17: 1988): 224.

13. Riggs, "Intimations," 63.

14. Ibid., 67–68.

15. Gaines, "Ménage," 58.

16. Lapeyre, "Lecture aliénée," 132.

17. Ibid., 138.

18. Gallop, *Daughter's Seduction*, 120–21.

Bibliography

Albanese, Ralph Jr. *Le Dynamisme de la peur chez Molière: une analyse socio-culturelle de Dom Juan, Tartuffe et L'Ecole des femmes.* University, Miss.: Romance Monographs, 1976.

———. "Argent et réification dans *L'Avare.*" *L'Esprit Créateur* 21, no. 3 (fall 1981): 35–50.

———. "*Le Malade imaginaire,* ou le jeu de la mort et du hasard." *Dix-septième siècle* 154 (1987): 3–15.

———. "Images de la femme dans le discours scolaire républicain (1880–1914)." *The French Review* 62, No. 5 (1989): 740–47.

Apostolides, Jean-Marie. "Molière and the Sociology of Exchange." Translated by Alice Musick McLean. *Critical Inquiry* 14, no. 3 (1988): 477–92.

Aristotle. *Poetics.* Translated by Leon Golden. Englewood Cliffs, NJ: Prentice-Hall, 1968.

Bauer, Dale, and Susan Jaret McKinsky, eds. *Feminism, Bakhtin and the Dialogic.* Albany: State University of New York Press, 1991.

Beauvoir, Simone de. *Le Deuxième Sexe.* Vol. 1. Paris: Gallimard, 1949.

Beckerman, Bernard. *The Dynamics of Drama.* New York: Drama Book Specialists, 1979.

Bergson, Henri-Louis. *Le Rire.* 1900. Reprint, Paris: Presses Universitaires de France, 1978.

Berk, Philip R. "The Therapy of Art in *Le Malade imaginaire.*" *The French Review* 45, Special Issue no. 4 (spring 1972): 39–48.

Berlan, Françoise. "L'Ingénuité d'Agnès. Etude d'un champ lexical dans *L'Ecole des femmes.*" *L'Information grammaticale* 24 (1985): 20–27.

Boileau, Nicolas. *L'Art poétique.* 1674. Reprint, Paris: Larousse, 1972.

Borgerhoff, E. B. O. *The Freedom of French Classicism.* Princeton: Princeton University Press, 1950.

Bray, René. *Molière, homme de théâtre.* Paris: Mercure de France, 1954.

Brody, Jules. "Esthétiques et société chez Molière." In *Dramaturgie et société: Rapports entre l'oeuvre théâtrale, son interprétation et son public aux XVIe et XVIIe siècles.* Edited by Jean Jacquot, Elie Konigson, and Marcel Oddon. Paris: CRNS, 1968: 307–26.

Cairncross, John. *Molière, bourgeois et libertin.* Paris: Nizet, 1963.

Chasseguet-Smirgel, Janine. *Sexuality and Mind: The Role of the Father and the Mother in the Psyche.* New York: New York University Press, 1986.

Cholakian, Patricia Francis. "The 'Woman Question' in Molière's *Misanthrope.*" *The French Review* 58, no. 4 (March 1985): 524–32.

Ciccone, Anthony. "Metalanguage and Knowledge in Molière's *Le Bourgeois gentilhomme*." *Degré Second* 6 (July 1982): 41–64.

Cixous, Hélène. "Castration or Decapitation?" Translated by Annette Kuhn. *Signs: Journal of Women in Culture and Society* 7, no. 1 (Autumn 1982): 36–55.

Corrigan, Robert, ed. *Comedy, Meaning and Form.* San Francisco: Chandler Publishing, 1965.

Dandrey, Patrick. "Structures et espaces de communication dans *L'Ecole des Femmes.*" *Littérature* 63 (1986): 65–89.

Defaux, Gérard. *Molière ou les métamorphoses du comique: de la comédie morale au triomphe de la folie.* Lexington, Ky.: French Forum Publishers, 1980.

Dens, Jean-Pierre. "*Dom Juan:* héroïsme et désir." *French Review* 50, no. 6 (May 1977): 835–41.

Derrida, Jacques. "All Ears: Nietzsche's Otobiography." In *The Pedagogical Imperative, Teaching as Literary Genre.* New Haven: Yale University Press, 1982.

Dickson, Jesse. "Non-sens et sens dans *Le Bourgeois gentilhomme.*" *French Review* 51 (1978): 341–52.

Doubrovsky, Serge. "Arnolphe ou la chute du héros." *Mercure de France* 343 (1961): 111–118.

Dryden, John. "Preface to *An Evening's Love.*" In *Four Comedies.* Edited by L. A. Beaurline and Fredson Bowers. 1671. Reprint, Chicago: The University of Chicago Press, 1967: 183–92.

Dunmore, John. "The Impotence of Dom Juan." *New Zealand Journal of French Studies* 4, No. 2 (1983): 5–16.

Ekstein, Nina. "*Le Misanthrope* and *Tartuffe*: Two Critiques of Verbal Portraiture." *Revista di letteratura moderne e comparate* 42, no. 2 (April–June 1989): 137–152.

Eustis, Alvin. *Molière as Ironic Contemplator.* Paris: Mouton, 1973.

Felman, Shoshana. "*Don Juan* ou la promesse d'amour." *Tel Quel* 87 (1981): 16–36.

———. *The Literary Speech Act.* Translated by Catherine Porter. Ithaca: Cornell University Press, 1980.

Force, Pierre. "What Is A Man Worth? Ethics and Economics in Molière and Rousseau." *The Romanic Review* 80, no. 1 (1989): 18–29.

Freud, Sigmund. *Jokes and Their Relation to the Unconscious.* Edited and translated by James Strachey. 1905. Reprint, New York: W. W. Norton and Company, 1968.

Frye, Northrop. *Anatomy of Criticism.* Princeton: Princeton University Press, 1971.

Fumaroli, Marc. "Aveuglement et désabusement dans *Le Malade imaginaire.*" In *Vérité et illusion dans le théâtre au temps de la Renaissance.* Edited by M. T. Jones-Davies. Paris: Touzot, 1983: 105–14.

Gaines, James F. "Ménage versus Salon in *Les Femmes savantes.*" *L'Esprit Créateur* 21, no. 3 (fall 1981): 51–59.

———. "*L'Ecole des femmes:* Usurpation, Dominance and Social Closure." *Papers on French Seventeenth Century Literature* 9, no. 17 (1982): 607–25.

Gallop, Jane. *The Daughter's Seduction: Feminism and Psychoanalysis.* Ithaca: Cornell University Press, 1982.

———. *Thinking Through The Body.* New York: Columbia University Press, 1988.

―――. *Around 1981: Academic Feminist Literary Theory.* New York: Routledge, 1992.

Gossman, Lionel. *Men and Masks: A Study of Molière.* Baltimore: Johns Hopkins University Press, 1963.

Greenberg, Mitchell. "Suréna's Melancholy and the End of the Ancien Régime." In *Actes de Baton Rouge.* Edited by Selma Zébouni. Paris: Biblio 17, 1986: 124–39.

―――. *Corneille, Classicism and the Ruses of Symmetry.* Cambridge: Cambridge University Press, 1986.

Gross, Nathan. "Values in *Le Bourgeois gentilhomme.*" *L'Esprit créateur* 15 (spring-summer 1975): 105–18.

―――. "The Dialectic of Obligation in Molière's *Dom Juan.*" *Romanic Review,* 65 (1974): 175–200.

Guicharnaud, Jacques. *Molière: une aventure théâtrale.* Paris: Gallimard, 1963.

Gutwirth, Marcel. "Molière and the Woman Question: *Les Précieuses ridicules, L'Ecole des femmes, Les Femmes savantes.*" *Theatre Journal* 34, no. 3 (October 1982): 344–59.

―――. "Dom Juan et le tabou d'inceste." *Romanic Review* 77, no. 1 (1986): 25–32.

Hegel, G. W. F. *The Philosophy of Fine Art.* Vol. 4. Translated by F. B. P. Osmaston. 1820. Reprint, London: G. Bell, 1920.

Hoffman, Paul. *La Femme dans la pensée des Lumières.* Paris: Ophrys, 1977.

Howarth, William D. "Une Pièce comique tout à fait achevée: Aesthetic Coherence in *Les Femmes Savantes* and *Le Tartuffe.*" In *Form and Meaning: Aesthetic Coherence in Seventeenth-Century French Drama.* Edited by William D. Howarth. Amersham, England, Avebury, 1982: 142–55.

Huizinga, Johan. *Homo ludens.* 1950. Reprint, Boston: Beacon Press, 1955.

Irigaray, Luce. *Speculum of the Other Woman.* Translated by Gillian Gill. Ithaca: Cornell University Press, 1985.

―――. *This Sex Which Is Not One.* Translated by Catherine Porter. Ithaca: Cornell University Press, 1985.

Jackson, G. Donald. "Gestes, déplacements et texte dans trois pièces de Molière." *Papers on French Seventeenth Century Literature* 11, no. 20 (1984): 37–59.

Johnson, Roger, Editha S. Newmann and Guy T. Trail, eds. *Molière and the Commonwealth of Letters: Patrimony and Posterity.* Jackson, Miss.: The University Press of Mississippi, 1975.

Jones, Dorothy F. "The Treasure in the Garden: Biblical Imagery in *L'Avare.*" *Papers on French Seventeenth Century Literature* 15, no. 29 (1988): 517–28.

Kelly, Joan. *Women, History and Theory.* Chicago: The University of Chicago Press, 1984.

Kennedy, William. "Comic Audiences and Rhetorical Strategies in Machiavelli, Shakespeare, and Molière." *Comparative Literature Studies* 21, no. 4 (1984): 363-82.

Knutson, Harold K. *Molière. An Archetypal Approach.* Toronto and Buffalo: University of Toronto Press, 1976.

Kris, Ernst. *Psychoanalytical Explorations in Art.* 1935. Reprint, New York: International Universities Press, 1952.

Kristeva, Julia. *Desire in Language: A Semiotic Approach to Literature and Art.* New York: Columbia University Press, 1980.

————. "Women's Time." Translated by Alice Jardine and Harry Blake. *Signs: Journal of Women in Culture and Society* 7, no. 1 (autumn 1981): 13–35.

Lamb, Charles. "Notes on Thomas Middleton's *A Fair Quarrel.*" In Vol. 1 of *The Works of Charles and Mary Lamb.* Edited by E. V. Lucas. 1818. Reprint, London: Methuen, 1912: 45–46.

————. "On the Artificial Comedy of the Last Century." In *Lamb as Critic.* Edited by Roy Park. 1822; 1823. Reprint, Lincoln, Nebr.: University of Nebraska Press, 1980: 62–68.

Lapeyre, Elisabeth. "*Les Femmes savantes:* une lecture aliénée." *French Forum* 6, no. 2 (May 1981): 132–139.

Lawrence, Francis. "Dom Juan and the Manifest God: Molière's Antitragic Hero." *PMLA* 93 (1978): 86–94.

Leiner, Wolfgang, ed. *Onze études sur l'image de la femme dans la littérature française du dix-septième siècle.* Tübingen: Narr, 1984.

LePage, Raymond. "Brian Bedford's *Tartuffe:* The Erotic Violence of Hypocrisy." *Theatre Journal* 34, no. 3 (October 1982): 389–96.

Magné, Bernard. "*L'Ecole des femmes* ou la conquête de la parole." *Revue des Sciences humaines* 145 (janvier/mars 1972): 125–40.

Marsh, Rufus K. "Alceste, *Honnête Homme* or *Faux Honnête Homme?*" *Stanford French Review* 5, no. 1 (spring 1981): 21–34.

Mauron, Charles. *Psychocritique du genre comique.* Paris: José Corti, 1964.

McKenna, Andrew. "*Tartuffe,* Representation and Difference." *Papers on French Seventeenth Century Literature* 16, no. 30 (1989): 77–93.

Mehlman, Jeffrey. "How to Read Freud on Jokes: The Critic as Schadchen." In *New Literary History* 6, no. 2 (1975): 439–61.

Meredith, George. "An Essay on Comedy." In *Comedy.* Edited by Wylie Sypher. 1877. Reprint, Garden City, NY: Doubleday, 1956: 3–57.

Molière. *Comedies.* Translated by Donald M. Frame. Oxford: Oxford University Press, 1968, 1985.

Montbertrand, Gérard. "Territoire et société dans *L'Avare* et *Tartuffe* de Molière." *French Literature Series* 15 (1988): 7–17.

Moore, Will G. *Molière, A New Criticism.* Oxford: Clarendon Press, 1949.

Morel, Jacques. "A Propos de la 'Scène du pauvre' dans *Dom Juan.*" *Revue d'histoire littéraire de la France* 72 (1972): 938–44.

Mossman, Carol A. "The Restitution of Paternity in Molière's *Le Malade imaginaire.*" *The South Central Review* 3, no. 1 (spring 1986): 50–56.

Olson, Elder. *The Theory of Comedy.* Bloomington: Indiana University Press, 1975.

Orwen, Gifford. "*Tartuffe* Reconsidered." *French Review* 16, no. 5 (April 1968): 611–15.

Peacock, Noel. "Lessons Unheeded: The Dénouement of *Le Misanthrope.*" *Nottingham French Studies* 20, no. 1 (1990): 10–20.

Pelous, J.-M. "Les Problèmes du temps dans le *Dom Juan* de Molière." *Revue des Sciences humaines* 38, no. 152 (octobre-décembre 1973): 555–63.

Pineau, J. "Harpagon ou la terre aride." *Revue d'Histoire du Théâtre* 38, no. 4 (1986): 406–17.

Pruner, Michel. "La notion de dette dans le *Dom Juan* de Molière." *Revue d'histoire du théâtre* 26 (1974): 254–71.

Richter, Jean Paul. "Über die Humoristische Dichtkunst." Vol 5 in *Werke*. 1804. Reprint, München: Carl Hanser, 1963: 124–44.

Riggs, Larry. "Context and Convergence in the Comedy of *Le Misanthrope*." *Romance Notes* 5, no. 1 (fall 1984): 65-69.

———. "The Issues of Nobility and Identity in *Dom Juan* and *Le Bourgeois gentilhomme*." *French Review* 59, no. 3 (February 1986): 399–409.

———. "Ethics, Debts and Identity in *Dom Juan*." *Romance Quarterly* 34, no. 2 (May 1987): 141–46.

———. "Intimations of Post-Structuralism: Subversion of the Classicist Subject in *Les Femmes savantes* and *Le Tartuffe*." *Literature Interpretation Theory* 2, no. 1 (July 1990): 59–75.

———. "Molière's 'Poststructuralism': Demolition of Transcendentalist Discourse in *Le Tartuffe*." *Symposium* 44, no. 1 (spring 1990): 37–57.

Scherer, Jacques. *Structures de Tartuffe*. Paris: Société d'édition d'enseignement supérieur, 1974.

———. *La Dramaturgie classique en France*. Paris: Nizet, 1976.

Schlegel, August Wilhelm von. *A Course of Lectures on Dramatic Art and Literature*. Translated by John Black. 1808. Reprint, London: H. G. Bohn, 1846.

Sedgwick, Eve Kosofsky. *Between Men: English Literature and Male Homosocial Desire*. New York: Columbia University Press, 1985.

Shapira, Charlotte. "La Séduction face au ciel dans *Don Juan* de Molière." *Neohelicon* 11, no. 1 (1984): 345-56.

Shaw, David. "Egoism and Society: A Secular Interpretation of Molière's *Dom Juan*." *Modern Languages* 59, no. 3 (September 1978): 115–25.

———. "*Les Femmes savantes* and Feminism." *Journal of European Studies* 14, no. 1 (1984): 24–38.

Spingler, Michael. "The King's Play: Censorship and the Politics of Performance in Molière's *Tartuffe*." *Comparative Drama* 19, no. 3 (fall 1985): 240–57.

Tobin, Ronald. "Fusion and Diffusion in *Le Bourgeois gentilhomme*." *French Review* 59, no. 2 (December 1985): 234–45.

———. "Don Juan, ou le principe du plaisir." In *Littérature et gastronomie: huit études*. Tübingen: Biblio 17, 1985: 21–63.

Van Laan, Thomas. *The Idiom of Drama*. Ithaca: Cornell University Press, 1970.

Vernet, Max. "Economie, histoire, littérature." *Oeuvres et Critiques* 16, no. 1 (1990): 61–72.

Vialet, Michèle. "*Le Bourgeois gentilhomme* en contexte." *Papers on French Seventeenth Century Literature* 17, no. 32 (1990): 51–58.

Walker, Hallam. *Molière*. New York: Twayne Publishers, 1971.

Wolfe, K. Willis. "Pouvoir de pédant, volonté de femme: le renouvellement moliéresque d'une tradition comique." In *Actes de Davis*. Edited by Claude Abraham. Paris: Biblio 17, 1988: 221–27.

Zwillenberg, Myrna K. "Arnolphe, Fate's Fool." *Modern Language Review* 68 (1973): 292–308.

Index